NIETZSCHE'S ETHICS
AND HIS
WAR ON 'MORALITY'

Nietzsche's Ethics and his War on 'Morality'

SIMON MAY

CLARENDON PRESS · OXFORD

OXFORD

UNIVERSITY PRESS

Great Clarendon Street, Oxford OX2 6DP

Oxford University Press is a department of the University of Oxford.
It furthers the University's objective of excellence in research, scholarship,
and education by publishing worldwide in

Oxford New York

Athens Auckland Bangkok Bogotá Buenos Aires Calcutta
Cape Town Chennai Dar es Salaam Delhi Florence Hong Kong Istanbul
Karachi Kuala Lumpur Madrid Melbourne Mexico City Mumbai
Nairobi Paris São Paulo Singapore Taipei Tokyo Toronto Warsaw

and associated companies in Berlin Ibadan

Oxford is a registered trade mark of Oxford University Press
in the UK and in certain other countries

Published in the United States
by Oxford University Press Inc., New York

© Simon May 1999

The moral rights of the author have been asserted

Database right Oxford University Press (maker)

First published 1999

All rights reserved. No part of this publication may be reproduced,
stored in a retrieval system, or transmitted, in any form or by any means,
without the prior permission in writing of Oxford University Press,
or as expressly permitted by law, or under terms agreed with the appropriate
reprographics rights organization. Enquiries concerning reproduction
outside the scope of the above should be sent to the Rights Department,
Oxford University Press, at the address above

You must not circulate this book in any other binding or cover
and you must impose this same condition on any acquirer

British Library Cataloguing in Publication Data

Data available

Library of Congress Cataloging in Publication Data

May, Simon.
Nietzsche's ethics and his war on 'morality'/Simon May.
Includes bibliographical references and index.
1. Nietzsche, Friedrich Wilhelm, 1844–1900—Ethics.
I. Title.
B3318.E9M38 1999 170′92—dc21 99–28678
ISBN 0–19–823846–0

1 3 5 7 9 10 8 6 4 2

Typeset by Hope Services (Abingdon) Ltd.
Printed in Great Britain
on acid-free paper by
Biddles Ltd.,
Guildford & King's Lynn

Preface

This book addresses a need inadequately met by the expanding literature on Nietzsche's philosophy: namely, for an investigation of his ethics of 'life-enhancement' which reveals his complexity as both revolutionary and conservative. For Nietzsche is a thinker who not only repudiates traditional conceptions of god, guilt, asceticism, pity, and truthfulness, but also retains a severe ethic of discipline, conscience, 'self-creation', generosity, and honesty. As a result of his strident style and the sheer diversity of his disciples—from the political right to the political left, from Existentialists to Postmodernists, from Nazi ideologues to Students of 1968, not to mention the many artists and thinkers who have found inspiration in his writings—it has been easy to lose sight of the subtlety with which he 'revalues' values such as altruism or truthfulness, and of how he is at once ancient, in his concern with the good and the virtuous, and modern, in his obsession with autonomy and his exaltation of the will.

Part I of this book undertakes a broad survey of Nietzsche's ethic and its opposition to traditional 'morality', as conceived by him. It includes a critical examination of his conception of values, his standard for the evaluation of values, his analysis of fundamental concepts and values of 'morality'—such as altruism, responsibility, and universal duties—and the new ethical ideal he espouses. Part II illustrates this survey by presenting a detailed case study of Nietzsche's revaluation of the *value* of truth—perhaps the most fundamental and original of his attempts at a revaluation of all values, but also the least studied by his admirers and critics alike.

In attempting to show that Nietzsche's attack on 'morality' (and the divine) is far more nuanced than is usually supposed, I argue that his inquiry into the value of guilt, bad conscience, truth, resentment, revenge, asceticism, and God reveals that all of the latter can have 'life-enhancing' as well as 'life-denying' functions—and, insofar as they are life-enhancing, can survive a thoroughgoing 'revaluation of all values'. For example, in revisiting Nietzsche's conception of guilt, I suggest that guilt retains a central and, indeed, valuable role in his ethics of the self-responsible individual; and that he wishes to abolish only guilt that is structured by moral notions and values, or by conceptions of indebtedness towards an original source of human life and power—notably god(s). And in studying Nietzsche's scattered but pathbreaking inquiry into the value of truth—which encompasses not just what truths are valuable, but for whom, and when over the course of a life—I propose that, though Nietzsche rejects an unconditional valuation of truth (on six distinct grounds), truth remains, for him, of indispensable value as a safeguard against a panoply of life-denying errors upon which, in his opinion, 'morality' is parasitic. This entire analysis of Nietzsche's critique of 'morality' is based on a discussion of his conception of values, especially the sense in which they are 'determined' (by our individual history), 'objective' (as conditions for attaining certain ends), and yet, in our choice of them, influenceable by reasons—features which may come as a surprise to those accustomed to viewing Nietzsche as, variously, an Emotivist, Existentialist, or Irrationalist.

Though I am critical of Nietzsche's self-defeating conception of justice, of his core assumption that 'life-enhancement' demands world-affirmation (or, conversely, that the 'devaluation' of 'temporality' or 'becoming' or 'world' necessarily stifles human flourishing), of his aim completely to de-deify the world, and of the impossible and undesirable autonomy of the *Übermensch*, I conclude that his inquiry into many of the key values and concepts of traditional morality is highly illuminating, both philosophically and psychologically, and is of particular value to those engaged in contemporary ethics and critiques of 'modernity'.

SM

Acknowledgements

I am particularly indebted to Professor Bernard Williams, Monroe Deutsch Professor of Philosophy at the University of California, Berkeley, and Fellow of All Souls College, Oxford, Dr Christopher Janaway, Senior Lecturer in Philosophy at Birkbeck College, University of London, and Dr Alan Thomas, Lecturer in Philosophy at the University of Kent at Canterbury, for thoroughly reviewing all chapters with me at various stages in their preparation, and for giving so generously of their time. Thanks are also due to Professors Malcolm Budd of University College London and David Cooper of Durham University for their detailed comments. I am grateful to Professor Jennifer Hornsby for a Departmental Fellowship at Birkbeck College, University of London, which helped me to prepare this book for publication, and to Dr Anthony Grayling of Birkbeck College and Professor David Wiggins, Wykeham Professor of Logic at Oxford, for their generous encouragement and advice. I greatly appreciate the valuable research assistance provided by Amber Carpenter and Sonia Memetea, respectively of King's College, London, and St Anne's College, Oxford. Finally, I thank Peter Momtchiloff, Philosophy Editor at Oxford University Press, and Robert Ritter, my assistant editor, for their confidence in this work—and for their patience throughout.

Contents

PART II. FROM OLD TO NEW: NIETZSCHE'S
REVALUATION OF THE VALUE OF TRUTH—A CASE
STUDY

Contents

A Note on Sources

My primary source material is Nietzsche's published works in the English translation of Walter Kaufmann, which is widely cited in the secondary literature and is, on the whole, authoritative.

Extracts from Nietzsche's notebooks, collected under the title *The Will to Power* (the *Nachlass*), are cited only where they manifestly sum up themes that pervade his published writings. Though these notebooks contain a wealth of fascinating ideas, some of which are more closely and calmly argued than the corresponding published material, this does not justify the decision, notably and notoriously by Heidegger, to treat them on a par with those works which Nietzsche himself approved for publication.

In general, I focus upon Nietzsche's 'mature' writings—*The Gay Science, Beyond Good and Evil, On the Genealogy of Morals, Thus Spoke Zarathustra, Twilight of the Idols,* and others published after 1882—because here we find the richest exposition of his attack on traditional 'morality' and of the ethic which he himself espouses. I use earlier works, such as *The Birth of Tragedy, Human, All Too Human,* or *Daybreak,* purely as sources of supplementary material, or to demonstrate the origin, or length of gestation, of Nietzsche's later ideas.

A full list of primary and secondary sources is given in the Bibliography.

List of Abbreviations

Primary sources are cited in the text by abbreviation and by section number, and their full publication details are given in the Bibliography. Please note that references to *Ecce Homo* follow the abbreviations used in the Index of Kaufmann's translation, and that references to *Thus Spoke Zarathustra* follow the abbreviations used in the Contents pages of Kaufmann's translation. In order to minimize the inconvenience of referring to footnotes, most references to Nietzsche's works are incorporated into the text. (By contrast, all references to secondary sources are entered in footnotes—with full publication details for the first citation, and a shortened form of the title for subsequent citations. Full details of all secondary sources are given again in the Bibliography.)

A	*The Antichrist*
BGE	*Beyond Good and Evil*
BT	*The Birth of Tragedy*
CW	*The Case of Wagner*
D	*Daybreak: Thoughts on the Prejudices of Morality*
EH	*Ecce Homo*
GM	*On the Genealogy of Morals*
GS	*The Gay Science*
HAH	*Human, All Too Human*
P	Preface
TI	*Twilight of the Idols*
TL	*On Truth and Lies in a Nonmoral Sense*
WP	*The Will to Power*
Z	*Thus Spoke Zarathustra*

PART I

The New Ethic versus the Old:
Nietzsche versus 'Morality'

1

Introduction and Methodology

We believe that morality in the traditional sense . . . must be overcome. (*BGE*, 32)

1.1 OVERVIEW OF THE BOOK

1.1.1 Summary of aims

My aims in this book are threefold. The first is to scrutinize Nietzsche's subtle critique of certain key concepts and values of traditional Judaeo-Christian morality and its secular embodiments—a critique that, I will argue, is far from uniformly hostile to that morality. Throughout I take traditional 'morality' to be simply one type of ethics, despite its claims to universal validity.[1] And I take 'ethics' to be concerned with two general questions, to which the traditional 'morality' examined by Nietzsche supplies a very particular set of answers: namely, what is the 'good' life for agents? And what are the best means—virtues, values, and practices—for attaining it? How I regulate my behaviour towards others is, on this definition, only one aspect of the good and its attainment.

My second aim is to piece together the non-moral ethics, or 'immoralism', that Nietzsche advances in place of those aspects of traditional morality—in both its religious and secular manifestations—that he rejects as 'life-denying'. Again, my interpretation is marked by its insistence on the subtlety of many of Nietzsche's key ethical views, both in what they repudiate and in what they advocate. At the same time, an attempt to mine what is philosophically valuable in Nietzsche's ethics should not obscure his more repugnant claims, for example on the value of cruelty; and, in Chapter 6.5, I

---

[1] In Chapter 6.1, I summarize the six principal elements of the morality rejected by Nietzsche—i.e. I define the target at which he takes aim.

draw attention not only to their obvious inhumanity but also to the inescapable danger they pose to the success of Nietzsche's own ethic of 'life-enhancement'.

Finally, my third aim is to understand in more detail the *kinds* of arguments employed by Nietzsche to undermine the old morality and, moreover, to what extent they succeed in 'revaluing' its traditional values. In order to render this third task manageable, without sacrificing the detail that makes it useful, I have limited myself to a case study of the revaluation of just one traditional value, namely the value of truth. This is, however, central to Nietzsche's axiology; and though Nietzsche's conception of truth has received considerable attention in the secondary literature, his pathbreaking, and much more interesting, treatment of its value has, by comparison, been surprisingly neglected.

Part I addresses itself to the first two of these aims, while Part II is dedicated to the third.

This emphasis on Nietzsche's ethics is fully in keeping with his overriding concern with that subject. This concern has three grounds. First, flourishing is, for him, the only unconditioned end in relation to which the worth of all values, ends, practices, *and* concepts is to be judged. Thus, the life-value of a concept is always more important to him than its truth-value (e.g. *BGE*, 4). Second, many of our actual ethical projects and practices have, Nietzsche holds, done us terrible harm over more than two millennia—and we must therefore uncover both the reasons for our attraction to them and the guises in which they persist despite our conviction in their demise. And third, it is our 'highest' values that father our specific philosophical systems and not, as much of the 'tradition' would have it, vice versa (*BGE*, 6).[2] As a result, Nietzsche's thinking on a subject such as epistemology or metaphysics is driven by the question of what ethical values and practices its axioms proceed from and, in turn, promote—and cannot be otherwise understood. In short, to Nietzsche's famous pronouncement that 'only as an *aesthetic phenomenon*' is 'existence and the world . . . *justified*'[3] we might add that only as an ethical phenomenon can human life be *explained*.

---

[2] Throughout, I use the term 'value' to refer only to what Nietzsche calls our 'highest' values—those, such as truthfulness, pity, self-denial, and meekness, that have, for better or worse, endured (in some cases for millennia) and contribute to defining the identity of individuals or societies. By contrast, passing whims, needs, and wants, which in colloquial speech are, sometimes, also called 'values', are of little interest to him.

[3] See *BT*, 5 and 24.

1.1.2 *Approach to Part I*

In comparing Nietzsche's 'immoralism' with what he takes to be the principal features of traditional morality, as I attempt to do in Part I, I have paid particular attention to two points:

First, I have avoided the vague question: 'is Nietzsche rejecting one particular morality or all morality?', where it is seldom clear either what these terms denote or whether it is the author's definition of them or Nietzsche's that is under discussion. Instead, I address the question: 'what particular ethical concepts (or uses thereof) is Nietzsche rejecting or, by contrast, supporting?'. What is immediately obvious is that he is not rejecting all *ethics*—and that, for him, a worthwhile life must be disciplined by clear ends and the practices they demand.

Second, Nietzsche accepts many of the values, concepts, and attitudes which feature in traditional Christian or secular morality—such as 'altruism' and 'truthfulness', 'responsibility' and 'soul', 'asceticism' and 'guilt', 'pity' and 'god'—provided they can have life-enhancing functions. The case study of the value of truth in Part II is intended to illustrate this claim in detail.

Nonetheless, as will become apparent in the course of Part I, this notable absence of absolute repudiations from a philosopher who is often seen as a caricature of stridency does not rescue Nietzsche from a larger problem: namely, what philosophical principle or psychological process could he posit to justify his core assumption that the radical devaluation of temporality or 'becoming' necessarily results in the stifling of human flourishing and hence in what he calls 'descending' or '*décadent*' life? Nietzsche's concept of 'life-denial' clearly cannot be employed to justify this assumption without circularity, for it already employs that same assumption as a standard for determining what is life-denying (and life-enhancing). Moreover, he does not explain how his claim that cultural vitality is depressed by the devaluation of 'becoming' is to be squared with the obvious artistic creativity of historical Christendom.

Chapters 3, 4, and 5 effectively constitute a commentary on, respectively, the three parts of Nietzsche's *On the Genealogy of Morals*, perhaps his central ethical work and certainly his most closely argued. In Chapter 6, I summarize what I take to be the six key elements of the 'morality' which he rejects; and I suggest that 'becoming what one is' is the ideal which best embodies Nietzsche's new ethic.

1.1.3 Approach to Part II

In Part II, I choose one particular value—that of truth—for a detailed case study of just how Nietzsche's ethic differs from traditional morality, and thus of how he 'revalues' one of the latter's 'highest' values. I have chosen the value of truth for four reasons. First, for the old morality, this value is regarded both as constitutive of the Good and as vital to attaining it. Second, truth remains highly valued in Nietzsche's new ethic and, therefore, illustrates well the contrast between old and new. (Indeed, his seemingly paradoxical intent is to undermine the unconditional valuation of truth in order to be *more* truthful about its value.) Third, a commitment to truth is, for Nietzsche, the principal engine of the 'revaluation' of traditional values. For, on the one hand, it discredits what he sees as the essential postulate of the old morality—notably the idea that values and standards could have groundings that transcend time, contingency, and individual human needs and practices. And, on the other hand, it is central to confidence in a new ethic—i.e. to regarding it as 'life-enhancing' and its presuppositions as intelligible. Finally, until Nietzsche, the value of truth or truthfulness seems to have been taken for granted by religion and science,[4] rationalists and anti-rationalists alike. Even those who devalued science and reason and elevated art and unreason often did so on the grounds of 'science's' supposedly inferior access to the true and 'authentic'—i.e. in the name of truthfulness itself.

As to Nietzsche's conception of truth, I interpret this as basically empirical[5]—an interpretation warranted not so much by his terminally vague utterances on the nature of truth as by the fact that his entire genealogical project assumes that propositions about the life-value of our concepts, values, and practices can be true or false in a roughly conventional sense. Moreover, as I argue in Chapter 7.3 and 7.4, this interpretation is consistent with Nietzsche's 'perspectivism', with his belief that truth can be inaccessible (e.g. truth about the precise significance of our actions), and with his view that what we have called 'truth' is, sometimes, illusion (e.g. the postulates of Platonic metaphysics).

---

[4] Here, and henceforth in this book, 'science' is to be taken in the broadest sense of the disciplines encompassed by *Wissenschaft*.

[5] Empirical in the sense, outlined in Chapter 7.3–4, that what may be deemed 'true' is not simply dictated by convention, utility, or other 'impositions' of the knower, but is also disciplined by a world which is held to exist independently of actual knowers.

1.2 EXEGETICAL DIFFICULTIES

Nietzsche's works, whether by design or default, do not allow of uncontroversial interpretation. They obey, with singular fidelity, his own insistence that an artist cannot be mimetically represented, but only brought 'to life again'.[6] An interpretation of Nietzsche, more than of almost any other philosopher, should be prefixed by the word 'neo-', as it is inevitably both one-sided and readily pressed into the service of the perspective of a particular interpreter.

There are two main reasons for this exegetical difficulty. First, Nietzsche's *own* philosophy of 'perspectivism' invites and condones radically divergent interpretations (e.g. *GM*, III, 12). Second, there is the imprecision of his style: the short aphorisms, the joking and suggestiveness, the contradictions (less frequent than is sometimes supposed), the obsession with paradox—the latter sometimes prompting the defiant feeling that not everything dear to Western man can be an inversion, perversion, or repudiation of reality. Here one is not helped by Nietzsche's much-quoted assertion that profundity loves masks; for he often gives us no way of distinguishing his mask from his face. Nonetheless, Nietzsche's inconsistency and assertiveness constitute no decisive reason for dismissing him, both because, as Philippa Foot rightly observes,[7] there is a remarkable underlying unity to his writings, and because Nietzsche supplies us with a wealth of hypotheses and ideas which, even in their embryonic or sketchy form, enable us to look afresh at many of the deepest issues in ethics and psychology. Indeed, the ultimate reason for studying Nietzsche is, I suggest, to extract the new concepts and philosophical tools he bequeaths us, even if they are frequently unsystematic or inconsistent with one another.

To be sure, some Nietzschean terms, such as 'will to power', '*Übermensch*', 'self-overcoming', and 'Eternal Return', are exegetical minefields which cannot be crossed with any great confidence. But in, for example, his conception of 'value', of the 'sovereign' and the 'reactive', of 'free will', of 'bad conscience', of the 'ascetic ideal', of what it means to move 'beyond good and evil', and of the value of

---

[6] *HAH*, 126, under 'Assorted Opinions and Maxims'.

[7] Philippa Foot, 'Nietzsche's Immoralism', in R. Schacht (ed.), *Nietzsche, Genealogy, Morality: Essays on Nietzsche's* Genealogy of Morals (Berkeley and Los Angeles: University of California Press, 1994), 3.

truth in an age of '*décadence*', Nietzsche does, I will argue, provide philosophically useful nuggets, supported by arguments,[8] which can be extracted from the texts with a considerable degree of confidence. And, essentially, my ambition here is selectively to mine just such nuggets, rather than to seek a coherent interpretation which aspires to see off all exegetical challenges.

[8] Nietzsche does not, in general, take Rorty's view (e.g. when speaking of traditional concerns like the nature of truth) that we should '*say* little about these topics, and see how we get on' or that '[i]nteresting philosophy is rarely an examination of the pros and cons of a thesis' (Richard Rorty, *Contingency, Irony, and Solidarity* (Cambridge: Cambridge University Press, 1989), 8–9). Nietzsche's distaste for 'refutations' is more a lack of interest in final, logical disproofs directed at traditional epistemological problems; but he is very much interested in 'pros and cons' in ethical matters—such as the value to us of our values.

2

Foundations: Nietzsche's Conception of Values

Nietzsche's conception of the nature, function, and grounding of values is the cornerstone of his whole approach to ethics. To elucidate that conception—and related concepts, especially 'will' and 'power'—is crucial to understanding both his criticism of traditional morality and the ethic which he espouses in its place.

2.1 THE NATURE AND FUNCTION OF VALUES

There are three essential points about Nietzsche's conception of a value:

1. Values—that is, the 'highest values' that concern Nietzsche—are 'physiological demands for the preservation of a certain type of life' (*BGE*, 3)—or, as he puts it in a passage from the *Nachlass* that excellently, albeit cumbersomely, sums up his published views: 'The standpoint of "value" is the standpoint of conditions of preservation and enhancement for complex forms of relative life-duration within the flux of becoming' (*WP*, 715).

There are two main points here: that value is a 'standpoint' (roughly, its subjective nature), and that it is a 'demand' or 'condition' (roughly, its objective nature).

That valuing is a 'standpoint' means, as Heidegger observes,[1] that it takes the world in a particular way, both in the sense of seeing and of the thing seen—i.e. both in the sense of a particular way of seeing the world, and in the sense of a particular aspect of the world seen. It is, in other words, imbued with the 'perspectivism' which, for Nietzsche, informs all perception and cognition—'perspectivism' denoting the partial (in both senses of the word: i.e. desire- or value-laden and

---

[1] See Martin Heidegger, 'The Word of Nietzsche: "God is Dead" ', in *The Question Concerning Technology and Other Essays*, trans. William Lovitt (New York: Harper & Row, 1977), 72.

incomplete) perspectives and understanding which we necessarily have of everything in the world.[2]

Moreover, that a ('highest') value is a 'demand' or 'condition' means that it is in no sense an arbitrary whim. Nietzsche underlines this point by describing these demands as 'physiological'—a word often used by him to denote what is stubbornly factual about life and human beings, what can only be falsified or ignored or revalued, but never eradicated as a presence. Indeed, a value, on this definition, is objective in perhaps the most interesting sense of that term: namely, as a *necessary condition* for the success of a particular type of life (and thus of the 'type' of person suited to that life). In other words, values are objective in that each type of life—such as the musical, the philosophical, or the religious—is, when successful, empirically correlated to particular 'highest' values. This empirical correlation is, in Nietzsche's metaphor, like the relationship of a tree to its fruit: 'our values, our yeas and nays . . . grow out of us with the necessity with which a tree bears fruit . . . evidence of *one* will, *one* health, *one* soil . . . ' (*GM*, P, 2).

If, for Nietzsche, values correlate to facts about the type of person one is, then he can be nothing like an 'Emotivist'.[3] Even where he makes Emotivist-sounding statements, like 'moralities are . . . merely a *sign language of the affects*' (*BGE*, 187), the important point is that the (ruling) affects are not arbitrary impulses, but 'tell a story' about the type of person that nature, nurture, and life-circumstances have made one and the type(s) of life to which one is therefore suited. Thus, a person's 'morality bears decided and decisive witness to *who he is*—that is, in what order of rank the innermost drives of his nature stand in relation to each other' (*BGE*, 6; cf. *A*, 57). In short: Nietzsche is an ethical naturalist, in that he correlates (but in no sense reduces) ethical values, motivations, and practices to pre-ethical facts about the human beings who espouse them—facts which, importantly, extend beyond the nature or 'types' of these individuals to include the crucial circumstances of chance and neces-

---

[2] 'There is *only* a perspective seeing, *only* a perspective "knowing" . . . ' (*GM*, III, 12). I return to the relation between valuing and perspectivism in Chapter 7.3.1.

[3] This empirical correlation is missed even by such a subtle author as Alasdair MacIntyre when he characterizes Nietzsche as an Emotivist in *After Virtue: A Study in Moral Theory* (2nd edn., London: Duckworth, 1985), 22. It is also not properly captured by those who regard as quintessentially Nietzschean the idea that 'there is nothing, either good or bad, but thinking makes it so' (Shakespeare, *Hamlet*, Act II, Scene ii), such as J. P. Stern in *Nietzsche* (London: Fontana Press, 1978), 60.

sity and thus historical context within which they have to live their lives and seek their goods. And this empirical correlation can, of course, only be established *ex post* by examining the lives of individuals, or communities, or even whole epochs, and attempting to understand the effects of their actual ethical values and practices. Nietzsche measures these effects in terms of his standard of 'life-enhancement' (or its opposite, 'life-denial')—terms that are explicated in Chapter 3. His attempt to explain the ethical in terms of the pre-ethical is conducted, as we will see, by means of 'genealogies' (fictional or real) of ethical practices and the various ends that they are 'interpreted' as serving.

2. As is well known, Nietzsche explicitly connects valuing and the seeking or attainment of power. For example: 'Values and their changes are related to increases in the power of those positing the values' (*WP*, 14). Even the life-denying ascetic ideal is merely a means for gaining power over life (*GM*, III, 13). In general, *all* attempts to exert power presuppose an 'interpretation', informed by one's values, that gives purpose and justification to a particular way of securing power: 'all events in the organic world are a subduing, a *becoming master*, and all subduing and becoming master involves a fresh interpretation' (*GM*, II, 12).[4] There are three points worth noting here. First, scientific or philosophical theorizing is not, on this account, the only form of mastery that involves interpretation: political authority, individual self-control, and even artistic forms all presuppose, and, in that sense, are, particular interpretations of the world. Second, there is no hard-and-fast distinction between interpretation and action: the one always involves the other. Third, Nietzsche does not mean that all power, and hence all human transactions, involve *exploitation*. For Nietzsche's notion of power is very broad, meaning essentially 'form-giving' (e.g. *GM*, II, 18), i.e. the in-forming of 'becoming' (which, for him, characterizes all events, desires, and the like) with structure and organization. Indeed, this imposition of value-laden form upon 'becoming'—i.e. upon the ungraspable complexity of actions and events in their actual historical setting—is given a name by Nietzsche: 'will to power'. And our 'highest' forms have for us the splendour and eternal value that we

---

[4] The absolute identity between interpretation and power is even clearer in the original German, where Nietzsche says that 'alles Überwältigen und Herr-werden ein Neu-Interpretieren, ein Zurechtmachen ist'. The 'ist' is, of course, the 'is' of identity, a better rendering of Nietzsche's meaning than Kaufmann's 'involves'.

call 'Being': 'To impose upon Becoming the character of Being—that is the supreme will to power' (*WP*, 617).[5]

'Being', here, is whatever is, for us, supremely valuable, splendid, and powerful; no metaphysical assumptions are made about its permanence or its distinctness from 'becoming'. It is free, in other words, of what Nietzsche takes to be the traditional philosophical supposition that '[w]hatever has being does not become' and 'whatever becomes does not have being' (*TI*, III, 1). In sum, 'will to power' denotes the securing of power over the world and, to that extent, it is expressed through the valuing and interpretation that characterize all (human) life. Or, as Zarathustra puts it in his typically oracular manner: 'A tablet of the good hangs over every people. Behold, it is the tablet of their overcomings; behold, it is the voice of their will to power' (*Z*, I, 15).[6]

3. Finally, these conditions for the preservation and enhancement of life that Nietzsche calls 'values' can be considered at three levels of ascending generality: the purely individual (Nietzsche's ultimate concern), 'types' of people (for example, the 'philosopher' or the 'artist'), and the human in general. In the second category, we find, for example, that asceticism is crucial to the philosopher's success (*GM*, III, 7); and in the third that prolonged discipline is necessary for any human flourishing. Indeed, Nietzsche calls discipline a 'moral [i.e. universal] imperative of nature' (*BGE*, 188)—for imposing which he is even prepared to praise Christianity (*BGE*, 188 and 263). Discipline, he insists, is a value common to every successful ethic.[7]

Nietzsche's emphasis on the universal value of discipline suggests two points. First, it confirms that he does not object to seeing one's values as universally valuable, where one considers them essential to

---

[5] This citation is much employed by Heidegger in his discussion of 'Will to Power' as a 'metaphysical' doctrine. (See Martin Heidegger, *Nietzsche*, ed. David Farrell Krell (San Francisco: Harper & Row, 1979–87; reprinted as HarperCollins Paperback edn., 1991), vols. i–iv; for example, i. 19–20, ii. 201–4, and iii. 156–7 and 245–6.) My use of it does not reflect agreement with, or even adequate understanding of, Heidegger's discussion, and I concur with Krell's comments on the latter in ii. 257 n. 2.

[6] Note that all references to chapters of *Thus Spoke Zarathustra* follow the abbreviations used in the contents pages of Kaufmann's translation.

[7] Jaspers emphasizes that Nietzsche's whole attack on conventional morality (or moralities) is undertaken 'not in order to remove men's chains, but rather to force men, *under a heavier burden*, to attain to a higher rank'. (Karl Jaspers, *Nietzsche: An Introduction to the Understanding of his Philosophical Activity*, trans. Charles F. Wallraff and Frederick J. Schmitz (Tucson, Ariz.: University of Arizona Press, 1965), 140—my italics.)

any human flourishing—an observation which, though hardly surprising, is worth making in view of the widespread opinion that Nietzsche opposes all universalization. (By contrast, universalization is, in no sense, constitutive of a value for Nietzsche; and universal prescriptivity in a Kantian sense, far from being a logical or necessary feature of a morality, is, for him, itself merely another value— of interest to those who seek to rein in the strong and dissolve the unique.)

Second, though values, for him, clearly cannot be disinterested (*BGE*, 220)—any supposedly 'impartial' standards being, from a psychological point of view, merely value-laden products of the lust for permanence and, from a philosophical point of view, wholly unintelligible—the pursuit of one's 'highest' values may well require the suspension or suppression of interests, desires, or perspectives that interfere with them. The motive for this disciplined disinterest—i.e. the motive for the 'higher' values that demand it—is, of course, thoroughly interested, which is why, for Nietzsche, the concerns of a morality are always the highest and strictest form of prudence.

2.2 'WILL'

Nietzsche's definition of 'the supreme will to power', which we cited above, has a notable feature: that 'will to power' is presented as the *achievement* of stamping Becoming with the character of Being—not as the *intention* of doing so. In other words, 'will to power' is the securing of power over the world, not a 'striving for power', where the 'striving' and the 'power' are related as cause and effect.

This distinction is crucial, not only for explicating the concept of 'will to power' but for the wider reason that it reflects Nietzsche's repudiation of the dualism of will and its effect, of actor and his action, thinker and his thought, subject and its property. These pairs are all products of the 'atomistic need' (*BGE*, 12; cf. *GM*, I, 13)— i.e. the need for enduring continuants and constants which we construe in order to avoid the pain of 'becoming', flux, change, and extinction;[8] and Nietzsche's rejection of them collectively is a paradigmatic example of the way he thinks in terms of 'families' of

---

[8] But what is this 'securing of power' and how is it to be identified if there is, as it were, no 'securer'? How, in other words, does Nietzsche propose that we escape the 'ownership' function of the concept of 'subject' or 'self'? I only raise this question here, but do not attempt to answer it.

concepts united by a certain (ultimately ethical) *function* to which they are all dedicated. The 'will' in will to power is, therefore, not a *causa sui* that is the efficient cause of our actions and can be known by direct introspection, as it is in certain traditional religious and philosophical accounts;[9] it is simply a term that denotes 'something *complicated*, something that is a unit only as a word' (*BGE*, 19). That 'something' is actually a whole 'complex of sensation and thinking' which, in its detailed make-up, is largely unknowable (ibid.). We can refer to it, however, because it is permeated by 'a ruling thought' (though the latter cannot be detached from the willing 'as if any will would then remain over') and is experienced epiphenomenally as the 'affect of the command' (ibid.; cf. *GS*, 347). Similarly, 'freedom of the will' is merely the epiphenomenal 'affect of superiority in relation to him who must obey' (*BGE*, 19): it is the joyful consciousness of being at the stronger, and hence commanding, end of a gradient of force. The traditional conception of 'free will' essentially misinterprets this commanding as brought about by the deliberate causal agency of willing, and as exemplifying (or presupposing) absolute 'freedom'.

In sum, what has been called a 'free' will is simply a strong will, and what has (equally absurdly) been called an 'unfree' will is actually a weak will (*BGE*, 21): 'The "unfree will" is mythology; in real life it is only a matter of *strong* and *weak* wills' (ibid.). The idea of a deliberate causal agency of willing that could, as it were, have 'done otherwise' in any given situation is, Nietzsche suggests, invented by traditional morality because it greatly enhances the possibility of blame;[10] whereas his conception of willing, while it allocates an ethically indispensable role to responsibility, guilt, and blame, does so in quite a different manner, which we will explore in Chapter 4 (especially sections 4.2.4 and 4.4). Thus, Nietzsche, as it were, takes all the way one aspect of Kant's revolutionary picture of human beings—that which sees them as natural objects determined by other natural objects and thus, ultimately, by their own history; while he naturalizes the other aspect—that of free agents transcending the phenomenal order—eliminating Kant's metaphysical understanding of freedom, autonomy, and will,[11] to leave a con-

---

[9] For example, Schopenhauer's (*BGE*, 19).

[10] Bernard Williams emphasizes this point in his 'Nietzsche's Minimalist Moral Psychology', in Schacht (ed.), *Nietzsche, Genealogy, Morality*, 237–51.

[11] Indeed, stripping away the metaphysics from Kant's conceptions of freedom, autonomy, and will helps one to realize just how much Nietzsche's own conception of this trio owes to Kant (with, in key respects, Schopenhauer as intermediary). For an interesting

ception of the free person as one able to master, in virtue of a sufficiently strong set of dominating drives, all distractions to 'promising himself'—distractions which crucially include *ressentiment* and the moral values it generates, notably pity. These claims will be elaborated in detail in Chapters 3 and 4, but the point now is to show how the conception of willing presupposed by 'will to power' is quite opposed, in Nietzsche's view, to that presupposed by morality—and thus how 'will to power' is basic to Nietzsche's 'immoralism'.

2.3 'POWER'

In discussing Nietzsche's conception of value (and 'will to power') thus far, we have actually employed the term 'power' in two distinct ways, which Nietzsche himself does not explicitly distinguish and which are easily conflated. They are: power as an explanatory concept; and power as a standard of value. 'Will to power' is, I suggest, the concept that unites the explanatory and the valuational ways in which 'power' is used in Nietzsche's philosophy.[12]

The explanatory claim is that the drive for power accounts for all our settled values and urges, including those that are self-effacing, self-denying, or self-destructive; in other words, that psychology is to be understood 'as morphology and *the doctrine of the development of the will to power*' (*BGE*, 23). This claim seems to go together with what looks like an essentialist, but ultimately obscure, view that will to power is 'the essence of life' (*GM*, II, 12), that 'life itself is *will to power*' (*BGE*, 13), that we inhabit 'a world whose essence is will to power' (*BGE*, 186; cf. *WP*, 1067).[13]

The valuational claim says that (for Nietzsche) power is a standard of value. Thus, when Nietzsche asks 'What is good?', he answers:

perspective on Nietzsche's 'German' version of autonomy and its relationship to 'modernity', and specifically on his Kantian dimension, see Robert B. Pippin, *Modernism as a Philosophical Problem* (Oxford: Basil Blackwell, 1991), esp. chapter 4. Yet, though Nietzsche stands with one foot firmly on the post-Kantian ground of 'autonomy', with the other he is on ancient territory—a point to which I return in Chapter 10.1.1.

[12] I illustrate the explanatory use of 'will to power' in Chapter 5 (especially 5.2–3), using the 'ascetic ideal' as my main example, while I treat the valuational use in Chapter 3 (especially 3.1–2) through a discussion of Nietzsche's standard of 'life-enhancement'.

[13] 'Will to power' seems unintelligible unless its extension is restricted to *human* valuing, acting, and psychology—a restriction which only some of Nietzsche's references to this concept evince (e.g. *BGE*, 13 and 23; *WP*, 254, 681, 688).

'Everything that heightens the feeling of power in man, the will to power, power itself' (*A*, 2). And in the *Nachlass* he adds: 'The ascent on this scale [of force] represents every rise in value . . . ' (*WP*, 710).

These distinctions immediately raise two important questions: first, how are these uses of the term 'power' related? And second, does the seeming essentialism of Nietzsche's concept of 'will to power' contradict his tirade against metaphysics in general and the 'thing-in-itself' in particular? (And is it therefore inconsistent with his doctrine of 'perspectivism'?)

As to the first question, Nietzsche's espousal of power as a 'highest' value is grounded not in his perception of the basic character of human valuations as evincing a drive for power—i.e. in the 'explanatory' claim about power—but rather, like all valuation, in 'physiological' conditions for the preserving or flourishing of a particular kind of person or life (in this case, Nietzsche's own). This means that, in one sense, his ethics is unencumbered by a 'fact/value' distinction—i.e. insofar as facts about a 'type' of person or life correlate empirically to a corresponding set of values that will preserve just such a type (so that such facts function as explanations for espousing the corresponding values or as reasons for acting in the ways endorsed by those values). But, in another sense, he cannot overcome a 'fact/value' distinction: for the 'fact' that, say, an individual seeks power (or possesses any other motivation, such as seeking comfort) does not entail that maximizing power (or that other motivational goal) will be one of his or her 'highest' values. (Thus, Schopenhauer can regard the striving 'will' or human suffering as a universal fact, but this does not entail that he values its maximization: the contrary is, of course, the case.) This latter point is very important in reading Nietzsche: for we must beware of attributing to him the assumption that 'life-enhancing' values necessarily affirm how the world actually is, in the sense, for example, that power must be a highest value if the striving for power is a universal feature of human life; or, conversely, that values which deny how the world actually is necessarily deny life. Indeed, we will see (especially in Part II) that Nietzsche regards error and falsification as often essential to a flourishing life and that, in principle, he only opposes the way 'morality' falsifies or denies the world's basic character insofar as such falsification or denial results in an impoverished life. (In practice, however, he, too, sometimes seems prone to assume erroneously that if values or beliefs radically falsify or deny the world—for example, those structured metaphysically—they necessarily impoverish life.[14])

Turning now to the second question—whether the essentialism of 'will to power' contradicts Nietzsche's opposition to metaphysics in general and the 'thing-in-itself' or innate essences in particular—I do not believe it does. For 'will to power' makes no appeal to essence as something entirely *distinct* from its qualities or effects, namely in being unconditioned and featureless. Instead, 'will to power' is essentialist in quite a different sense, namely in being a proposition on which Nietzsche expects unanimous agreement among those whose perspectives are not distorted by the illusions of 'morality' which, as he sees it, aim to deny just such a claim. And, we should note, 'perspectivism' is essentialist in exactly the same way—i.e. that, from Nietzsche's perspective, *any* agent not under the sway of such illusions (e.g. that there is wholly impartial truth or reason) will identify perspectivism as essential to explanations of *all* human cognition, valuing, and judging.

That, as a claim to truth, 'perspectivism' cannot itself be more than a perspective does not count as an objection to the main point I am making here—i.e. that there are some items that, according to Nietzsche, would be seen (as true or existing) from any perspective that did not seek to 'devalue' life, power, or 'the world'; and, by contrast, that there are other items where such consensus could not be expected—for example, the 'truths about "woman as such"' that Nietzsche insists are only '*my* truths' (*BGE*, 231). The class of items on which Nietzsche seems to expect unanimity from those not in the grip of errors fostered by 'morality' embraces the core group of interlinked concepts that is needed to explicate 'will to power': notably 'valuing', 'will', 'power', 'rank order' (of 'souls' or 'types'), and, of course, 'perspectivism'. Indeed, one of Nietzsche's principal reasons for valuing truth is, as I will argue in Chapter 10, precisely to sweep away those falsifications of reality that obstruct such unanimity and that are integral to 'morality'. Sweeping them away is, therefore, part and parcel of the project to 'overcome' morality.

---

[14] This erroneous assumption—in effect, that world-denial is necessarily life-denying or, conversely, that life-enhancement necessarily presupposes world-affirmation (see e.g. *BGE*, 56)—is taken up again in Chapters 5.5, 6.4, and 10.5.

2.4 THE HISTORICAL DETERMINATION OF VALUES

The foregoing discussion leads to a crucial point about the individual's 'will to power': namely, that he cannot 'choose' the values it expresses, except within narrow bounds and in a restricted sense of 'choosing'.

The narrow bounds follow from Nietzsche's proposition that an individual's possible values are limited by the particular 'type' of person he is—that 'his morality bears decided and decisive witness to *who he is*' (*BGE*, 6). The restricted sense of 'choosing' follows from Nietzsche's deterministic conception of 'willing'. Both these ideas have already been mentioned in this chapter.

Thus, the range of values we are capable of pursuing expresses the 'type' of person we are—our 'nobility', our 'strength', our 'taste', our capacity for 'discipline', and other features which subsequent chapters will enlarge upon. And the type of person we are is simply a given: it is a function of nature, nurture, and life-circumstances and so, for Nietzsche, of unfathomably complex historical conditioning (to which he often gives the name 'breeding'[15]). Our nature is that inner 'granite of spiritual *fatum*' which sets for us certain 'predetermined . . . questions' that guide our thoughts and actions, and which disposes us to 'predetermined . . . answer[s]' (*BGE*, 231). Nurture (when sufficiently prolonged and powerful) is, according to Nietzsche's Lamarckian manner of thinking, actually one with nature, since it inscribes itself into our inherited characteristics: thus, '[o]ne cannot erase from the soul of a human being what his ancestors liked most to do and did most constantly' (*BGE*, 264). For example, an enduring morality is one form of nurture whose power accumulates as a result of '*obedience* over a long period of time and in a *single* direction' (*BGE*, 188). Finally, the decisive life-circumstances are, in the main, those that bring about (or refer back to) great suffering and so *demand* a response from the individual.[16]

These constraints of nature, nurture, and decisive life-circumstances constitute a broad personal *telos* that limits us to a certain range of

[15] For example, Nietzsche asks whether to 'breed an animal *with the right to make promises* . . . is not . . . the real problem regarding man' (*GM*, II, 1). Here, the 'breeding' is, in keeping with Nietzsche's Lamarckism, the result not merely of selective propagation, but also of training and the life-circumstances that further it (notably socialization, as we will discuss in Chapter 4.2.2 and 4.2.4).

[16] Thus, Nietzsche says of '*great* suffering' that 'only *this* discipline has created all enhancements of man so far' (*BGE*, 225; cf. *BGE*, 270, and *TI*, IX, 38).

possible values and 'destinies'.[17] This range is fixed (which is why Nietzsche finds the idea, associated with some forms of relativism, that there is *nothing* binding about values beyond the force of local conventions as 'childish' as the traditional moral conviction that worthwhile values must be *universally* binding—*GS*, 345). But which particular values we pursue from within this predetermined stock is driven by the circumstances of life. Among these circumstances is, we should note, the encountering—whether sought or fortuitous—of reasons, truth, and learning that have a bearing on our 'choice' of values. That reason or truth or learning 'changes us' is not only explicitly stated by Nietzsche (e.g. *BGE*, 231); it is implicit in his whole genealogical project, with its expectation that if we see *why* we pursue the valuations, practices, and assumptions that we do, the latter will either be confirmed—though perhaps *'for other reasons than hitherto'* (*D*, 103)—or else undermined. Moreover, reasons, truth, and learning—about the real functions of our values—are crucial motors of the millennial 'revaluation of all values' so dramatically predicted and advocated by Nietzsche.[18] Thus, to claim *either* that he is an 'irrationalist', who diagnoses or wishes to see all human decisions as purely impulsive and as lacking any form of reckoning, *or* that his determinism is incompatible with a central role for reason (and hence deliberation) in the outcome of moral choices, would be essentially to misunderstand his whole philosophical project.[19]

But, one surmises, reason and truth can be so powerful only because we are receptive to them in three ways. The first is that we have a prior general commitment to truth as a 'highest' value. This commitment to truth is not fortuitous—both because, like any 'highest' value, it must

---

[17] J. Ibanez-Noe discusses the notion of a *telos* in Nietzsche's thinking, in 'Nietzsche and the Problem of Teleology', *International Studies in Philosophy*, 29/3 (1997), 37–48.

[18] For a useful study of the scope of this revaluation, see E. E. Sleinis, *Nietzsche's Revaluation of Values: A Study in Strategies* (Urbana, Ill.: University of Illinois Press, 1994).

[19] Nietzsche's allowance of such a role for reason and, as I argue in Chapter 7.3–5, for truth-claims that are a property of sentences that perspectively describe, and are revisable by, a world 'out there' is only one aspect of his work; another is, of course, his passionate critique of the idea of rooting values (and moral obligations) in a conception of reason that lies beyond contingency. These two aspects of his work may set up the kind of dilemma for Nietzsche to which Habermas refers when he says that Nietzsche's 'theory of power cannot satisfy the claim to scientific objectivity and, at the same time, put into effect the program of a total and hence self-referential critique of reason that also affects the truth of theoretical propositions' (Jürgen Habermas, *The Philosophical Discourse of Modernity*, trans. Frederick Lawrence (Cambridge, Mass.: MIT Press, 1987), 104–5). I will not, however, pursue the implications of this dilemma here.

be a condition for our enhancement or preservation as individuals if we are genuinely to espouse it and because, in the particular case of the value of truth, it has been 'bred' into us over two millennia by our two philosophically dominant traditions: the Socratic-Platonic and the Judaeo-Christian. In other words, the authority of a value (or the 'interpretations' that give voice to it) is inescapable if, in general, the ethical tradition in which one is located[20] and, in particular, the type of person one is strongly predispose one to it. The second type of receptivity is that we have *specific* drives and needs which will be satisfied by acting in the ways suggested by *just those* reasons—in other words, that we have what Bernard Williams calls 'internal reasons'[21] for choosing as we do from our range of possible values. (Obviously Nietzsche makes no appeal to any dispassionate process of practical reasoning—i.e. one that appeals to rules that are taken as unconditioned by our needs and interests.) And the third is that we possess the strength to choose—remembering that, for Nietzsche, choosing depends not on a 'free will' as *causa prima* (which is a fiction), but on a *strong* will (*BGE*, 21). Now all three types of receptivity are, in turn, products of the nature, nurture, and previous circumstances that have made us what we are—in short, of our individual history. That individual history is, in turn, indissolubly conditioned by its membership in a particular ethical community with a particular history—a point underlined by two central Nietzschean presuppositions: that the individual self (just like any object) can be intelligibly conceived only as a collection of qualities that lacks anything like a metaphysical continuant standing outside history or time; and that every quality is linked, directly or indirectly, to every other, with the result that the self or an object *is*, in a crucial sense, its history.

In other words, the past, on this line of thinking, overwhelmingly determines both the menu of possible values we could pursue and the actual values that we do 'choose'.[22] We are therefore not free to change 'at will' our highest values, or the 'interpretations' that they

---

[20] Nietzsche's conception of the power of ethical tradition, and especially of our Socratic inheritance, is illuminatingly explored by Randall Havas in *Nietzsche's Genealogy: Nihilism and the Will to Knowledge* (Ithaca, NY: Cornell University Press, 1995).

[21] Bernard Williams, 'Internal and External Reasons', in *Moral Luck: Philosophical Papers 1973–80* (Cambridge: Cambridge University Press, 1981), 101–13.

[22] See, for example, *TI*, where Nietzsche says that the individual is 'the whole single line of humanity up to himself' and castigates modern man for lacking 'the will to tradition, to authority' (see *TI*, IX, 33 and 39 respectively).

express; and the idea that we can do so through great moments of choice of a conventionally voluntaristic nature (or, perhaps, of an Existentialist sort, enacted by a freely self-determining consciouness that is unconditioned by anything, even its own past), is, for Nietzsche, nonsense.[23] All such change is the outcome of deep-rooted and largely subconscious drives acting over a long period, rather than of voluntary conscious decisions.[24] (We are, as Nietzsche memorably puts it, 'in the phase of modesty of consciousness'—*WP*, 676; cf. *GS*, 354–5.) Indeed, even 'rational thought', he says, 'is interpretation according to a scheme *that we cannot throw off*' (*WP*, 522—my italics). In short, Nietzsche espouses a kind of secular Calvinism, a broad 'predestination' of souls, according to their particular history and rank (see, for example, *A*, 57), which leaves little room for the individual to do anything about his inherited weaknesses, unless aided by decisive life-circumstances—prominent among which, in this epoch of *décadence*, is the encountering of Nietzsche's own genealogies.[25]

Now maximally to affirm, through the kind of life we lead, the reality of our nature, nurture, and life-circumstances, and hence of our individual past, is, for Nietzsche, not the antithesis of personal freedom but its precondition. 'Freedom of the will'—which, for him, means mastery of ourselves and thus of circumstances—is unattainable without maximally expressing what he calls the 'necessity'[26] of our own nature. Moreover, to develop the self-discipline to 'promise' ourselves, and so to live out our highest axiological allegiances, however hard the truths and tasks they entail, is also to be self-responsible (*GM*, II, 2).

---

[23] Thus, it is, I submit, a serious error for a distinguished thinker, like Kolakowski, to see Nietzsche as an Existentialist who 'proclaims that man can liberate himself totally, from everything, can free himself of tradition and of all pre-existing sense, and that all sense can be decreed by arbitrary whim' (Leszek Kolakowski, *Modernity on Endless Trial* (Chicago: University of Chicago Press, 1990), 72). Indeed, it is a principal theme of this book that, for Nietzsche, the attempt to free oneself 'totally' from one's history or 'type' is not only doomed to fail, but is undesirable because it denies reality in precisely the way in which traditional 'morality' seeks to (e.g. *A*, 15).

[24] Graham Parkes discusses the subconscious nature of drives in *Composing the Soul: Reaches of Nietzsche's Psychology* (Chicago: University of Chicago Press, 1994), esp. 293–9.

[25] For a valuable explication of Nietzsche's determinism and how it sits with his individualism, see Richard Schacht, *Nietzsche* (London: Routledge & Kegan Paul, 1983), esp. 304–12 and 335–8.

[26] *BGE*, 213. See also *TI*, V, 'Morality as Anti-Nature'; *TI*, VI, 'The Four Great Errors', especially section 8, where Nietzsche talks about the 'fatality of [one's] essence', that '[o]ne is necessary, one is a piece of fatefulness'. This is also what Zarathustra calls 'my *own* necessity' (*Z*, III, 12, section 30).

By contrast, when we resent and oppose that necessity—for example, by seeking (an imaginary) freedom from, or transcendence of, it—we are unfree and irresponsible. For Nietzsche, a decisive feature of morality is to deny our determination by history—not, as it were, through a simple misunderstanding, but through its central ambition to transcend temporality and suffering, an ambition which demands an absolute and unhistorical grounding for human life and ethics.[27]

In other words, whether or not Nietzsche regards history in general and an individual's history in particular as contingent (in that they comprise series of events that could have been otherwise),[28] the important point is that *for us*, who are conditioned by them, they constitute 'necessity' (in that they determine the reality of our nature, nurture, and life-circumstances). Thus, what may be contingent as one's history is necessity as one's fate; and only by maximally expressing—i.e. 'willing'—that necessity can one be free.[29]

This account of our highest values as determined by our individual history, rather than by 'free will', and of freedom as willing, rather than escaping, the 'necessity' expressed by that history, has a seemingly problematical consequence: namely that if that history happens to determine, in an individual or culture (such as ours), precisely the moral values which Nietzsche opposes, then he seems, perversely, to demand that we should 'will', rather than repudiate, those very values—i.e. that we should enthusiastically confirm what he regards as a life-denying ethic. In fact, this seeming problem holds the clue to how Nietzsche thinks morality will be 'overcome': for the answer is that only by *really willing*—i.e. living out—the values of morality can the latter's life-denying functions become apparent to us, and thus serve as reasons for their own abandonment, in just the way that, as I will show, only a genuine commitment to valuing truth unconditionally enables those who espouse this key value of morality to discover that such unconditionality is inimical to flourishing. Moreover, the standards against which the functions of 'morality' will be found inimical to flourishing may well be drawn from morality itself—again,

---

[27] For example, Nietzsche criticizes the 'Egypticism' of the philosophers' 'lack of historical sense' (*TI*, III, 1).

[28] His doctrine of 'Eternal Return' clearly suggests uncontingency; but it is unclear whether he posits it as a cosmological theory or simply hypothetically, as a test of life-enhancement.

[29] For an excellent formulation of this point and how it is made in *Thus Spoke Zarathustra*, see Peter Berkowitz, *Nietzsche: The Ethics of an Immoralist* (Cambridge, Mass.: Harvard University Press, 1995), 208–10.

in just the way that the unconditionality of the 'will to truth' is, as I will show, found wanting by its own standard of truthfulness. In other words, even if one's history has bequeathed one a life-denying ethic, it is only by uncompromisingly willing that ethic—i.e. in Nietzsche's terms, by 'becoming what one is'—that one can 'overcome' it. This means that, just as one's inheritance of an ethic is the product of a certain history, so one's 'overcoming' of it can only occur at a particular historical moment—i.e. one at which that ethic has been sufficiently lived through for its nature to become overwhelmingly apparent to the individuals or cultures which espouse it.[30] As a result, the particular set of values and practices that is denoted by the term 'morality' can be overcome neither at just any time in the history of morality, nor simply at the behest of a philosopher like Nietzsche, but only by an epoch that has really made them its own—that has, to use Nietzsche's terminology, really 'willed' its own 'necessity'. Thus, to the extent that the modern scientific spirit is, far from being incompatible with religious morality, actually an extreme refinement of that morality's ascetic idealism, modern science has, in just this sense, really made the essence of morality its own—and so has laid the basis for the overcoming of morality.

2.5 AFFIRMING THE NECESSITY OF HISTORY: THE VALUE OF TRUTH

As I have just indicated, Nietzsche's paradoxical suggestion is that morality is overcome only by being affirmed. Specifically, what he finds most 'life-denying' about morality—its espousal of the unconditioned (and thus of the anti-historical and non-perspectival)[31]—is overcome only by affirming unconditionally one of morality's highest values, namely that of truth. By doing so, one comes to see the falsity of, *inter alia*, two crucial presuppositions of morality, as Nietzsche sees them: first, that highest values (including that of truth itself) can be unconditioned by the specific history and needs of the individual and, second, that values construed as unconditioned can

---

[30] Again, this point owes much to discussions with Bernard Williams and to Randall Havas's *Nietzsche's Genealogy*.

[31] Nietzsche's rejection of the unconditional may be found in, for example, *BGE*, 30, 31, and 198, and *A*, 11. But it applies only to himself and others capable of significant life-enhancement; and to that extent his rejection of the unconditional is not itself unconditional (see e.g. *BGE*, 61; *WP*, 287, 894). I return to this point in Chapter 8.1.1.

be conducive to human flourishing. And I want to suggest that, for Nietzsche, the *primary*—and indispensable—value of truth lies in the 'negative' task of clearing away those falsehoods perpetrated by morality that, in his view, obstruct our capacity to live by a 'life-enhancing' ethic, rather than to fulfil the 'positive' role of defining the good and choosing our values. Though Nietzsche's philosophy leaves open such 'positive' roles for practical reason—for example, in guiding our insight into the possible goods prescribed or licensed by our nature, nurture, and circumstances, in helping us to choose between these possible goods or to arrange them into a hierarchy, and in guiding our thoughts and actions towards accomplishing them—such deliberation can, in general, only be one influence among the many which, together, determine which values we actually pursue, whether explicitly or implicitly. Moreover, as I will argue, Nietzsche is distinctly sceptical of the value of attempting to understand exactly who we are or to devise blueprints for our 'self-realization'. This is partly because it is impossible to know what is best in us as individuals (*BGE*, 249);[32] partly because it is impossible to judge the ethical significance of our individual actions (e.g. *GS*, 335); and partly because self-knowledge can actually obstruct self-realization.[33]

Now in the specific case of the value of truth, overcoming morality presents a double (apparent) paradox. The first paradox is that the moral attitude to the value of truth—i.e. that the value of truth is unconditioned—is overcome, Nietzsche suggests, by affirming that very attitude. For to be unconditionally truthful about the value of truth is to conclude that, since we need much untruth, truth is *not*, in fact, unconditionally valuable to our flourishing. And the second paradox is that since, historically, it is our *moral* tradition that has ascribed such a high value to truth, to be more truthful about the value of truth is, in a sense, to respect more fully the reality of one's membership in this tradition.[34]

[32] Presumably because our past (nature, nurture, and life-circumstances) is too complex to be able to identify *the* most flourishing life that it permits—and because one's nurture and life-circumstances are constantly changing.

[33] For example, Nietzsche says: 'To become what one is, one must not have the faintest notion *what* one is' (*EH*, II, 9).

[34] Randall Havas makes a similar point when he speaks of 'obedience' to one's culture—'culture' being defined by him as 'a form of life in which sense is made'. Havas's notion of 'obedience' is vivid and instructive. (See, for example: *Nietzsche's Genealogy*, 9, 14, 52–65.)

2.6 CONCLUSION

In sum, for Nietzsche, which values an individual pursues and their value to her are determined by who she is—i.e. by her nature, nurture, and decisive life-circumstances, and so by her individual history. Among these life-circumstances is the encountering of reasons and truths which, for an individual (or epoch) that is receptive to them, may change the values she (or it) espouses. Yet the complexity and unpredictability of life-circumstances, and of the workings of nature and nurture, mean that which highest values actually govern an individual's life, rather than are merely entertained by her, can best be known (to her or others) *ex post*, rather than in advance.

On this view, any idea that an individual's highest values are either arbitrary preferences or freely chosen, or that their value can be 'grounded' in considerations that are independent of who that individual is, would be absurd, because denying of the fact of their determination by her preservation-enhancement needs and her ethical inheritance (and so by the whole history that has made those needs and inheritance what they are). Hence, a strong individual is, for Nietzsche, a mixture of the passive and the active: she is passive insofar as she submits to the 'necessity' of this historical determination; and she is active inasmuch as she 'wills' that necessity and so strives to express the particular configuration(s) of power that it permits.

We now need to move beyond this consideration of Nietzsche's conception of values and the authority for values to an understanding of the supreme standard by which he evaluates values. Though this standard is, famously, 'life-enhancement',[35] the criteria by which it is to be gauged are, strangely, seldom addressed rigorously in the secondary literature, though to understand them is clearly essential to analysing Nietzsche's new ethic and how it differs from traditional morality.

---

[35] Synonyms for life-enhancement are: 'life-promoting' (*BGE*, 4) or 'superabundance' of life (*GS*, 370). Its opposite is the 'denier' of life (e.g. *GM*, III, 13) or the *décadent* (e.g. *EH*, I, 1–2).

3

'Life-Enhancement': Its Degrees and Types

3.1 'LIFE-ENHANCEMENT': THREE CRITERIA

Though Nietzsche himself, true to his distaste for definitions, does not clearly explicate criteria[1] for 'life-enhancement', the valuations and practices that he deems life-enhancing in his works do, I suggest, consistently exemplify one or more of the following three criteria: 'power', 'sublimation' (of power), and the sort of 'form-creation' that invites love of world and life. Maximal life-enhancement will maximize all three criteria at once.

For example, raw power alone is exemplified by the pure 'beast of prey' that Nietzsche sees at the core of all 'noble races' (*GM*, I, 11)—though only as one of their traits. Sublimation of raw power—i.e. a combination of the first two criteria—is manifested by the desire for knowledge, in all of which there is a 'drop of cruelty' (*BGE*, 229). Indeed, what Nietzsche values in the 'slave', as we will see, is precisely his capacity to sublimate his power into intelligence. Form-creation that evinces high degrees of power, but not sublimation, is demonstrated by the 'organizers who build states' (*GM*, II, 18). Yet the types of life that Nietzsche most values maximize all three criteria; and of these types three stand out in his writings: the creation of values that affirm life, the creation of great art, and the creation of an autonomous character with 'style'.[2] They are, when highly developed, of roughly equal value to Nietzsche—though his supreme sort of human being has a disposition to all three types of life. In this chapter, I discuss the role of these key concepts—as well as others such as 'master' and 'slave'—in Nietzsche's critique of traditional morality.

---

[1] Of course, such criteria, just like all our highest standards or values, can, given Nietzsche's conception of the latter, best be known *ex post*.

[2] For the meaning of 'creation' see 3.1.3 below.

3.1.1 'Power' as a criterion of value

Power, we recall from Chapter 2.3, is advanced by Nietzsche not merely as an essentialist claim and explanatory concept, but also as a standard of value. 'Good' is '[e]verything that heightens the feeling of power in man, the will to power, power itself' (*A*, 2). By contrast, 'bad' is '[e]verything that is born of weakness' (*A*, 2; cf. 57). Here, we should note, power is deemed good not just as an efficient force, but also as an experience. For the phenomenology of power is essential to that self-reverence (typical of the 'master') without which human beings relapse into destructive resentment.[3] Thus, a 'slave'-type may, in fact, have more efficient power, of whatever kind, than a 'master'-type; but if he *feels* powerless he will be prey to all the envy and anger that are, for Nietzsche, embodied in both the ('reactive') manner of valuing and the particular values of traditional 'morality'.

Two points should be noted at once. First, the problem of defining and measuring 'power' would be very great even if it referred simply to efficient force or political control or, in general, statable 'outcomes'. But this problem seems insuperable if all human behaviour in its inexhaustible variety, including such activities as knowing and self-discipline, is to be explained in terms of power. And if 'power' also refers to the *experience* of power, then these difficulties of calibration are further compounded. Although Nietzsche speaks of value as directly correlated to a 'scale of force' (*WP*, 710), it is hard to see what such a common scale of force might be.

Second, power cannot be Nietzsche's only criterion of life-enhancement, because if all our 'highest' values, including those he repudiates as life-denying, can be explained as strategies for gaining power, then he must (at least *ex post*) have other criteria for differentiating their value.

3.1.2 'Sublimation' as a criterion of value

The degree to which power is 'sublimated' constitutes, I suggest, Nietzsche's second criterion of life-enhancement. 'Sublimation' (or 'spiritualization') of power is its employment for tasks that require

---

[3] This is a recurring theme not only in *GM* I, but in other places too. For example, in *GS*, 290, Nietzsche says: 'one thing is needful: that a human being should *attain* satisfaction with himself . . . Whoever is dissatisfied with himself is continually ready for revenge.'

complex and honed use of drives. It demands maximal receptivity, attunement, and discipline of one's senses and thoughts, rather than the crude, heedless eruptions of their raw 'instinctual' state. For example, '[a]lmost everything we call "higher culture"', Nietzsche famously suggests, 'is based on the spiritualization of *cruelty*, on its becoming more profound' (*BGE*, 229).[4] Philosophy itself is 'the most spiritual will to power' (*BGE*, 9). The brutality in us that all higher culture sees itself as having overcome is, Nietzsche claims, still alive and well, but its power is now shorn of coarseness, though not of force. 'That "savage animal" [in us] has not really been "mortified"; it lives and flourishes, it has merely become—divine' (*BGE*, 229).

Nietzsche is suggesting at least three very interesting propositions here. First, if culture does not extirpate or 'leave behind' barbaric instincts but, rather, depends on them as raw material for sublimation, then culture is no barrier to those instincts and may even, in some sense, keep them alive (a point I explore further in Chapter 6.5.3). Second, the disciplining of the drives that is involved in all sublimation can be employed either to suppress life—as in extreme asceticism—or to invigorate it—as in great philosophy, art, and the creation of a character with 'style', i.e. in all three types of life most valued by Nietzsche (a point to which I return in Chapter 5.2–5.3). Third, even knowledge is the result of such a sublimation of cruelty. For 'any insistence on profundity and thoroughness is a violation, a desire to hurt the basic will of the spirit which unceasingly strives for the apparent and superficial—in all desire to know there is a drop of cruelty' (*BGE*, 229; cf. 230).

The essential point here is the second: discipline, to the point of self-cruelty, is central to all 'higher culture'—providing that this self-cruelty hones and refines the 'instincts' rather than simply suppresses them, that it enhances the alertness and range of the senses rather than shrinks them. As Nietzsche puts it in the *Nachlass*:

I desire for myself and for all who live, *may* live, without being tormented by a puritanical conscience, an ever-greater spiritualization and multiplication of the senses; indeed, we should be grateful to the senses for their

---

[4] Graham Parkes suggests interesting parallels between Nietzsche's concern with transmutation of the passions and that of the Rinzai Zen tradition. See his article 'Nietzsche and East Asian Thought: Influences, Impacts, and Resonances', in B. Magnus and K. M. Higgins (eds.), *The Cambridge Companion to Nietzsche* (Cambridge: Cambridge University Press, 1996), 377. For other such parallels, see also Graham Parkes (ed.), *Nietzsche and Asian Thought* (Chicago: University of Chicago Press, 1991).

subtlety, plenitude, and power and offer them in return the best we have in the way of spirit.[5] (*WP*, 820)

Sublimation, as expressed in Nietzsche's three favoured types of life, can therefore be so life-enhancing because it enables us to harness to creative ends drives (and the values they express) whose violence might otherwise annihilate or paralyse us, and, moreover, to accommodate a great variety of opposing drives (and the values they express) whose coexistence might otherwise be impossible. By contrast, traditional 'ascetically ideal' morality deals with such drives simply by extirpating or crushing them. Thus, it is only through sublimation that Nietzsche's highest man—the one who can harness and integrate the maximum number and variety of drives—is possible. 'Greatness', Nietzsche says, depends upon 'how *far* one could extend [one's] responsibility', one's 'range and multiplicity', one's 'wholeness in mani-foldness' (*BGE*, 212; cf. *WP*, 966). Sublimation is crucial in enabling us to maximize the 'range and multiplicity' of talents and drives at work in a whole personality or in the service of a single objective.

3.1.3 'Form-creation' as a criterion of value

Power and sublimation are, however, insufficient as criteria of 'life-enhancement' because they can be forcefully expressed in 'slavish' values and practices, like those structured by the ascetic ideal, that repudiate life and shrink experience (though Nietzsche clearly has more respect for life-denying values when they do satisfy at least these two criteria). A further criterion is needed; and this is supplied, I suggest, by 'form-creation' that invites love of world and life.

Now, for Nietzsche, the types of form-creation that most power-fully 'seduce' us to life are valuations that glorify it, works of art that beautify it, and an own character that is pleasing to ourselves. The first is achieved through 'genuine' philosophy; the second by the cre-ative artist; and the third by giving 'style' to one's character. These three activities represent the types of 'will to power' that Nietzsche most values ('types' that, like 'master' or 'slave', can coexist in one 'soul'). The more one succeeds in these areas the more one enhances life; and one enhances it maximally by combining all three (as Goethe did). In all three cases, 'creation' denotes neither arbitrary fiat nor conventional voluntarism, but rather expressive acts that

---

[5] Elsewhere, Nietzsche defines 'spirit' as 'care, patience, cunning, simulation, great self-control, and everything that is mimicry' (*TI*, IX, 14).

arise out of willing the *necessity* of 'what one is'—acts that, as we discussed in Chapter 2.4, reflect the agent's past and, above all, his 'rank' (*BGE*, 213; cf. *BGE*, 221, 228, 257). In this sense Nietzsche, as we saw, equates creativity with 'freedom of the will' or 'necessity' (*BGE*, 213). I will now briefly summarize each of these three types.

The 'genuine' philosopher is, for Nietzsche, a creator or legislator of values (*BGE*, 211)—though not necessarily a builder of 'systems', for most of the latter simply give voice to established values. To 'create' values is to posit an ethic that constitutes, in fact, the legislator's own conditions for preservation and enhancement (*BGE*, 213). But those values are *not* purely solipsistic: they 'determine the Whither and For What of *man*' (*BGE*, 211—my italics)—or, at least, of those of equivalent 'rank'. Indeed, that they are not solipsistic is entailed by the 'objectivity' of Nietzschean values: for others of the same type will share, with the legislator, at least certain 'conditions for preservation and enhancement'—i.e. certain 'core' values.

Let us note five further points about the ('genuine') philosopher. First, he is a commander of himself before everything else: he cannot 'command' others unless he is able to will his own values ('naturalistically', of course, and not through anything like Kantian reason). For this task the philosopher will need protracted solitude (*BGE*, 44). Second, he is also a severe critic 'of his time' (*BGE*, 212): for he must discredit the old values to make way for the new. Third, though he is a critic, he has little to do with Kantian-type 'critiques', which, in their fixation with finding ultimate grounds for knowledge, values, and beauty, never, according to Nietzsche, touch on the 'real' questions, namely those concerning the creation (and, to that end, the evaluation) of values. Fourth, he displays two cardinal virtues: courage and self-respect—just the two virtues that, Nietzsche claims, the typical 'scholar' lacks.[6] And, fifth, he necessarily values truth— at least about the 'conditions' that maximally enhance life (and that, therefore, protect against '*décadence*'[7])—which, in turn, demands honesty about the fundamental character of existence, a point to be discussed again in Chapter 10.1.1 and 10.2.1.[8]

---

[6] *BGE*, 205–7, 227. See also my further discussion of this point in Chapter 10.1.2.

[7] Nietzsche claims that he himself, unlike (the artist) Wagner, could resist *décadence* only because of the 'philosopher in me' (*CW*, P).

[8] Truth-formulation is, for Nietzsche, form-giving in a neo-Kantian sense of seeing the world as 'a something', where the 'something' is informed by the perspectivism referred to in Chapter 2.1 (though, of course, the parameters of that perspectivism are dictated by one's nature and interests rather than by any deducible 'categories').

The artist, for his or her part, is, above all, one who creates 'the great seduction to life' (*WP*, 853, II)—which also means away from life-denying pessimism and its morality. The extension of 'artist' varies widely in Nietzsche's works: there are places where it embraces any individual who can induce others to master life— including men of religion (*BGE*, 59), philosophers (ibid.), and ascetic priests (*GM*, III, 20); and others where it is restricted to creators of tragedy, music, sculpture, and the like (e.g. *GM*, III, 4–5). These types of individual and activity are all artistic in that they 'falsify' reality by selectively representing, transfiguring, perfecting, and thus beautifying it (for a particular 'taste', of course), and so render existence affirmable, despite its horror. For in art, Nietzsche claims, 'the *lie* is sanctified and the *will to deception* has a good conscience' (*GM*, III, 25).[9] Artists are motivated by the intoxication (*Rausch*) of love that makes whatever it fastens on, including the lover himself, into a work of art, thus enabling it to be experienced as valuable, beautiful, and whole.[10]

Yet the 'pure' artist differs greatly from the philosopher (or the 'priest'). For the pure artist, unlike the philosopher, cannot and must not create values or dedicate himself to seeking propositional truth. He cannot do so because he is incapable, *qua* artist, of taking up the independent positions needed to create values or seek propositional truth. And he must not do so because to be creative he is necessarily and 'to all eternity separated from . . . the actual' ('von dem . . . Wirklichen abgetrennt') and 'forbidden . . . to lay hold of' it.[11] This estrangement of the artist from the 'actual'—and his concomitant unreflectiveness (at least in the sense of reflecting upon propositional formulations)—have, as I read Nietzsche, up to three distinct objects: the 'inner' nature and character of the individual artist himself, including the wellsprings of his creativity; the overall (ethical)

---

[9] If Nietzsche is suggesting that it is constitutive of art to falsify reality—in the sense that art must present a complete illusion if it is to succeed—this would seem to me to be unfounded. But, on the whole, it seems that what Nietzsche means by the 'lie' or 'deception' of art is not total falsification, but rather the selective illumination and magnification of particular aspects of reality, thus enabling closer proximity to the latter than most experience of, or propositions about, it allow. See, for example, *GS*, 78.

[10] See, for example, *TI*, IX, 8–10; *WP*, 808. For a discussion of the resemblances of Nietzsche's and Plato's conceptions of love, see Martha C. Nussbaum, 'The Transfigurations of Intoxication: Nietzsche, Schopenhauer, and Dionysus', *Arion*, 1/2 (May 1991), 75–111.

[11] *GM*, III, 4. This fascinating suggestion is further discussed in Chapters 5.7, 6.4, 8.1.2, and 10.3.2.

value of his work; and, perhaps, 'external' reality in general.[12] Like
'the whole world of Greek art and poetry' which 'never "knew" what
it did' (*GS*, 369), the creative artist must remain in the realm of the
'superficial' (*GS*, P, 4), free of the search for 'profound' truths or
fixed meanings. Artists, Nietzsche implies, would lack this flexibility
to escape the immobilizing horizons of values, judgements, and
truths if they possessed the philosopher's urge and aptitude for the
definitive, the conceptual, and the independent standpoint. In these
ways, then, art and philosophy are antithetical.

On the other hand, the power and the need to falsify artistically
may depend on having *first* perceived the world in all its terrible,
unfalsified reality. One has the power to rearrange the elements of
reality—i.e. to be an artist—only if one has first really *seen* them.
And one needs art as a counterforce to the horror and ugliness of
such insight—'lest we *perish of the truth*' (*WP*, 822). For with
Nietzsche, truth and beauty are no longer one, as with Plato, but can
be diametrically opposed: beauty is needed to redeem the ugliness of
truth—i.e. both to justify and to transcend that ugliness by making
oneself and the world seem more perfect, beautiful, and strong as a
result of having once seen it. Thus art, insofar as it is beautiful and
enables us to falsify reality with a good conscience, actually helps us
to *sustain* our truthfulness, where honesty alone—especially about
the pervasiveness of error—would 'lead to nausea and suicide' (*GS*,
107). This, Nietzsche says, is the ground of our '*ultimate gratitude to
art*' (ibid.)—and it is extremely important to be clear that his claim
is not that we need art in order to avoid truth altogether, or as an
alternative form of life to one that values truth, or to aestheticize
existence by seeing it 'as' a work of art, but, exactly to the contrary,
that we need art in order really to be able to face the truth, in order
to seduce to life those who have been shaken by genuine insight into
its horrors. The gruesome fate of someone who possesses only an
exceptional capacity to look truthfully at the world—and no counter-
balancing capacity for art—is exemplified by Hamlet: 'In this sense
the Dionysian man resembles Hamlet: both have once looked truly
into the essence of things, they have *gained knowledge*, and nausea

---

[12] The first two senses in which the artist must be, to a high degree, unreflective if he
is to be creative seem reasonable to me. The third—that he must be estranged from external reality in general—I find unconvincing, even if this estrangement is taken to relate only
to propositional truths about that reality. However, I advance the third only tentatively as
something Nietzsche might be construed as saying in *GM*, III, 4, as well as elsewhere.

inhibits action . . . Knowledge kills action; action requires the veils of illusion: that is the doctrine of Hamlet . . . ' (*BT*, 7).

In short: philosophy enables us (propositionally) to know existence; and art enables us to affirm it. Truth creates a need for art; and art makes the pursuit of truth bearable. Though art is ethically opposed to truthfulness, insofar as it is innately fiction-creating, it is psychologically supportive of truthfulness, in that it enables us to live with the truth.[13] In this sense, then, art and philosophy, falsification and truthfulness, are complementary.

Yet the point that the artist must first have seen deeply into reality if he is (selectively) to re-present or falsify it is one on which Nietzsche appears to be divided, and not just between his early and late works. In one late work, as we have seen, he suggests that the artist is necessarily estranged from 'the actual', condemned to the 'eternal "unreality" and falsity of his innermost existence', forbidden 'actually to *be*' and incapable of an independent, courageous stand in relation to values, and hence of creating them (*GM*, III, 4–5). Whereas in another—*BGE*, 59—he claims that the degree to which one needs to falsify artistically is in direct proportion to how far one has reached beneath 'surfaces', to the truth—and suffered from it (i.e. really, honestly, seen it). These views seem reconcilable only if, as I have suggested, one takes the terms 'artist' and 'philosopher' as types that, though ethically conflicting, can coexist within one person. Thus, the philosopher in him formulates and grasps truths about the deep nature of reality and has the independence to create his own values (or at least to take his own stand in relation to them); while the artist is separated from that reality and is merely the 'valet'[14] of values created by others. This reading is supported by *BGE* 39, where Nietzsche speaks of Stendhal, the artist, as a 'philosopher'—where 'the concept "philosopher" is not restricted to the philosopher who writes books'—and praises him as the 'last great psychologist'. The 'strength of a spirit', Nietzsche there says, should be measured both by how much truth it can endure and by how much it *therefore* needs to falsify what it sees—i.e. by its being both philosopher and artist.

This brings us to the third type of 'form-creation' most valued by Nietzsche: namely, giving 'style' to one's own character. This,

---

[13] If so, once truth is accepted as *intrinsically* valuable (however that comes to be), this, *ipso facto*, confers value upon art.

[14] *GM*, III, 5.

Nietzsche makes clear, demands both truthfulness (knowing one's strengths and weaknesses) and falsification (creating a work of art out of the whole):

> To 'give style' to one's character—a great and rare art! It is practised by those who survey all the strengths and weaknesses of their nature and then fit them into an artistic plan until every one of them appears as art and reason and even weaknesses delight the eye. (*GS*, 290)

The point of making a work of art out of one's character is to make oneself affirmable—just as the point of beautifying the world in general is to make it affirmable. As Nietzsche very rightly says: 'Whoever is dissatisfied with himself is continually ready for revenge . . . For the sight of what is ugly makes one bad and gloomy' (ibid.). Ethically, to give 'style' to one's character is, therefore, a precaution against *ressentiment* and, so, against 'morality'.

But to make a pleasing whole out of one's character is not the same as, and does not commit Nietzsche to advocating, the creation of a coherent 'narrative' out of one's life. Differently put: to give style to one's *living* is not the same as giving style to one's *life*. For a literary narrative is authored by an agent who, however sketchily, foresees an overall shape to his characters' lives, which, in their key elements, he knows or conceives in advance. Whereas, a Nietzschean individual not only cannot know 'what' he is prior to the experiments of actual living, but should not seek, before he has experienced and attempted a great deal, to know who he is. Thus, in a key idea,[15] Nietzsche says: 'To become what one is, one must not have the faintest notion *what* one is' (*EH*, II, 9).[16] Because this inevitable and necessary, even if temporary, ignorance of one's nature and potentiality is not always true of the author of literary characters or of the latter themselves, the analogy between a literary individual and Nietzsche's conception of a real life, though powerful, is not perfect.[17]

In sum, the ancient tension between art and philosophy is continued by Nietzsche, though with a new twist: art and philosophy are,

[15] To which we will return in Chapters 6.2.1, 8.6, and 10.4.2.

[16] Note that all references to *Ecce Homo* follow the abbreviations used in the index of Kaufmann's translation.

[17] Nonetheless, some parallels drawn by, say, Nehamas between literary characters and Nietzsche's conception of a lived life are strong, such as that, for both, no detail is inconsequential and each life is its own justification. See Alexander Nehamas, *Nietzsche: Life as Literature* (Cambridge, Mass.: Harvard University Press, 1985), 163–4.

in principle, equally valuable; neither must be regarded as essentially subordinate to the other; and this is epitomized by the creation of one's own character, which demands both art and truth. The inescapable tension between the artist and the philosopher as types (and between art and philosophy, in terms of the values internal to them) persists: for the genuine philosopher values highly (certain) truths,[18] is committed to conceptualization, and can stand independently vis-à-vis values, whereas the artist aims at illusion, avoids conceptualization, and is necessarily incapable of that ethical independence. For these reasons, art and philosophy are not finally reconcilable in a synthesis and will remain, as Heidegger vividly puts it,[19] in 'raging discordance'. Yet art and philosophy are equally valuable because each provokes an essential need for, and so confers value on, the other. The artist needs the philosopher to create, or endorse, or make vivid the values of the culture within which he lives and, where necessary, to protect that culture from the life-denying falsehoods that lead to *décadence*.[20] Indeed, art will be the big winner from the liberating 'revaluation of all values', which only the truth-seeking of philosophy can bring about. Whereas philosophy—insofar as it genuinely looks into the 'abyss' of reality—needs the beautifying illusions of art lest it 'perish of the truth'. For art constitutes the best counterforce against world-denying pessimism and the greatest stimulant of the will.[21]

That Nietzsche, at least in his later works,[22] ranks art and philosophy equally is quite consistent with the possibility that sometimes an individual or culture needs to attach priority to one or the other—for example, times of *décadence* when the priority is for philosophy to expose the life-denying function of values or to create new ones, or of despair when art is needed to 'seduce' one back to life. Yet there is no question that Nietzsche values supremely a life in which all three types of form-creation are present, a life which, like Goethe's, seeks '*totality*' and fights 'the mutual extraneousness of

---

[18] See Chapter 10, which identifies the kinds of truths valued by the (life-enhancing) philosopher.

[19] Heidegger, *Nietzsche*, vol. i, trans. David Farrell Krell, chapter 19, *passim*.

[20] This latter point will be discussed in detail in Chapter 10.

[21] Art '*arouses the will*' says Nietzsche (*GM*, III, 6), in pointed distinction to Kant and especially to Schopenhauer.

[22] Julian Young gives a good account of the movement in Nietzsche's conception of the value and role of art and artists from his early books to his last works. See Julian Young, *Nietzsche's Philosophy of Art* (Cambridge: Cambridge University Press, 1992).

reason, senses, feeling, and will' (*TI*, IX, 49).[23] The virtues of Dionysus, the artist, also encompass those of the philosopher—'daring honesty, truthfulness, and love of wisdom' (*BGE*, 295). And the goal to which Nietzsche commits himself as the 'reason' and 'warranty' of his whole life is 'to see as beautiful'—which only the artist can do—'what is necessary in things'—which only the philosopher (or *Wissenschaftler*, broadly conceived) can establish (*GS*, 276). Such a life triumphally overcomes, even though it cannot eliminate, the ancient feud between art and philosophy.

3.2 NIETZSCHE'S EVALUATION OF VALUES AND CONCEPTS

I have claimed, thus far, that the values of which Nietzsche most approves will maximally fulfil three criteria: first, they can be employed to maximize one's power; second, this power will be maximally refined or 'sublimated' (as in the man of knowledge); and, third, this sublimated power will be maximally deployed in the creation of 'forms' that 'seduce' to life—i.e. that invite love of life. Conversely, the values of which Nietzsche most disapproves will minimize one's power, will express power of the crudest kind (e.g. the bland materialism of the 'last man'; the boisterous nationalism of Bismarckian Germany), and will inhibit the creation of forms (e.g. by making them seem bad or pointless).

Now the evaluation of traditional moral values using three separate criteria, themselves of such great inner heterogeneity, is bound to be a very complex business, which will issue neither in clear condemnation of those values, nor in clear approval. First, there is, prima facie, no reason why any given value or, in general, any particular ethic, should not produce a high score by one criterion and a low score by another, and so be subject to different judgements depending on which criterion is uppermost in one's mind at any one time or on how one sums the three. Thus, the 'ascetic ideal' generally scores highly in terms of power, highly in terms of sublimation, and poorly in

---

[23] On Nietzsche's Goethe, see, for example: Erich Heller, *The Importance of Nietzsche: Ten Essays* (Chicago: University of Chicago Press, 1988), chapter 2; and Karl Schlechta, 'The German "Classicist" Goethe as Reflected in Nietzsche's Works', in J. C. O'Flaherty, T. F. Sellner, and R. M. Helm (eds.), *Studies in Nietzsche and the Classical Tradition* (2nd edn., Chapel Hill, NC: University of North Carolina Press, 1979), 144–55.

terms of form-creation (except in the hands of the 'priest' who uses it to dominate the 'herd'). Creators of states, on the other hand, score well in terms of power, badly in terms of sublimation, and well in terms of form-creation. Second, one cannot assess the performance of a value on any of these criteria in the abstract; one can do so only in relation to the features of a particular type of life or person, because values are conditions 'for the preservation of a *certain type* of life' (*BGE*, 3—my italics). Thus, a given value may enable one type of person to find power and enhance his life, while achieving the opposite for another. Third, any given value may also score very differently depending on how life-enhancing are the functions it serves. Thus, pity is bad when, *inter alia*,[24] it has the 'insane' aim of abolishing suffering—insane because suffering is inseparable from living, because suffering is, in large part, both cause and effect of our growth in power and creativity and 'sovereignty',[25] and because the state of undisturbed '[w]ell-being' which such pity seeks 'makes man ridiculous and contemptible'. By contrast, pity is good when it has the '*converse*' object: namely, those who resist suffering, those who cannot bear to be (or to witness others being) 'broken, forged, torn, burnt, made incandescent, and purified'. In this contrast, Nietzsche says, we have 'pity *versus* pity' (*BGE*, 225, *passim;* cf. *GS*, 338; *A*, 7).[26]

Thus, what we traditionally call 'values', such as pity, generosity, or thrift, are, for Nietzsche, just vague notions. Something is fully a value only if it is specified in terms of its functions (and the motives they express) in the life of a particular type of individual. As a result, much contradiction in Nietzsche's writings may be attributable not to simple inconsistency on his part (though there is patently a good deal of that) but to the fact that different emphases on these three criteria, or combinations of them, will produce genuinely different evaluations of traditional values. For all his strident language, there

---

[24] Other features of 'bad' pity are: the presumption to understand the suffering of the pitied (which is extraordinarily difficult to do), and so the denial of his or her individuality; and the urge to protect oneself from the suffering of others, rather than to help them grow in strength.

[25] 'Sovereignty' carries with it the '*right to make promises*' (*GM*, II, 1–2). Thus, pity potentially threatens the sufferer's capacity to acquire that crucial 'right'—and so endangers the creation of the 'autonomous' individual, the breeding of whom is, Nietzsche suggests, 'the real problem regarding man' (*GM*, II, 1).

[26] For a valuable discussion of Nietzsche's critique of pity, see Martha C. Nussbaum's article 'Pity and Mercy: Nietzsche's Stoicism', in Schacht (ed.), *Nietzsche, Genealogy, Morality*, 139–67; and David E. Cartwright, 'Kant, Schopenhauer, and Nietzsche on the Morality of Pity', *Journal of the History of Ideas*, 45/1, 1984, 83–98.

is, in fact, almost no value (e.g. altruism) or motivation (e.g. *ressentiment*) or even morality (e.g. Christianity) that Nietzsche condemns outright. Indeed, many of his apparent contradictions necessarily arise from the very consistency with which he subjects values to the three separate, though linked, criteria discussed above. Hence these are contradictions from which no amount of sympathetic exegesis can or should rescue him.

Now Nietzsche's evaluation of *concepts* proceeds just like his evaluation of values: the primary standard is always life-enhancement rather than epistemological probity. This is clearly illustrated in his attack on the concept of 'God' (and its underlying Platonic metaphysics), which takes place at three levels of progressively deeper significance. The first employs conventional positivist arguments that God cannot be empirically verified or falsified, or that what is said about him is literally meaningless, or that the characteristics attributed to him are incoherent (e.g. omnipotence), or that Christianity has made testable claims that have failed to materialize (such as redeeming 'evil' or containing suffering), or, indeed, that the Gospels may be inaccurate or fictional (this being, for Nietzsche, and I would strongly agree, the most uninteresting of all attacks on traditional Christianity). The result of these arguments—which concern the standard fare of theology, for and against which passions have raged for centuries—is atheism. This is just what Nietzsche refers to when he says that people turn to atheism today as a result of having 'thoroughly refuted' certain predicates of God—such as 'the father', 'the judge', 'the rewarder', his 'free will', his urge to 'hear' us, his capacity to 'help' us, or his 'clear communication' (*BGE*, 53; cf. *A*, 15).

Ultimately, however, Nietzsche considers this level of attack very limited, for two reasons. First, though it has undermined the 'theistic satisfaction' which the 'religious instinct' sought, it has left that instinct itself untouched. Indeed, 'the religious instinct is . . . in the process of *growing* powerfully' (*BGE*, 53—my italics), precisely from a desperate urge for new satisfactions to replace the terrifying loss of the old—an observation strikingly confirmed by modern cults of nationalism, pop idols, 'holism', and other substitutes for the 'theistic satisfaction'. Second, the positivistic spirit[27]—though it has helped to destroy a life-denying system of belief—is itself a sign of

---

[27] i.e. a spirit that concerns itself only with what is real, useful, verifiable, etc.

a workaday, dry nature, compared to which Nietzsche much prefers the transcendental instincts of Platonism—a point that excellently illustrates my contention that Nietzsche is always more concerned with whether arguments arise from (or serve) a spirit of nobility or life-enhancement than with their epistemological claims, so much so that he may condemn such arguments, if they evince an opposing spirit, even when they generate exactly the conclusions for which he labours himself. Thus, he says:

the charm of the Platonic way of thinking, which was a *noble* way of thinking, consisted precisely in *resistance* to obvious sense-evidence—perhaps among men who enjoyed even stronger and more demanding senses than our contemporaries, but who knew how to find a higher triumph in remaining masters . . . over the motley whirl of the senses—the mob of the senses, as Plato said. In this overcoming of the world, and interpreting of the world in the manner of Plato, there was an *enjoyment* different from that which the physicists of today offer us . . . 'Where man cannot find anything to see or to grasp, he has no further business'—that is certainly an imperative different from the Platonic one, but it may be the right imperative for a tough, industrious race of machinists and bridge-builders of the future, who have nothing but *rough* work to do. (*BGE*, 14)

I have quoted this remarkable passage at length because here Nietzsche disdains the very positivistic attack on Platonism that he himself employs, and admires (with whatever ironic undertones) the very Platonic transcendentalism that elsewhere he so strenuously criticizes. And he does so precisely because such people repudiate metaphysics in the name of a workaday ethic that Nietzsche finds every bit as dreary as the metaphysical guilt of the Christianity it replaced. As he says in the same passage, 'visual evidence and palpableness' fascinate, persuade, and convince 'fundamentally plebeian tastes'. The vulgar, who are too busy for God, are the first to forget him (*BGE*, 58). If one does 'sacrifice God for the nothing' and instead 'worship the stone, stupidity, gravity, fate' (*BGE*, 55), then Nietzsche wishes to do so out of an altogether nobler spirit.

This nobler spirit fosters the second and, for Nietzsche, decisive, type of argument against Christian 'dogma', namely that it engenders weakness, degradation, and despair—and that its claim to foster love, light, and life is simply *false* (and is detected as such by its own 'will to truth'). Beliefs like the divine purposiveness of nature and life are rejected not on sceptical grounds but because of their 'mendaciousness, feminism, weakness, and cowardice' (*GS*, 357). In short: 'What is now decisive against Christianity is our taste,[28] no longer our reasons' (*GS*, 132). Its proper prosecutors are moralists, not epistemologists. Indeed, Nietzsche says in a much-neglected passage: 'If one were to *prove* this God of the Christians to us, we should be even less able to believe in him'—for 'we experience what has been revered as God, not as "godlike" . . . not merely as an error but as a *crime against life*' (*A*, 47).[29]

Yet Nietzsche's first two lines of attack on the religious instinct—namely, on the coherence of Christianity's basic axioms and on the belief that these are life-enhancing—still leave intact what he sees as the psychological bedrock of that instinct: the 'atomistic need' (*BGE*, 12), which underlies, for example, the Christian notion of the 'soul'. This 'need', to which we already referred in Chapter 2.2 (and which is further discussed in Chapters 7.3.2 and 10.2.1), employs two basic concepts: the hard-core subject separable from various types of predicate, such as predicates of thought or action (for human beings) or effect (for inanimate objects); and the essential equality of subjects in each animate or inanimate category, whose differences are fully determined by their predicates. The atomistic need reveals itself ethically as egalitarian democracy, universal rights, freedom of the will, and essential guilt; scientifically in particle theories and the reifying of 'cause and effect'; logically in concepts like *causa sui* or the 'it' or 'I' or 'logical person'; and grammatically in the subject-predicate structure. It is, perhaps, because the atomistic need is the ultimate foundation of the religious urge, because it is the need that will survive long after God is 'dead' and all claims made on his behalf discredited, and because it residually manifests itself in such inconspicuous and hence, for Nietzsche, dangerous, ways as the 'subject' of grammar and the 'particle' of physics, that it is the only motive, value, or concept *as such* that I could discover against which Nietzsche is explicitly willing to fight 'relentless war unto death'. (As I have suggested, he is more ambivalent in his attitude towards the other values and concepts employed by Christianity, like altruism,

---

[28] 'Taste' here denotes, roughly, the kinds of projects, people, manners, and the like that someone of a given ethical and aesthetic orientation is collectively attracted to or repelled by.

[29] In Chapter 5.5, I will argue that, although ethical arguments against a particular conception of God are indeed far more powerful than an epistemological or ontological line of attack, Nietzsche's pursuit of the former type of argument needs to be substantially qualified.

the unconditional, pity, and asceticism itself, which, as he presents them, are also susceptible of life-*enhancing* functions.)

3.3 NIETZSCHE'S EVALUATION OF THE MANNER OF VALUING: 'MASTERS' AND 'SLAVES'

So far we have considered how Nietzsche assesses the value of specific values or concepts of traditional morality, such as pity or God. And we have seen how this critique depends on the three criteria of life-enhancement which I have reconstructed from his writings.

But Nietzsche's critique of morality goes further than this. He is also concerned with the general *manner* in which we value—that is, with whether these values arise in a *sovereign* way or, rather, as a *reaction* to our fear or envy of others. And it is my contention that the famous terms 'master' and 'slave' denote, respectively, the sovereign and reactive manner of valuing.[30]

The characteristics of the sovereign individual, or 'master', can be simply stated. He has no interest in universalizing his values. He expects others like him (even if they are enemies) to share his values because they are the same type of person, not because they are human as such. His conception of 'good' is not shaped by a reaction of envy or fear towards another whom he dubs 'bad' (*GM*, I, 11). Finally, by being courageous enough to recognize his own nature (and that of his 'type') as the sole ground of his values, he has no need to project the latter onto some external authority, be it transcendent or secular. Thus, the primary meaning of 'master', in its pure conceptual form, concerns not the domination of others (which 'slaves' attempt too) but rather a relationship to oneself—namely, that of sovereign self-legislation (culminating in the capacity to 'promise' oneself—*GM*, II, 1–2). To the extent that such sovereignty

---

[30] I deliberately use the term 'sovereign', rather than 'active'. First, 'sovereign' better describes the noble person's capacity to live 'in trust and openness with himself' (*GM*, I, 10) than does 'active' and is also closer in meaning to the masterly ideal of 'autonomy' that Nietzsche introduces in *GM*, II, 1–2, which is essentially the self-mastery to 'promise oneself'. Second, the term 'active' usually denotes the opposite of 'passive'; and yet, as mentioned in the next paragraph, passivity is also a crucial feature of the master, in his submission to the reality of his own historical determination. Third, the 'slave' is also active in the search for power, indeed crucially so; for with his very persistence he is able to overwhelm the masters.

includes a phenomenology of consciously submitting to one's own nature and its historical determination, rather than craving external (and, specifically, absolutely authoritative) guidance, the master may be seen as 'passive'. But to the extent that the master fully and courageously wills his own 'necessity' and, moreover, in an age of *décadence*, seeks uncompromisingly to abandon all life-denying ways of employing values (including the false beliefs on which such employment is parasitic), he is active.[31] There is, therefore, an ideal combination of activity and passivity which characterizes a healthy individual's relationship to his 'will to power'.

By contrast, the 'reactive' individual, or 'slave', 'needs, physiologically speaking, external stimuli in order to act at all' (*GM*, I, 10). These stimuli, the triggers of all his most enduring valuations and practices, concern the strength in others—or, importantly, in himself—that he fears. In response, he experiences 'reactive' affects like 'hatred, envy, jealousy' (*GM*, II, 11) and attempts to neutralize strength by dubbing it 'evil' and shameful. Thus, the reactive spirit never defines itself for itself, but always against something higher and stronger which it interprets, and so resents, as the cause of its oppression and suffering. This interpretation moralizes suffering by ascribing it to failure to respect unconditional maxims, a failure which, in the Christian story, is, in turn, held to originate in essential (or 'original') guilt—located within ourselves as well as within others. The resentment of one's (perceived) weakness that fuels these attitudes Nietzsche calls '*ressentiment*'.

Ressentiment has, I suggest, three principal features which distinguish it from mere 'resentment': first, its object of hatred is universal in scope, embracing, at the limit, all of existence; second, it thoroughly falsifies that object in order to render the latter inescapably blameworthy—which, at the limit, means that it falsifies the whole character of existence; and, third, since such universal resentment is impossible to satisfy, its revenge must be, at least in part, imaginary.[32]

[31] That one's own longevity, or that of others, may be curtailed as a result of this intensive living is not a concern of Nietzsche, who, for 'higher' types, could be said to favour the maxim: 'affirm uninhibitedly those values which maximize your own sovereign life-enhancement.'

[32] A substantially different, and very interesting, account of *ressentiment* is given by Gilles Deleuze in *Nietzsche and Philosophy*, trans. Hugh Tomlinson (London: Athlone Press, 1983), 111–24—though Deleuze, here as elsewhere, takes great liberties with Nietzsche's texts. Perhaps the subtlest critique of Nietzsche's conception of *ressentiment* and its nourishment of Christian morality is by Max Scheler in *Ressentiment*, trans. W. Holdheim (New York: The Free Press, 1961).

As to its universality, *ressentiment* casts blame not merely on specific objects of fear, such as the 'masters' of *GM* I, or, self-reflexively, the agent himself,[33] but also on the whole world, including such very general features of it as time, space, and contingency. Blame is universal for two distinct reasons: first, because the slave's rage is directed at the suffering which, in and of its very nature, existence generates; and, second, because to repudiate the world as a whole, which is the *only* domain in which 'masters' can find value, is the best strategy for undermining anything that they could possibly live for.

In order to achieve this wholesale devaluation—i.e. to make it credible (to himself as well as to his target, the master), first, that strength and, indeed, existence itself are guilty, and, second, that such guilt can be punished or avenged—the man of *ressentiment* falsifies not only the nature of the master but also the very character of existence. For example, he assigns whatever he resents to a corrupt and corrupting realm called the 'phenomenal' (in contrast to a truly 'real' domain transcending it altogether); he posits a god who saves the weak and damns the strong; and he invents all sorts of philosophical concepts, like 'essence' and metaphysically 'free will', so that those who possess strength can be made to feel constitutively 'guilty' and yet still capable of 'choosing' to repudiate, however imperfectly, what they inescapably are. The favoured ideal which structures these fictions is, of course, the 'ascetic ideal', which, in its limiting form, demands that the whole of 'phenomenal' existence be transcended for the sake of a metaphysical realm, such as God or Truth (see Chapter 5.3). With the aid of such fictions, the slave is able both to despise and to take revenge upon his enemies *'in effigie'* (*GM*, I, 10)—and, at the limit, he hates not merely the masters in effigy, but also the world in effigy. Collectively, Nietzsche calls the ethic parasitic on these fictions 'Christian morality'.

Now these particular fictions not only enable blame to be directed at an effigy, but also permit hatred to become 'spiritual'—i.e. channelled into high ideals rather than brutally enacted. The spiritualization of hatred (*GM*, I, 7) is vital to the 'slave' for two reasons: first, revenge against the 'masters' is best achieved by revaluing their values, rather than by attempting a direct assault; and, second,

---

[33] Insofar as the agent himself instantiates what he blames: e.g. that he is 'phenomenal' or that he is interested in 'this world'. I return to this point in Chapter 4.3 in discussing the moralization of guilt.

revenge against existence or time itself cannot be enacted and must be imaginary. (We should note that neither of these reasons for spiritualizing hatred depends upon the contingent historical fact of the 'masters' being politically or socially dominant. Even if the master-type were of equal or lesser strength both reasons would stand because the master would still be resented for his sovereign nature and his life-enhancing values.)

Ressentiment is, I suggest, philosophically interesting not only in the way suggested by Nietzsche—i.e. in that it *generates* the revolutionary values and fictions of 'morality'—but, even more so, in that it *presupposes* a revolution in values: i.e. in that a radically new ethical outlook is necessary for resentment to become *ressentiment* and for slaves to acquire the conception, let alone the ambition, of final escape from allotted social roles and inevitable suffering. This is an outlook in which human inequality and suffering—even if, or perhaps precisely if, explicable in terms of natural chance and necessity—have become, to a crucial degree, unacceptable; and in which the expectation exists of ultimately overcoming both these conditions. It conceals a world-picture with two essential postulates and values: first, the postulate that human beings are, in some essential sense, equal and the corresponding value that they should, to this extent, be treated as equal; second, the progressivist postulate that ultimate freedom from chance and necessity—and the 'undeserved' suffering they engender—is possible and the corresponding value that such freedom is the supreme good.[34] In the first case, fixed social roles no longer have divine or other unchallengeable foundations, and the expectation exists of abolishing certain social disadvantages. In the second case, suffering has become 'The Problem of Suffering' and the expectation exists of ultimately abolishing all suffering. What one might call 'universalism' is central to both: in the first case, the idea that human beings have properties in common that transcend those endowed by birth or luck, and moreover that the former properties count for more than do the latter; in the sec-

---

[34] At the limit, both postulates exemplify the 'atomistic need'. For quality-less 'subjects' are not only absolutely equal—in that they have no qualities to distinguish them—but also (metaphysically) sheltered from contingency and flux. One instance of such a 'subject' is 'soul atomism', as taught by Christianity (*BGE*, 12). This concept of the soul is central to any explication of the Christian belief in the essential equality of individuals (before God) and in the possibility of an other-worldly life free of suffering. In terms of what *ressentiment* presupposes, however, no metaphysical story about a distinct domain where such freedom is to be found is yet necessary.

ond case, that worldly existence or suffering as a whole—rather than the particular objects or events that make it up—has a meaning or a value or a nature.[35] It seems to me that Nietzsche's 'slaves' (unlike, perhaps, all others in world history) have *already* undergone this very complex philosophical revolution before they, as it were, come on stage; and that the question of how they armed themselves with these two philosophical prerequisites for their rebellion—i.e. with the two postulates and values just mentioned—is at least as important as the ethical strategy by which they subsequently subdue the 'masters'. Yet this question is not given due recognition by Nietzsche's account of the slaves' rebellion.[36]

3.4 IS 'MASTER/SLAVE' COEXTENSIVE WITH 'LIFE-ENHANCEMENT/LIFE-DENIAL'?

Now the question arises: how are 'master' and 'slave', the 'sovereign' and 'reactive' modes of valuing, related to 'life-enhancement' and 'life-denial' as I have defined them? The answer is complex. 'Master' and 'life-enhancement' are, I suggest, not identical concepts, and nor are 'slave' and 'life-denial'. To explain why this is so—and hence why Nietzsche's attitude to 'masters' is far from one of simple approbation (or his attitude to 'slaves' one of total condemnation)—will help us better to illuminate the ethic he advances in place of 'morality'. Central to such an explanation are the following six points:

1. The 'slave'-type, just like the 'master', is capable of both power and sublimation—i.e. of satisfying the first two criteria of life-enhancement—and, to a lesser extent, of form-creation. As to power,

[35] Though Nietzsche, of course, firmly rejects—*contra* Schopenhauer—the possibility of any overall valuation of life from some standpoint external to it (e.g. *GS*, 346; *TI*, II, 2; *TI*, V, 5), seeing even the impulse to reach such a judgement as a symptom of *ressentiment*, he cannot legitimately reject general valuations of, or statements about, existence as a whole from an internal standpoint—i.e. one not appealing to a standard that supposedly transcends time and contingency—as this is precisely what his affirmations of 'Eternal Return' and '*amor fati*' are. The question, then, is whether it would be more life-enhancing to be free even of this 'intrinsic' type of collective questioning, answering, and valuing.

[36] Nor, as Martha Nussbaum remarks, does Nietzsche's brilliant analysis of revenge account for the fact that noble characters can be driven to it—by betrayal of precisely those virtues, such as trustingness, which the 'slaves' lack (Martha C. Nussbaum, *The Fragility of Goodness: Luck and Ethics in Greek Tragedy and Philosophy* (Cambridge: Cambridge University Press, 1986), 417–18).

the whole point of 'slave morality' is that it is a successful formula for attaining power, a fact of which its impresarios, the 'priests', are all too aware (e.g. *GM*, III, 11). As to sublimation, slave morality is, as just discussed, the spiritualization of revenge—i.e. the channelling of revenge into high ideals that serve two purposes: first, to subdue the 'masters' by revaluing their values; and, second, to enable any revenge over and above that revaluation to be imaginary—which the insatiable nature of *ressentiment* requires it to be. In addition, the 'slave' can weakly satisfy the third criterion of life-enhancement: for insofar as *ressentiment* gives birth to new, albeit world-denying, values (*GM*, I, 10), and so makes living bearable for those who might otherwise be too weak or despondent to tolerate it, it is itself form-creating.

2. Conversely, the 'master'-type can promulgate slavish values, as the ascetic priest does. Indeed, the possibility of a sovereign manner of valuing that generates life-denying values may offer a clue to Nietzsche's complex attitude to Socrates (and, indeed, to Schopenhauer), whom he seems both to vilify and to admire. I suggest, in short, that Nietzsche venerated Socrates' manner of valuing—which was nobly sovereign in almost exactly Nietzsche's sense—while repudiating *some* of his specific values, and especially the supreme value placed on absolute and timeless standards,[37] which he sees as inaugurating the fateful Western road to *décadence*.

3. The distinction in value between master and slave must, therefore, turn on the third criterion of life-enhancement, namely 'form-creation' that invites *love* of world and life. The creation of radically individual forms—whether in the shape of new life-affirming values, of great art, or of a unified character with 'style'—demands a breadth of talent, power, and individuality that the 'reactive' emotions simply cannot supply. Though the slave may be capable of form-creation (such as that expressed in 'giving birth' to moral values or in routine philosophy, science, or art) that modestly seduces to life or that reflects a temperate attachment to the world, form-creation that passionately engages with the world requires different orders of courage and individuality—i.e. those of the 'master'. In this sense only, life-enhancement is always masterly.

4. Though 'form-creation' that invites love of world and life is itself always 'masterly', Nietzsche interestingly suggests that slavish

---

[37] For example, the idea that there is one timeless standard in relation to which all courageous acts are to be judged courageous.

traits are crucial to motivating it—and especially to generating its variety and subtlety. For the slave's feeling of vulnerability, the gnawing question mark he (in contrast to the master) places over his identity and power, and his restless dissatisfaction with his lot, can all provide decisive impetus to the highest realms of thought and art and self-mastery—in other words, to maximal life-enhancement. He, unlike the master, is a painful problem to himself; and in his search for relief from the pain and for a solution to the problem he is driven to feats of thought, imagination, self-discipline, and artistry for which the self-assured master simply lacks comparable motivation. Thus, all three features of the reactive spirit—namely *ressentiment*, bad conscience, and the ascetic ideal (principal themes of, respectively, the three essays of *On the Genealogy of Morals*)—which, when taken to extremes, are unrelentingly life-denying, are, in more moderate form, inducements to philosophy, autonomy, and truthfulness. *Ressentiment* first made men '*interesting*' (*GM*, I, 6), it has made them '*cleverer* than any noble race' (*GM*, I, 10), and its instincts have been '*instruments of culture*' (*GM*, I, 11). Bad conscience has fostered 'memory' and been the 'womb of all ideal and imaginative phenomena' (*GM*, II, 18; cf. my Chapter 4.2.3). And the ascetic ideal has structured the West's unique commitment to truth (e.g. *GM*, III, 24; cf. Chapter 5.3). The essential point here is that though the activity of form-creation is 'masterly', its genesis is crucially dependent upon the slave's phenomenology of self-doubt.[38] This hypothesis is excellently exemplified by the following passage:

Supposing that . . . the *meaning of all culture* is the reduction of the beast of prey 'man' to a tame and civilized animal, a *domestic animal*, then one would undoubtedly have to regard all those instincts of reaction and *ressentiment* through whose aid the noble races and their ideals were finally confounded and overthrown as the actual *instruments of culture*; which is not to say that the *bearers* of those instincts themselves represent culture. Rather is the reverse not . . . *palpable*! These bearers of the oppressive [i.e. slavish] instincts that thirst for reprisal . . . represent the *regression* of mankind! (*GM*, I, 12).

[38] That '*ressentiment*', 'bad conscience', and the 'ascetic ideal' might have a common role both in enforcing slave values and in generating the sovereign, cultured individual constitutes two important linkages between the three essays of *GM*. What determines whether, in any individual or society, this trio is life-denying rather than life-enhancing is, first, the preponderance of slave drives over master drives and, second, the power of the 'priestly type' to mobilize the slave drives behind 'morality' (e.g. *GM*: I, 6–7; III, 9–11; III, 17–22).

5. Nietzsche is, therefore, inescapably ambiguous towards both 'slave' and 'master' moralities: neither of them, alone, can maximize life-enhancement. Most fertile individuals or cultures are, he suggests, a composite of both: 'in all the higher and more mixed cultures there also appear attempts at mediation between these two moralities . . . and at times they occur directly alongside each other . . . within a *single* soul' (*BGE*, 260).[39] Masters, for their part, need slave instincts in order to maximize life-enhancement—i.e. to achieve the most powerful and sublimated expressions of form-creation—for three reasons suggested in the previous paragraph: (*a*) slave traits provide something to be 'overcome'; (*b*) they themselves supply much of the motivation for that overcoming, motivation which arises from the urge to be rid of vulnerability; and (*c*) the overcoming fosters crucial skills, such as abstract thought, self-discipline, and the creation of beauty. Without slave instincts, the masters' expression of power would, therefore, remain crude and unreflective; while slave instincts uncontrolled by mastery would be marked by pure, formless *ressentiment*.[40] Indeed, Nietzsche suggests, 'today there is perhaps no more decisive mark of a "*higher nature*", a more spiritual nature, than that of being . . . a genuine battleground of these opposed values' of 'good and bad' versus 'good and evil' (*GM*, I, 16)—i.e. the opposed value-systems of 'master' and 'slave'.

6. Finally, this discussion shows that, whatever Nietzsche's 'historical' story may suggest, slavishness and *ressentiment* should not be automatically correlated with weakness or lack of talent. The slave is, above all, someone in possession of the philosophical presuppositions of *ressentiment* which we discussed earlier—presuppositions which make him feel appallingly vulnerable and resentful, whatever his actual strengths. In theory, therefore, such a person could be

[39] Thus, on Nietzsche's account, if people with an overtly 'masterly' disposition adopt slave morality, they do so not only because they are coerced or because they unthinkingly internalize the moral norms of their society, but also because they possess a partly 'slavish' soul.

[40] Nietzsche's ethical views sometimes exemplify a version of Aristotle's theory of 'the mean'—in the sense that too little and too much of something are both life-denying, while the right amount is life-enhancing. This is true, for example, of the ratio of master to slave in an individual, which we have just discussed, as well as of 'bad conscience' and the ascetic ideal—i.e. for all three of the main concepts of *On the Genealogy of Morals*. Thus, too little ascetic denial results in psychic dissipation or crudity; too much in an overall denial of one's life-possibilities; and the right amount in the person capable of autonomy, beauty, and imagination. That moderation—in this specific sense only—may be better exemplified for Nietzsche than for Aristotle himself (for whom the 'theory' is notoriously tricky) would be a nice irony from the philosopher of Dionysian intoxication!

gifted and powerful. This is confirmed, in practice, by the fact, as Nietzsche describes it, that so many geniuses have succumbed to the slavish interpretation of life, among them Plato, Kant, Pascal, and the later Wagner. To be a malcontent one does not need to be ungifted, nor to be sovereign must one be one of nature's talents; and if Nietzsche's concept of *ressentiment* had supposed otherwise it would have been rooted in an obvious psychological error.

In sum: Nietzsche's ideal of man cannot be assimilated to his picture of the original masters, with their 'disgusting' murderers, arsonists, and rapists (*GM*, I, 11)—even if he does admire their unabashed expressiveness. His ideal life is attained only by the (unending) fight against slavishness in order to impose 'a form upon oneself' (*GM*, II, 18), to discipline oneself, like Goethe, 'to wholeness' . . . 'in the *faith* . . . that all is redeemed and affirmed in the whole', and to ensure that one '*does not negate any more*' (*TI*, IX, 49, *passim*). Nietzsche seems unequivocally to repudiate slavishness only where it scores negatively by all three criteria mentioned earlier—empowerment, sublimation, and form-creation that seduces to life: that is, only where its sole aim or result is to suppress, deny, and devalue life, one's own and others'. But to suggest that Nietzsche's critique of morality is limited to such outright condemnation, or that he sees 'slave' impulses as leading exclusively to morbid *ennui* and the suppression of all vitality, would be to underestimate the complexity and analytical power of his master/slave dualism.

3.5 THE SCOPE OF 'MASTER' AND 'SLAVE' CATEGORIES

The reactiveness of the 'slave' and the sovereignty of the 'master' manifest themselves, Nietzsche suggests, across a very broad spectrum of human activity—reaching into areas that are generally regarded as having little to do with the subject-matter of morality—above all, in dominant manners of thinking in epistemology, science, and psychology. Five examples will suffice to illustrate this point about the scope of Nietzsche's typology:

1. Philosophies which assume that the value of actions (e.g. of altruism) is determined 'from the point of view of those to whom they were done, that is to say, those to whom they were *useful*' (*GM*,

I, 2) are reactive. Such reactive philosophies underlie utilitarian thinking, Darwinism and its concept of 'adaptation', and, indeed, the whole of technical-industrial civilization to the extent that it depends on 'calculating prudence' or 'a calculus of utility' (*GM*, I, 2).

2. Aesthetics has been largely preoccupied with the perceiver, rather than with the creator, of art; e.g. Kant's third Critique (*GM*, III, 6).

3. The value placed on consciousness is also symptomatic of reactiveness. Consciousness, because it '*has developed under the pressure of the need for communication* . . ., does not really belong to man's individual existence but rather to his social or herd nature; . . . it has developed subtlety only insofar as this is required by social or herd utility' (*GS*, 354).

4. The enterprise of modern science and its unconditional valuation of truth are manifestations of the ascetic ideal (*GM*, III, 24–5), which is, in turn, a paradigmatic expression of the reactive spirit. In addition, certain key concepts of the individual sciences, such as physics and physiology, are essentially reactive, insofar as they embody the democratic assumption of ' "nature's conformity to law" ' (*BGE*, 22; cf. *GM*, II, 12). And this is a disguised expression of:

5. The 'democratic instincts of the modern soul' (*BGE*, 22) and the resulting egalitarian (and revolutionary) element in modern nation-states—which is also thoroughly reactive in spirit.

One could summarize these points in a formula: 'slave reactiveness—i.e. *ressentiment*—is the dominant form or structure of our thought and sensibility'. It is expressed not merely by individuals but by entire civilizations and manners of thinking. It is the common feature of apparently opposed enterprises, such as religion and science—which, to that extent, are continuations by different means of the same fundamental values and motives (a point to be developed in discussing the ascetic ideal in Chapter 5.3). It generates a metaphysics of permanence (the postulates of the 'atomistic need')—as we discussed above—which manifests itself in an ontology of substance-attribute, in a science of atomism and mechanism, in a psychology of will-action, and in an ethics of slave morality.[41] By contrast, Nietzsche advocates a metaphysics (in the sense of postulating a fun-

---

[41] The connection between some of these manifestations of 'reactive' metaphysics is made in, for example, *GM*, I, 13 and *BGE*, 12.

damental concept in terms of which everything else may putatively be explained but which itself may not be explained in terms of anything else) of 'will to power'/valuing, which manifests itself in an ontology of force or effect, in a science of energy/field theories, in a psychology of actions and events, and, when the 'atomistic need' has been thoroughly overcome, in an ethics of life-enhancement.

The point of alluding to these very wide implications of Nietzsche's concept of *ressentiment* is to show that, for him, 'slave morality' is associated with an entire way of conceiving and relating to the world, and is not restricted to the kinds of concerns traditionally taken to fall within the scope of morality, such as our duties and obligations towards each other.

3.6 'MASTER' AND 'SLAVE' AS TYPOLOGY RATHER THAN HISTORY

The discussion thus far suggests at least four reasons why Nietzsche's account of masters and slaves is more interesting as a typology of drives than as an account of some original type of person or society. First, he is primarily concerned with individuals who are a composite of these drives (and where to extirpate one or the other would be impossible, even if desirable). Second, in the interaction of these drives within a single individual we find that slave traits generate 'life-enhancing' capacities (such as for thought, discipline, and art) that are not necessarily present in the historical slaves. Third, 'slave' and 'master' are intended to apply to *manners* of thought and being, exemplifiable across a broad range of human activities, rather than simply to historical individuals. Fourth, the historical story by which slavish '*ressentiment* itself becomes creative and gives birth to values' (*GM*, I, 10) is, as we suggested in closing section 3.3, less interesting than what is presupposed philosophically by the very possibility of *ressentiment*—which only conceptual, rather than historical, analysis can establish. Thus, *ressentiment* is associated with certain values (particularly, essential equality), with certain questions (notably, 'why is there suffering at all?'), and with certain aims (above all, to abolish suffering and inequality). For 'slaves' to experience their inferiority as so unacceptable, their expectations must already have been armed by such values, questions, and aims.

Moreover, none of these four points, we may note, depends upon the accuracy of Nietzsche's account in *GM* I of the historical nobles and slaves (although it is questionable whether, for example, the Homeric heroes, whom Nietzsche so admires, bear much resemblance to his unreflecting 'nobles', with their forgetfulness of insults and inability to take enemies, accidents, or misdeeds seriously (*GM*, I, 10)). Instead, the value of these conclusions is primarily philosophical and psychological. Indeed, in concluding Chapter 4.3, I will suggest that Nietzsche's genealogical accounts, of which that of the masters and slaves is a paradigm, are best taken as fictional; but that this does not prevent them from being valuable as ways of getting us to think, even if hypothetically, about the functions of our actual ethical practices and their motivations by relating them to possible earlier or more elementary practices and motivations in a manner which is free of the search for timeless 'groundings'.

3.7 CONCLUSION: 'GOOD/BAD' VERSUS 'GOOD/EVIL'

It is abundantly clear that Nietzsche retains a 'good/bad' distinction—in that he both sanctions the use of these terms as general concepts and himself espouses rigorous standards of good and bad. Hence, he says: 'it has long since been abundantly clear . . . what the aim of that dangerous slogan is that is inscribed at the head of . . . *Beyond Good and Evil.*—At least this does *not* mean "Beyond Good and Bad"' (*GM*, I, 17). As general concepts, 'good' and 'bad' (*schlecht*) simply denote what an individual, by his own sovereign standards, approves and disapproves of. Indeed, if values are necessary conditions for life and, as we recall from Chapter 2.1, empirically related to who we are as 'types', Nietzsche is committed to retaining a 'bad/good' distinction. And, because of that empirical relationship, 'good' and 'bad' do not denote arbitrary whims or thoughts. Thus, any critique of an ethic—such as Nietzsche's critique of the system of 'morality' that, as he sees it, is marked by the 'good/evil' distinction—can take place only from the perspective of the standards of a rival ethic—in this case Nietzsche's own standard of good and bad.

As we have already indicated, Nietzsche's good and bad are, respectively, life-enhancement and life-denial, for which we have reconstructed three criteria. And, as we also discussed, this standard does not lead Nietzsche to accept or reject (long-standing) values or practices as such—for example, pity or cruelty in themselves—but only the function for which they are employed. Thus, there are circumstances where he would disapprove of values which he generally links to the noble type—e.g. egoism—just as there are circumstances where he would approve of values which he primarily associates with the slave type—e.g. pity. What always determines whether Nietzsche approves of a particular value in a particular context is, first, the manner in which it is reached—i.e. whether it is reached by the sovereign choice of the noble type or whether by the reactive 'universalism' of the moral type—and, second, what purpose it serves—i.e. whether to enhance life and individuality ('ascending life'), or whether to deny life and individuality ('descending life'). If pity originates in sovereign choice and, in the context, enhances life, then Nietzsche would welcome it. If egoism had the reverse origin and purpose he would repudiate it:

Self-interest is worth as much as the person who has it: it can be worth a great deal, and it can be unworthy and contemptible. Every individual may be scrutinized to see whether he represents the ascending or the descending line of life. Having made that decision, one has a canon for the worth of his self-interest. (*TI*, IX, 33)

That he does not judge values or actions as good or bad in themselves is clear from the following passage from *Daybreak*:

I do not deny—unless I am a fool—that many actions called immoral ought to be avoided and resisted, or that many called moral ought to be done and encouraged—but I think the one should be encouraged and the other avoided *for other reasons than hitherto*. (*D*, 103)

The revaluation of all values—that 'act of supreme self-examination on the part of humanity' of its traditional moral convictions (*EH*, IV, 1)—is complete only when it becomes impossible (for those capable of life-enhancement) to think in terms of the old morality of 'good and evil'. And this seismic occurrence occurs not because the old values have been legislated away but because, under pressure from our commitment (or 'will') to truth, our old beliefs are fatally undermined in three ways. First, it becomes impossible to believe that the old morality enhances life. Second, the proposition that this, or any, morality receives unconditional validity from some absolute, timeless, impartial authority external to our own practices, values, and needs, such as God, Reason, or Nature, is held to be false—or at least unverifiable. (The discrediting of such an authority—or 'grounding'—for values is the wider meaning of Nietzsche's famous proclamation of the 'death of God'.) And, third, *ressentiment*—i.e. the psychological correlate of these traditional beliefs in morality and its grounding—is shown up for what it is: namely, as a vengeful attitude to a (sensible) world which we have devalued as such—with the unjustifiable presupposition that there is an independent, unhistorical point of view from which such a devaluation is possible. As we will discuss in Part II, it is one of Nietzsche's central axioms that to understand the truth about the functions of our most cherished values, theories, and practices can cause us finally to discard or replace them, and that truth is therefore a major, if not the major, catalyst of the coming 'revaluation of all values'.

4

Non-moral versus Moral 'Guilt' and 'Bad Conscience'

4.1 OBJECTIVES AND DISTINCTIONS

This chapter focuses on two sentiments—'guilt' and 'bad conscience'—that, as Nietzsche presents them, are central to both traditional morality *and* his new ethic of 'life-enhancement'.[1] This focus has four objectives:

(1) to explicate the non-moral, potentially life-enhancing, role played by these sentiments in the development of any society, of 'higher' culture, and, ultimately, of the 'sovereign' individual, the one who can maximally commit and command herself;

(2) to explicate the life-denying development of these sentiments in traditional morality and in producing the old ideal of self- and world-denial to which Nietzsche is so opposed;

(3) to understand what is involved in the crucial progression from non-moral to moral guilt and bad conscience—and to demonstrate that here, once again, Nietzsche's attack is not on a basic concept employed by Christian morality, such as 'guilt', but rather on the *use* to which it is put in life-denial;

(4) to explore how far that basic social form, the 'debtor–creditor relationship', is not only the historical 'origin' of the feeling of guilt, as Nietzsche suggests (e.g. *GM*, II, 4 and 8), but can also be used to model the nature of guilt.

I will argue that this relationship indeed successfully models the phenomenology of guilt, not only in the ordinary situation of an explicit contract between individuals, but also where the 'creditor' (or victim of a default) is taken to be a god or an ancestor or otherwise uncontracted in any conventionally reciprocal sense, or where the 'credit'

[1] The discussion in this chapter is based largely on the second essay of *On the Genealogy of Morals*.

cannot, even in principle, be calculated or repaid or voluntarily incurred. But I will also suggest that the debtor–creditor model has this explanatory fertility only if, like guilt itself, it presupposes a strong notion of personal accountability.[2] Whereas if it is taken to be just a mechanical transaction enforced by the threat of punishment, then it could not explain guilt. And if this is so, the conceptual distance between the debtor–creditor relationship and guilt is small in comparison with the conceptual leap represented by the appearance of a credible debtor–creditor relationship in the first place. But this is a leap which, I will argue, Nietzsche's genealogies do not address.

In order to draw the overall distinction between 'non-moral' and 'moral' forms of guilt and bad conscience, three points are in order:

First, the non-moral forms correspond to that normal intensity of guilty indebtedness and self-cruelty which, Nietzsche's arguments suggest, can be exhibited by an individual in any fairly developed society. In moral forms, by contrast, guilt is seen as defining a (human) world that must be 'transcended'. (This essentialism is, of course, the counterpart of the universal scope of *ressentiment*, which we discussed in Chapter 3.3.)

Second, guilt and bad conscience, in their general, non-moral forms, are phenomenologically quite different. Guilt, in its general form, is ethically experienced regret at one's failure (not necessarily intentional) to honour obligations to which one genuinely feels committed; whereas bad conscience, in its general form, arises from the cruel self-discipline needed to *avoid* guilty indebtedness to one's society. The general forms of these concepts do not necessarily lead to the moralized forms, though the latter obviously presuppose the former.

Third, the non-moral forms can be life-enhancing, whereas the moral forms are, according to Nietzsche, overwhelmingly life-denying. Guilt and bad conscience thereby exemplify my general thesis that all Nietzsche's 'slavish' categories—e.g. 'reactive' thought, *ressentiment*, the ascetic ideal—are potentially life-enhancing when they are sufficiently moderate to engage productively with 'masterly' traits, rather than overwhelming them with vengeful anger.

---

[2] Nietzsche suggests that a credible debtor–creditor contractual relationship *does* require that, for the debtor, the promise to repay is 'an obligation upon his own conscience' (*GM*, II, 5)—i.e. does presuppose an ethically charged notion of personal accountability.

This sharp distinction between general and moral forms of guilt and bad conscience helps us to analyse the tremendous differences between these forms as well as the questions posed by the transition from one to the other. Accordingly, the following discussion is divided into three sections: the first compares and relates these concepts in their general form; the second considers them in their specifically moralized form; and the third suggests some provisional conclusions—drawing on Nietzschean ideas but ranging beyond them.

4.2 THE NON-MORAL FORM OF 'GUILT' AND OF 'BAD CONSCIENCE'

On the debtor–creditor model, non-moral guilt and bad conscience both presuppose the agent's feeling of respect for the contractual relationship between debtors and creditors and for the discipline of promise-keeping that it demands.

4.2.1 The general form of 'guilt'

Guilt, in its most general form—that which appears in non-moral ethical codes—is a highly reflexive feeling of regret or inadequacy at failing to honour one's obligations, which one accepts, to a 'creditor'. The more substantial or stringent the obligation, the stronger the guilt. The position of 'creditor' can have different occupants, and Nietzsche, in the course of *GM* II (especially sections 19 and 20), suggests three main types, which, in order of increasing power, are: first, the individual with whom one has entered into some form of exchange of a classic debtor–creditor kind (such as trade); second, ancestors who are believed to empower the society, in return for which it owes them an increasing debt of gratitude; and, third, gods, whom Nietzsche depicts as the culmination of ancestor-worship.

This progression, all three stages of which occur, Nietzsche suggests, in 'prehistory' (*GM*, II, 19), and so are decidedly pre-moral, exhibits the interesting anthropological thesis that the power attributed to the creditor reflects the power of the society—so that to worship gods as its creditors is a sign of a society's strength rather than of its weakness (and, presumably, to concentrate all creditor-power in one god is the ultimate demonstration of one's confidence—at

least initially). For the first type of creditor—who is merely an individual—a complex society is not even needed. The creditor may, for
example, be another nomad. In the second phase, however, the society has developed real power, which it must attribute to someone,
and, given (one presumes) the belief that great power is unseen,
ancestors, who founded and empowered the tribe with untold sacrifices and accomplishments, are the best candidate for that attribution—though, if this is so, the question arises for the debtor whether
their credits can ever be repaid (*GM*, II, 19). In the third phase, the
society's triumphs outstrip even the empowering capacity attributable to great ancestors, so that only gods are seen as grand enough
to dispense such munificence. In the culmination of this phase, when
the tribe turns itself into an imperial ruler, all power is vested in one
god. 'Despotism', says Nietzsche 'always prepares the way for some
kind of monotheism' (*GM*, II, 20)—a deeply unconvincing hypothesis given that not one of the three great monotheisms originated
among imperial masters and that many empires, from the early
Roman to the Mongol, were polytheistic.

Nonetheless, as in the story of masters and slaves in *GM* I, the
palpable fictionality of Nietzsche's genealogy need not diminish the
importance of the conceptual *forms* he proposes. The form of guilt
which emerges from *GM* II may, in summary, be defined as a feeling of depressive, ethically charged inadequacy consequent upon failure to honour a debt to a recognized creditor—i.e. one to whom one
accepts the obligation of repayment—where (*a*) the position of creditor may have a variety of occupants, such as the three types suggested in the historical story, (*b*) the intensity of guilty indebtedness
(*das Schuldgefühl*) is proportionate both to the seriousness of the
obligation—i.e. how substantial and stringent it is—and to the perceived power of the creditor,[3] and (*c*) the debt need not have been
explicitly agreed with a creditor—as in most debts to ancestors and
gods or, indeed, in obligations which one feels towards oneself. This
basic account of guilt is, I suggest, very helpful; but we must be
alert to three sources of possible confusion which exist, or loom, in
GM II.

First, though 'debt' and 'guilt' are obviously related, they cannot
be straightforwardly equated. (The fact, to which Nietzsche points
in *GM*, II, 4, that they are denoted in German by the same word,

---

[3] The seriousness of the obligation and the perceived power of the creditor may, of
course, be related—and in the Judaeo-Christian tradition arguably are.

Schuld, may tempt one to suggest such a false equivalence.) 'Debt' denotes an obligation, which one may or may not be capable of discharging and which one may or may not recognize; whereas 'guilt' denotes a feeling consequent upon failure to discharge an obligation that one does recognize. Thus, not all debt engenders guilt: specifically, not debt that one can and does repay on time, or that one never recognized as repayable. Indeed, where debt exists on terms that are agreed and respected by both sides, it is a guilt-free transaction without which societies would be immobilized, if not impossible. In short, guilt is neither entailed by, nor equatable to, debt.

Second, Nietzsche cannot, therefore, be right to regard the feeling of guilt as simply a feeling 'of personal obligation' (*GM*, II, 8). Guilt is occasioned only by *failing* to honour what we take to be an obligation. Now that failure may occur not only for the conventional reason that a pre-agreed repayment schedule cannot be met, but also (as with debts to gods or ancestors) because the creditor's terms are not known or even knowable, or because repayment has no conceivable terminus. That a debt may confer strength on the debtor is therefore not inconsistent with the fact that his guilt at his inability to discharge it is necessarily experienced as impotence. (This feeling of impotence in all guilt is further discussed in the Endnote to this chapter.)

Third, a 'contractual relationship' between debtor and creditor, both conceived as 'legal subjects' (*GM*, II, 4), cannot be a simple mechanical transaction if it is to be useful as a model for blame and *Schuldgefühl*, but must itself be structured by a robust conception of accountability and responsibility. The limits of accountability may be a matter of convention—for example whether or not bad luck, such as everyday misfortunes or the unforeseeable workings of fate, is taken to mitigate one's accountability. But that a developed notion of accountability is in play here cannot be denied—or else the model would not work.

Two questions follow from this account of guilt in its basic form. First, what happens when guilt becomes moralized—i.e. when guilt becomes conceived as constitutive of life and as demanding to be 'transcended'? Second, why does guilty indebtedness not *decline* with the rise of atheism, i.e. with the disappearance of creditors possessing the power of gods? These questions are intimately related, for the particular conception of guilt that makes it a pillar of 'morality' (and that turns it into something essentially life-denying) *also* fortifies it against atheism.

To answer both questions, we need the concept of 'bad con-science'. The moralization of 'guilt'—and of 'obligation' or 'duty', which it presupposes since one feels guilty only when one disrespects what one regards as a duty—is, Nietzsche says, 'their pushing back into the conscience; more precisely, the involvement of the *bad* con-science with the concept of god' (*GM*, II, 21). But if we are to under-stand this obscure formulation, we must ask, first, what 'bad conscience', in its general form, is and, second, how exactly it is related to the moralization of guilt through this 'pushing back'. I will take these two questions in turn.

4.2.2 The general form of 'bad conscience'

Nietzsche's concept of 'bad conscience', in its general form, denotes the pain of regarding one's unsublimated 'masterly' passions, like '[h]ostility, cruelty, joy in persecuting' (*GM*, II, 16), as a perpetual source of potential guilt towards the rest of society, as constantly endangering one's social acceptance, and, thus, as making oneself a liability to oneself. The code of every society inevitably requires the individual to rein in these passions; but, before he has perfected this self-control, they will naturally strive to exert themselves externally, as they could do in a pre-social state. By thus threatening to flout the social code, they become a potential cause of both social rejec-tion and of guilty indebtedness towards society; and by needing to be forcibly reined in, they pit the individual against instincts of which, prima facie, he is proudest (because 'masterly'). This unpleasant combination of potential guilt towards society, liability towards oneself, and the need for self-aggression towards masterly instincts, is, I suggest, the 'bad conscience'.

Now Nietzsche actually advances two reasons why socialization of the individual leads to this turning inwards of his masterly passions—the one a pragmatic imperative, the other a quasi-'physiological' reflex. The pragmatic imperative is the need to secure the benefits of society by becoming gentle and calculable (*GM*, II, 2). Historically, this imperative arises because the context has changed from one where man roamed free to one where he is 'enclosed within the walls of soci-ety and of peace' (*GM*, II, 16). It is enforced by the incessant 'acts of violence' that forge a coherent society out of 'a hitherto unchecked and shapeless populace' (*GM*, II, 17). Such calculability demands, in turn, the ability to guarantee one's promises, i.e. to respect contracts and rules of justice and, should they be broken, to accept or make payment in kind, such as punishment in its many forms. In other words, becoming a citizen demands the *self-mastery* to participate in what is effectively a debtor–creditor relationship writ large, with the individual as the debtor and society, with its many benefits, as the creditor. By contrast, the reflexive reason for the inward-turning of masterly passions is simply an instance of the natural law that '[a]ll instincts that do not discharge themselves outwardly *turn inward*', i.e. that psychological forces hitting an obstacle head on are deflected directly back on themselves. This hypothesis might be called Nietzsche's 'law of the conservation of psychic energy'. It operates when these 'old instincts of freedom' suddenly run up against 'bulwarks' of a society, like its mores and punishments (*GM*, II, 16)—though whether this 'law' applies as much to the tender or possessive instincts, such as sympathy and love, as it does to the cruel and gregarious ones is open to question.

These remarks indicate why bad conscience is 'bad' and why it concerns 'conscience' and not 'consciousness'.

Bad conscience is 'bad' not in the sense that Nietzsche regards it as ethically bad, but because the agent experiences it as unpleasant. And the agent experiences it thus not merely because calculability demands painful self-cruelty, but, more profoundly, because, in being a potentially guilty debtor to society,[4] he has inescapably become a liability to himself. This great burden of self-consciousness lasts as long as his masterly instincts are seen as potential traitors to himself and to society, and, in place of the freedom to conquer, are assigned petty clerical tasks, such as 'inferring, reckoning, and co-ordinating cause and effect' (*GM*, II, 16). This is so *whether or not* he has actually transgressed or been punished, and whether he is the criminal or the judge. The tragedy of becoming a liability to himself visits the agent not because he has abused his powers or flouted society's norms, but just because, unless and until he has become a fully 'sovereign individual', one aspect of his nature—his outward-straining 'instincts of freedom'—is perpetually in potential conflict with another aspect—namely his inescapable commitment to that munificent creditor called 'society'.

---

[4] This guilt is, of course, still 'pre-moral' because it is not yet interpreted as an argument against human nature or life.

Moreover, what is bad here is 'conscience', precisely because what constitutes it is the always-looming guilt to which I have referred.[5] Since, as I have argued, guilt presupposes one's commitment to norms, and hence a developed notion of personal accountability or responsibility, bad conscience can be experienced only by someone who is genuinely committed to the social norms for the sake of which he represses his masterly instincts. It is because punishment does *not* bring about such genuine commitment (but rather only prudent or tactical obedience) that Nietzsche, interestingly, claims that punishment for breaking promises is *not* the 'soil' from which bad conscience, and its guilt, grow (*GM*, II, 14). Punishment, he insists, 'tames' but does not improve; it cultivates caution not remorse; thus, it actually hinders guilt rather than fostering it. (And the matter is viewed identically by the punishers, for whom the offender is merely 'an irresponsible piece of fate', rather than a 'guilty person'.)

Of course, punishment may foster the '*mnemotechnics*'—the capacity to remember—that is required for all promising and so for all 'calculability' (*GM*, II, 3). But the calculability of a person capable of 'bad conscience' is more than Pavlovian conditioning because it crucially involves one's *identification* with social norms which only a real sense of belonging to a society can instil. Violence and force may play their part in enforcing obedience to those norms (and, of course, in creating the society in the first place), but only a genuine sense of belonging to and needing the society can ensure the personal allegiance or responsibility towards its norms that is a condition for the possibility of guilt.[6]

---

[5] Nietzsche himself clearly equates bad conscience with 'the consciousness of guilt' (*GM*, II, 4). Indeed, because the possibility of guilt is central to the operation of bad conscience, *schlechtes Gewissen* is properly translated as 'bad conscience', rather than as 'bad consciousness'—as Danto insistently renders it (for example, in A. Danto, 'Some Remarks on *The Genealogy of Morals*', in Schacht (ed.), *Nietzsche, Genealogy, Morality*, 43). Moreover, *Gewissen* always means 'conscience' and never 'consciousness'; and had Nietzsche intended the latter he could have termed it *schlechtes Bewusstsein*—the sort of nausea that Zarathustra feels at the eternal recurrence of the 'small man' (*Z*, III, 13).

[6] Though punishment may not be the straightforward, proximate cause of genuine commitment to norms, it may, perhaps, feature in a detailed psychological account of how individuals come to recognize the authority of such norms—analogously to the way in which, for example, Bernard Williams argues that fear of the anger of a victim or viewer of one's actions plays a role in triggering guilty feelings about them. (See Bernard Williams, *Shame and Necessity* (Berkeley and Los Angeles: University of California Press, 1993), 219 and 221.)

4.2.3 General 'bad conscience' as 'active' or life-enhancing

Now it is important to note that, in its general form, 'bad conscience' can be life-enhancing—indeed, Nietzsche calls it '*active*' bad conscience (*GM*, II, 18), as we will see. This is so for both conceptual and practical reasons.

Conceptually, bad conscience has the *form* of a master. In terms of Nietzsche's master/slave dualism, bad conscience is actually a quintessential expression of active, 'form-giving', drives—i.e. of 'master' instincts—whose recalcitrant object is no longer other people but one's own unruly passions. (To suggest, as one might be tempted to, that bad conscience, being a response to social pressure, must be '*reactive*' would be to confuse a *precondition* for socialization with a *response* to socialization. Bad conscience, as such a precondition, is no more reactive than a language-speaker following the rules of a linguistic community. What he does with himself once socialized is another matter—and here he may be either active or reactive.)

Practically, there are two reasons why bad conscience is life-enhancing. First, the straightforward turning-inwards of the 'masterly' instincts is a strategy for the individual's preservation and, indeed, enhancement in a society; and unless Nietzsche holds, which he does not and could not, that socialization *per se* is life-denying (on the criteria reconstructed in Chapter 3.1), he cannot deem bad conscience itself to be life-denying.

Second, and much more interestingly, bad conscience can give rise to a series of major conceptual and ethical innovations. For, Nietzsche suggests, to direct violent cruelty against oneself rather than others, to burn into a great part of one's nature a 'no' to its outward expression, to become contemptuous of instincts of which one was 'formerly' proudest, to live with the contradiction of a freedom that is both restricted (externally) and enhanced (internally), creates a wholly new phenomenology: that of human nature as problematical and contradictory, that of oneself as a riddle to oneself, that of the tortured 'inner life' perpetually examining itself, that of a compromised 'outer' freedom versus a purer 'inner' freedom. In short: with the '*bad* conscience' we get 'the *internalization* of man', his creation of an inner, freer world, later christened 'the soul'. Nietzsche calls this state '*active*' bad conscience (*GM*, II, 16).

The *conceptual* correlate of this new phenomenology of contradictions is a world of polarities: free versus unfree, beauty versus ugliness, reason versus desire, knowledge versus opinion. For in this inner world of inescapable contradictions concepts embracing polar opposites become natural, such as beauty (necessarily opposed to ugliness) or the ideal (necessarily contrasted with its non-fulfilment). This, it seems, is the meaning of Nietzsche's statement that the self-cruelty of bad conscience is 'the womb of all ideal and imaginative phenomena', of 'strange new beauty and affirmation' and even of 'beauty itself' (*GM*, II, 18). Interestingly, beauty here originates from conflict and alienation and maturity, and not from wholeness and innocence, as almost every nostalgic fantasy would have it.

The *ethical* correlates of this new phenomenology are complex but, I suggest, include three that, in 'morality', are highly developed. First, the hallowed connection between freedom and morality may be established here since freedom, experienced primarily as some-thing internal, is pictured as a direct result of ethical discipline. Second, the quality of 'intentions' becomes important in ethical val-uations—for they are the warning signals of danger and must, there-fore, be watched and judged. Only by focusing on intentions can the individual isolate the horse before it has bolted (in the shape of socially proscribed actions). And third, this new world of polarities may also foster the *'faith in opposite values'* which, in its extreme form, Nietzsche regards as central to morality (*BGE*, 2).

In sum, Nietzsche's point here might be that this experience of being at war with oneself rather than only with others facilitates *all* thinking and acting and valuing that depend on polarities. Thus, it becomes natural to think in terms of ideals, in just the way that Plato, say, inaugurates, or of all things as either good or bad, and beautiful or ugly. And it also becomes natural to pursue values that in their very nature are self-contradictory—such as *'selflessness'* (*GM*, II, 18), i.e. the direction of the self against the self; indeed, not merely to pursue these values, but, in the new manner of thinking, to set them up as *ideals*. This may be why Nietzsche speaks of *'active* "bad conscience"' as *'pregnant with a future'* (*GM*, II, 16) and as an illness like pregnancy (*GM*, II, 19) which, though risky, can be the progenitor of a new life in which man, for the first time, is *'included* among the most unexpected and exciting lucky throws' of fate (*GM*, II, 16).

Despite this creativity and its attendant joys, the conscience *remains* 'bad' because one's 'calculability' is never perfect. Thus, great cruelty against oneself must be sustained; second, 'guilty indebtedness' to society (or other 'creditors' such as ancestors or gods) always looms; and, third, one still regards precisely the masterly drives of which one was 'formerly' proudest as one's greatest liability because their impulsiveness constantly threatens that calculability. Even if bad conscience stops short of the systematic self-loathing that characterizes its later, for example Christian, forms, these three feelings, taken together, cannot but be experienced as something alien, dark, and frightening.[7]

4.2.4 What is 'good conscience'?

Two obvious questions remain: what would 'good conscience' be, and why doesn't Nietzsche use this term? As to the first, 'good conscience' would, I suggest, be the exhilaration of being perfectly able to discharge any debts and, as a result, to *guarantee* one's own freedom (through power over oneself and external circumstances). And it would be good 'conscience', rather than 'consciousness', because it would carry with it a sense of what Nietzsche calls the '*right to affirm oneself*' (*GM*, II, 3) stemming from the capacity to be, under all circumstances, sovereign and unindebted.[8] There would no longer be a trace of that depressing sense, characteristic of bad conscience, that, despite painful self-control, one remains imperfectly sovereign and, to that extent, a continuing liability to oneself. (Clearly, good conscience would not result from the absence of debts *per se*—which could be assured simply by luck or cowardice.)

Now the person of 'good conscience' is, I suggest, precisely Nietzsche's '*sovereign individual*', his perfectly 'autonomous and supramoral' man who is the culmination of the long 'breeding [of] an animal with the right to make promises', and 'its ripest fruit' (*GM*, II, 2). He both fashions new forms out of himself, much like a sculptor moulding his bronze, and has perfected his powers of sustained willing and self-discipline—and hence is able to 'live out' his highest values to the full. 'Circumstances', which were once so constraining, are now malleable under the force of his power to do as he promises; society imposes no restraints upon the 'higher' matters that concern him—those internal and refined pursuits of the soul; he

---

[7] If, as Nietzsche repeatedly maintains, the first of these feelings—self-cruelty—occasions the same sadistic pleasure as externally directed violence (*GM*, II, 18)—this may mitigate the horror of the other two, but surely only marginally and intermittently.

[8] This feeling that one has the *right* to do something is just the sense in which one declares: 'I did it with a good conscience.'

is unoppressed by any system of punishment and rewards in virtue of his lordly ability to pledge himself. Thus, the ruthless conformism that socialization initially required—imposed by the whole 'morality of mores' that was needed to make men calculable—is the ladder that finally leads to the 'sovereign' individual, and that is discarded once he has been attained. Indeed, the initial indispensability of, and subsequent liberation from, this 'morality of mores' might be one good example of Nietzsche's obscure 'law of life' that '[a]ll great things bring about their own destruction through an act of self-overcoming' (*GM*, III, 27).

It is in this sovereignty to promise that Nietzsche sees the real (as opposed to imaginary) senses of 'freedom of the will' and 'responsibility'—concepts that, like 'guilt', he interestingly regards as arising historically from the accumulation of strength, rather than of weakness. And it is the innate awareness of this sovereignty, and of the 'extraordinary privilege of [this] *responsibility*', that Nietzsche calls '*conscience*' (*GM*, II, 2). Hence we may say, in brief, that when this awareness of sovereignty is punctuated by doubts the conscience is 'bad', and that when it is perfectly free of doubts the conscience is 'good'.

So why does Nietzsche nowhere refer in *GM* II to the individual of 'good' conscience? Because, I suggest, *infallibility* in controlling one's 'animal' nature, in committing oneself to ethical standards (individual or collective), and so in avoiding any possibility of guilty indebtedness or bad conscience, is unattainable. The 'end of this tremendous process' of self-mastery in the 'sovereign individual' (*GM*, II, 2)—which might also be seen as a culmination of the modern project of 'autonomy'—is, it seems to me, a theoretical endpoint, which can be approached but not reached. For an individual to be *perfectly* 'autonomous and supramoral' and 'like only to himself' is to be endowed with qualities previously attributed only to God. This man–god is, one surmises, as elusive as the 'dead' God; though, in taking the place of the old God, he presumably has, for Nietzsche, one great advantage over his predecessor: that he is not world-transcending, and that the path to him is not one of world-denial. (Moreover, the man–god's attainment is undesirable, even in terms of Nietzsche's own values, because he has nothing left to overcome and therefore nothing to live for. I will explain what I mean by this in Chapter 6.3.)

In other words, if perfect commitment to ethical standards (social or individual) is an unattainable goal, there can be no well-formed society whose members are altogether free from the possibility of bad conscience[9] and no individual altogether free from the possibility of guilt. The possibility of bad conscience will exist because there will always be a residual need for self-cruelty in taming those 'animal' instincts that crave free expression and resist socialization (even if the latter is restricted to one's own 'type' or 'caste'[10]); while the possibility of guilt will loom as long as the capacity to honour one's ethical commitments is imperfect—commitments which may be to one's entirely individual standards or ideals, as well as to wider social norms. In short, insofar as individuals feel themselves committed to ethical standards and to membership in societies, both guilt and the 'illness' of bad conscience are, though Nietzsche does not explicitly recognize this, necessarily universal[11]—a point to which I return in concluding this chapter. Thus, if Nietzsche wants to abolish *all* guilt or bad conscience—rather than, say, their *moralized* forms (and the linked notion of 'sin')—as part of creating a *'second innocence'* (*GM*, II, 20) of mankind, then he will *not* succeed.

I do not, however, think that such a final elimination of the possibility of guilt or bad conscience is part of his project. As to guilt, Nietzsche suggests that a 'second innocence', if it were to come about, would eliminate only one type of guilt (albeit the historically dominant type): namely that associated with religious belief and,

---

[9] Nietzsche makes it clear that even his 'noble races' or 'good men' of *GM*, I, 11, some of whom are portrayed as being quite undeveloped socially, do, *among themselves*, exhibit 'self-control' and 'the tension engendered by protracted confinement and enclosure within the peace of society'—i.e. do exhibit something like 'bad conscience'. Indeed, it is precisely in order to seek relief from this tension that they unleash it on those outside the tribe, where 'they savor a freedom from all social constraints' and 'go *back* to the innocent conscience of the beast of prey'. Note Nietzsche's use of the word 'conscience' here, in, I suggest, just the way in which he defines it in *GM*, II, 2—and his notion of going *back* to an innocent conscience from, presumably, a bad conscience. (The 'blond beasts of prey' of *GM*, II, 17, who lack bad conscience, do not count as a society, but are simply a 'pack'—though they create proto-states out of the peoples they conquer.)

[10] This is the sort of socialization that Nietzsche seems to commend (e.g. *A*, 57; *BGE*, 259; *GS*, 76. See also Chapter 6.5.1–2).

[11] Hence, it is implausible that the Greeks managed, for a long time, to 'ward off' the bad conscience by casting their gods as deifications of the very animal nature that is suppressed in bad conscience, a projection which, Nietzsche claims, enabled them both to ennoble this nature and to blame the gods for the troubles it caused (*GM*, II, 23). For one could not convincingly claim to be 'deluded by a god' *every* time one's nature got one into trouble, as distinct from those singular occasions on which one was manifestly not in 'one's right mind'; and the idea that 'the Greeks' blamed their gods in this way, or that their gods accepted the 'guilt' for man's wickedness, is, anyway, dubious—a point to which I return in Chapter 5.6.

specifically, with indebtedness towards god(s) who are held to be the absolute source of man's life, powers, and values—i.e. who are held to be mankind's 'origin, its *causa prima*' (*GM*, II, 20). Since, I suggest, the 'death' of God ultimately encompasses the discrediting of *all* belief in timeless, absolute, impartial standards, a 'second innocence' would, broadly construed, be the elimination of all guilt triggered by failure to respect such standards. Atheism, in the *simple* sense of not believing in a deity, is insufficient to abolish belief in such standards; and so such atheism will not, itself, lead to a 'second innocence'. (The prospect that it will do so, which Nietzsche teasingly holds out in concluding *GM*, II, 20, is immediately dashed by him in ending the first paragraph of the next section.) Only 'the *complete and definitive* [my italics] victory of atheism might free mankind of this whole feeling of guilty indebtedness towards its origin, its *causa prima*'—and such an ultimate victory entails, I suggest, the final overcoming of belief in *any* timeless or absolute or impartial standards. Thus, when Nietzsche claims elsewhere that guilt does 'not exist' (*GS*, 250), or that man is completely unaccountable for his actions and nature (*HAH*, 107), he can mean only two things: first, that the proposition that someone is 'guilty' or 'accountable' simply because he has failed to respect standards construed as impartial or normative (for example, as given by God, reason, or society) is a fiction, belief in which should be abolished; second, that we should abandon all moral interpretations of human nature that are advanced to explain such ascriptions of guilt—such as the notion of the essential corruption of man, to which I will presently turn.

This does not mean, however, that Nietzsche sees as either possible or desirable the elimination of guilt towards *any* ethical standards or ideals that the individual fails to respect—including standards which are self-legislated and life-enhancing. The elimination of such guilt would be impossible: for guilt is an entirely natural—indeed, inevitable—feeling on the part of the self-responsible individual who has failed to respect standards to which he or she is loyal. Moreover, to eliminate such guilt would be undesirable: for guilt plays a major role in inducing the individual to persevere with the arduous ethical ambitions that, for Nietzsche, are indispensable to life-enhancement. In short: what is key in Nietzsche's ethic, it seems to me, is not that the individual should never feel guilt, but that those standards, failure to respect which triggers guilt, should be life-enhancing and nature-affirming[12] and not, as with morality, the other way round.

As to bad conscience, Nietzsche concludes the second essay of *The Genealogy* not by calling for its abolition but, on the contrary, by demanding that the bad conscience now be directed against morality—and, by extension, against the moral conception of guilt and of bad conscience itself. The 'goal', if only one were 'strong enough' for it, is 'to wed the bad conscience to all the *unnatural* inclinations' that foster and are fostered by morality, rather than, as hitherto, to man's 'natural inclinations'. 'The attainment of this goal would require a *different* kind of spirit from that likely to appear in this present age': a spirit of '*great health*, . . . the *redeeming* man of great love and contempt, . . . Antichrist and antinihilist', to cite just a few of Nietzsche's paeans to this 'man of the future' (*GM*, II, 24, *passim*). In other words, bad conscience is not only residually present in this great figure, but is essential to his historic task.

The crucial next question, therefore, is what happens when, in a particular ethical community such as Nietzsche's 'Christians', the otherwise manageable 'illness' of bad conscience runs uncontrolled— i.e. what happens when it reaches that 'most terrible and most sublime height' (*GM*, II, 19) where the specifically *moral* form of bad conscience is born? This is a question which, as Nietzsche addresses it, is more about the 'what' than the 'why': that is, about what concepts (or functions or 'interpretations' of concepts) feature in the moral form of bad conscience (or guilt) that were absent in the premoral form; rather than about why the moral form and its new concepts (or their functions) appeared at all. Indeed, Nietzsche's response to this question is a classic instance of how he constructs a genealogical account—i.e. a real or fictional history of the changing functions or 'interpretations' of particular ethical concepts, values, and practices in the lives of communities.[13]

---

[12] 'Nature-affirming' in the sense of Nietzsche's hope that it will be possible to ' "*naturalize*" humanity' (*GS*, 109; cf. *BGE*, 230).

[13] In other words, in Nietzsche's method of genealogy an enduring practice (or 'procedure' or institution or value) is shown to receive a succession of functions or interpretations or 'meanings' (which may replace each other or be cumulative or, more likely, be a bit of both). Nietzsche's genealogical method, as portrayed in the second essay of *GM*, thus distinguishes between 'procedures', which he takes to be '*enduring*', and the 'meaning' attached to these procedures, which is '*fluid*' (*GM*, II, 13). At any given point in time, a practice is marked by a 'synthesis' of the various meanings that have historically attached to it—a synthesis that is 'hard to analyze' and, ultimately, 'totally *indefinable*'. Hence,

4.3 THE MORAL FORM OF 'GUILT' AND OF 'BAD CONSCIENCE'

Bad conscience and guilt are moralized, Nietzsche seems to suggest, when they are blamed on, or interpreted in terms of, some putatively innate corruption of human nature (or, more generally, of 'life' or 'the world') which one must therefore strive to suppress, extirpate, or 'transcend'. In the case of guilt, this supposed corruption is used to explain the belief that debts are both undischargeable and continually being incurred (say to gods or society). In the case of bad conscience, it is used to explain both the inevitable recalcitrance of one's 'animal' nature and the pain attendant on the effort to tame it. In both cases, guilt comes to be seen as constitutive of human nature— indeed, as one of its main defining features. The principal orchestrator of this new interpretation is, of course, none other than that fallen noble, the 'priest'.[14] His name for the corruption that is henceforth taken to be constitutive of humanity is 'sin' (*GM*, III, 20).

This conspicuousness of guilt is expressed in Nietzsche's image of the 'pushing back' of general guilt 'into the conscience' when it gets moralized (*GM*, II, 21). This image suggests the idea of many small 'islands' of guilt (arising from ordinary failures to repay debts) coalescing both with each other and with the much more permanent and fixed guilt (or potential guilt) of 'bad conscience' to form one leaden aggregate of guilty feeling, which then gets interpreted as 'essential' guilt before God. Moreover, this 'pushing back' of guilt into bad conscience suggests that, in the moralized state, they are phenomenologically one and the same—i.e. that, once moralized, general guilt and bad conscience are no longer experienced as distinct, but are melted into one experience of the individual as essentially guilty. Whether or not this attempt to interpret Nietzsche's idea of 'pushing back' is useful, it is clear that moralization is defined (critically though not exhaustively) by the idea that one's human

Nietzsche memorably says, 'only that which has no history is definable' (ibid.)—i.e. in terms of a fixed essential meaning.

[14] Nietzsche frequently suggests that the nobles and the priests are originally kin; for example, when he says 'how easily the priestly mode of valuation can branch off from the knightly-aristocratic and then develop into its opposite' (*GM*, I, 7). This is very much like a secular doctrine of the Fall. (And, as discussed in Chapter 5.3, Nietzsche regards the ascetic priest as 'among the greatest *conserving* and yes-creating forces of life'—*GM*, III, 13.)

nature is essentially and undischargeably guilty and *hence defective*.[15] Now we recall from our discussion of general guilt that the position of creditor can be occupied not only by one's society or god(s) but also by abstract objects such as ideals (which, particularly in their Platonic conception, act exactly like creditors to life, being the source of all its reality and truth). Hence the phenomenon, of which Nietzsche pointedly reminds us, that atheism does not abolish moralized guilt or bad conscience. For the same conceptual form obtains in a godless world: namely that some ineliminable characteristic of oneself always threatens to impede the honouring of one's obligations to a recognized higher authority, in this case an ideal.

Now it is a short step from this conceptual form to a still more general one: that life as such, or even 'the (phenomenal) world', is depraved and guilty before a higher authority from which it obtains, in some sense, its sustenance—and for whose sake it must be 'overcome'. But this concept is none other than the form of the 'ascetic ideal', to which the next chapter is devoted. And, I suggest, the ascetic ideal is one of two concepts by which guilt and bad conscience, in their moralized forms, are structured, justified, and (potentially) overcome.

The other such concept is metaphysical 'free will' and its associated dichotomy of the ' "doer" ' as distinct from his deeds (*GM*, I, 13). This embraces the idea that human beings have freedom of action that, at least in the moral sphere, is insulated from all contingency, and that through this they are perfectly responsible and causally efficient, so that their happiness follows from what they imagine to be their freely chosen virtues (rather than, as Nietzsche thinks is the case, the other way round).[16] Such a notion of 'free will' performs, I suggest, four functions in this context, the first two of which reinforce the notion of essential guilt, the latter two of which offer relief from it.[17]

First, 'free will' reinforces the notion of the debtor's ineliminable depravity by restricting the 'moral' self—the only agency capable of

---

[15] The converse—i.e. that human nature is defective and *hence guilty*—does not hold because phenomenologically, at least in Nietzsche's story, the guilt is prior: one incurs debts to society or gods, and then needs reasons for their being inexorable and undischargeable.

[16] These notions belong to 'The Four Great Errors' of morality advanced in *TI*, VI, 1–8.

[17] In terms of the aims of moral asceticism, these pairs of functions are, of course, entirely consistent. For the first establishes the reality of a guilty world, while the second offers the possibility of 'transcending' it.

perceiving and doing what is good or right—to a realm isolated from the contingent self, which latter, by contrast, is unfree to be good: i.e. is inescapably guilty.

Second, 'free will' rationalizes the idea that God is interested in *witnessing* all our actions—and hence that our guilt is noticed and reckoned. Indeed, long before the idea of freedom of action was employed by the divine creditor to blame and forgive the debts of man, it was, Nietzsche says, invoked 'to furnish a right to the idea that the interest of the gods in man . . . *could never be exhausted*', and so to avoid the appalling boredom for them of a wholly deterministic world (*GM*, II, 7). All the more entertainment would, therefore, be afforded to the Judaeo-Christian God, whose humans have unprecedented freedom to choose.

Third, 'free will' makes the notion of essential guilt more bearable by claiming to *guarantee* the possibility of 'willing' a change in behaviour, and thus of reducing, though never eliminating, guilty indebtedness to the creditor. (This is, however, a classic instance of a medicine that aggravates the sickness because one's inevitable failure, in practice, radically to change course—inevitable because the theory is flawed and hence the guarantee hollow—only confirms the problem of one's culpability from which free will was believed to offer relief).[18]

Fourth, if the deed is doubled (by dividing it into a 'doer' and an action that he 'does'), then the forgiveness of the deed must also be doubled, first time for the willing of it and then a second time for the deed itself. This offers further relief from guilt by enabling the doer to be forgiven even when his deed is condemned.

In sum, the 'ascetic ideal' and 'free will' are two crucial concepts in structuring an explanation of moral guilt. For they posit a realm that is essentially unfree and contingent, and thus inevitably prone to guilt; while positing another realm which is free and uncontingent, and thus offers hope of 'transcending' that burden. Clearly if the 'problem' of guilt is a phantom, then, to that extent, 'free will', in a roughly Kantian sense, loses much of its utility, even if it still possesses a residual role—perhaps, on this argument, equally bogus—in, for example, a general theory of action (and thus in informing concepts such as the 'intentional' or the 'voluntary').

---

[18] This idea of guaranteed freedom is, of course, employed by the 'slaves' in *GM*, I, 13 to insist that '*the strong man is free* to be weak'.

Yet to claim that these two concepts are, or were historically, central to structuring moral guilt is not the same thing as claiming that they are 'logically' presupposed by the concept of moral guilt on something like a Kantian transcendental argument. For the developmental stories of ethical concepts[19] or their functions told by genealogies attempt to explain one set of concepts or their functions only in terms of their *contingent* relation to an earlier or more elementary set, or higher order motivations for them in terms of more basic ones. Such explanations do not attempt either to *reduce* or *'logically'* to relate the later to the earlier concepts (or functions thereof) or the higher order to the more elementary motivations.[20] In other words, a genealogy, even if fictional, simply provides a way of thinking about the present functions and motivations of our ethical concepts, practices, and values by seeing them as contingent successors to possible earlier or more elementary functions and motivations in a manner which is free of the search for timeless 'groundings'. By re-presenting those functions and motivations in the light of such 'historical' explanation, the genealogist frees them up, as it were, from the immense authority of tradition and habit by which they are hallowed, so that their value to us may be reassessed in terms of our deepest ethical commitments. In addition, these (more or less) hypothetical patterns of explanation can then be tested against detailed historical or anthropological data. To qualify the role of genealogy in this way is, clearly, not to criticize it, but merely to state its proper, and, for ethics, very valuable, function.[21]

[19] Or of values or 'practices'.

[20] Nor, incidentally, do they assume that the meaning of a practice or concept, at any particular point in time, either *consists* of its developmental process up to that point or *necessarily* arises out of it. On the former, a practice embraces just those 'meanings' (or 'synthesis' thereof) that cleave to it at any given time, place, and context in which it is employed; but those meanings need not include *all* the meanings historically ascribed to it throughout the developmental process that genealogy has reconstructed. On the latter, Nietzsche, at least when he is doing genealogy, is too un-Hegelian and too insistent on the contingent relationship between the successive functions or meanings of practices at different historical times to see their developmental relationships as governed by an inherent logic or necessity.

[21] This general statement about the possible role of genealogies suggests that they can be employed to assess the functions and motivations of ethical practices not only in terms of specifically Nietzschean explanatory concepts (i.e. the 'will to power' which those practices supposedly disguise and serve) or standards of value (i.e. 'life-enhancement'), but also in terms of other explanatory concepts and standards of value. For further accounts of the genealogical method, see, for example: David C. Hoy, 'Nietzsche, Hume, and the Genealogical Method', in Yirmiyahu Yovel (ed.), *Nietzsche as Affirmative Thinker* (Dordrecht: Martinus Nijhoff, 1986), 20–38; and Michel Foucault's 'Nietzsche, Genealogy,

4.4 CONCLUSIONS

Nietzsche's conception of guilt and bad conscience suggests to me the following conclusions:

First, in a Nietzschean ethic, the possibility of guilt and bad conscience is central to any *description* of, respectively, ethically responsible individuals and a cohesive society. Indeed, the possibility of guilt exists wherever an agent feels genuine ethical commitments—i.e. a sense of personal accountability to standards (whether these are social or individual) which is not sustained simply by external threats, rewards, and monitoring and which, therefore, functions as an internal censor, as in any feelings of obligation structured by the debtor–creditor model.[22] To the extent that such commitment exists in pre-moral—or, in general, non-moral—societies (as it must do if they are to be ethical at all), *so too* does the possibility of guilt and bad conscience. Though 'morality' greatly intensifies these feelings, it surely does not invent them.[23]

Second, guilt and bad conscience are *valuable* to a Nietzschean ethic—insofar as guilt motivates the agent to respect his self-legislated, life-enhancing standards, and insofar as bad conscience is directed against 'morality' and creates the 'womb' for many of the cultural riches most prized by Nietzsche. Hence, the 'second innocence' conceived by Nietzsche will be free from certain sorts of guilt: especially from guilt dependent upon norms regarded as absolute or impartial; from guilt towards agents, such as gods, which are con-

---

History', in *The Foucault Reader*, ed. Paul Rabinow (New York: Pantheon, 1984), 76–100. (Foucault's account of genealogy, though bold and fascinating, invests it with an almost mystical power of historical insight and insufficiently recognizes the degree to which useful genealogies, including Nietzsche's own, can be fictional rather than painstakingly documentary.)

[22] On the debtor–creditor model, such a notion of personal accountability involves the idea that I have received a credit (or incurred a debt), that I am in a state to realize I have received it, and that only I (rather than some substitute) can acknowledge or repay it. Within this framework, the limits of accountability are then a matter of convention—such as whether they range beyond credits received under formal contract to those that are regarded as covered by implicit contract (e.g. taboos, rules of citizenship, or debts to gods), or as unilaterally extended (e.g. the power conferred by ancestors), and, within the latter, what counts simply as good luck that needs no reciprocation; whether they cover unintentionally incurred debts; what states of mind release the agent from repayment; what counts as repayment; etc.

[23] This conjecture is corroborated by Bernard Williams's discussion of the central role of such concepts in the ethics of Homeric Greece, in *Shame and Necessity*, *passim*.

ceived as the original source of the individual's life and power; and from moral explanations for guilt—for example, explanations which ascribe it to a 'fallen' nature or to the failure to exercise metaphysically 'free will'. But a 'second innocence' will not be free from *any* guilt—and, in particular, not from guilt arising from failure to respect self-legislated, life-enhancing standards. In short, to suggest that Nietzsche's ethic excludes, or seeks to overcome, 'guilt' *tout court* would be seriously to misunderstand it.

Third, the debtor–creditor model suggests just how varied can be the obligations which, when disrespected, occasion guilt. These can range far beyond an agent's formal obligations to other people to encompass all rules or norms which he or she regards as necessary to a flourishing life and thus as requiring respect. These rules could be either public or individual. And the object of the obligations they entail—i.e. the occupant of the position of creditor—could be the agent himself (resulting in guilt towards himself), or abstract objects like ideals, or unknown and unseen powers, such as ancestors, as well as many others. In sum: the crucial precondition for guilt—i.e. respect for certain ethical commitments or rules—could be generalized to range over all rules regarded by the agent as central to a good life.

Fourth, the value of 'bad conscience'—i.e. the kinds of goods that are attainable by disciplining the 'animal' in man—seems to depend critically on its intensity: too little bad conscience results in psychic dissipation or crudity; too much produces crushing guilt, self-disgust, and the paralysis of talent; while the right amount makes possible autonomy, beauty, and imagination. (Have we found here a successful application of Aristotle's 'theory of the mean'?—cf. Chapter 3.4, n. 40.)

Fifth, if the proximate cause of guilt is *not* punishment of the debtor, or his fear of punishment (which, as we discussed earlier, instils only prudence rather than guilt), but his experience of failing to respect an obligation to which he is, in some sense, wholeheartedly committed—i.e. to which he has 'promised' himself and, therefore, considers himself responsible—then guilt is not a 'reactive' emotion, as interpreters of Nietzsche sometimes claim,[24] but is, rather, quintessentially 'active'. Indeed, if, philosophically, guilt presupposes a notion of agent responsibility, one might hazard the

[24] For example, Randall Havas, in *Nietzsche's Genealogy*, 236, who claims that, for Nietzsche, responsibility and guilt are opposed in the sense of activity and reactivity.

suggestion that, psychologically, guilt can help reinforce the individual's feeling of agency and responsibility. This conjecture suggests that one reason for the frequent urge of human beings to accept guilt and responsibility where they have none is a deep-seated need to feel power over their lives, whether by influencing fate or by authoring events. It suggests, in other words, that accepting guilt may, on occasion, be the only way of attributing efficacy to oneself—and, as a corollary, that the pain of guilt may, in such circumstances, be less than the pain of irrelevance. Such self-attribution of guilt would, therefore, not so much *create* the feeling of being a victim, as arise *from* it (or from the urge to overcome it).

Finally, if, as I have argued, the debtor–creditor relationship can model the operation of guilt only by itself presupposing the concept of personal accountability—i.e. a strong sense that one's obligations are justified—then that relationship no more *explains* the conceptual leap to guilt than does, say, *ressentiment* explain the conceptual leap to the universalism of slave morality (see Chapter 3.3). For just as *ressentiment* explains the development of slave morality only because (so I argued) it is *already* structured by two of the principal presuppositions of the latter, namely universality of rights and of duties, so the debtor–creditor relationship successfully models guilt only because it already contains the latter's key presupposition, namely of personal accountability. In both cases, the 'revolutionary' concept— be it personal accountability or universalism of rights and duties— appears in the *explanans* as well as in the *explanandum*; but in both cases it is the appearance of this revolutionary concept that Nietzsche's genealogy does not account for. This is, however, no criticism of genealogy in general or of Nietzsche's genealogies in particular:[25] for every genealogy, whether fictional or real, must have *some* starting point at which the ethical concepts (or values and practices) whose development or successive functions and motivations it traces are simply taken for granted. Everything prior to this origin is left unexplained—and, in particular, why the relevant concepts or values which featured in it appeared at all. But this does not mean that further genealogical accounts could not, in principle, provide such explanations—although how far back they extend and whether any ultimate origin can be determined will, evidently, depend on the concept or practice under investigation. (Thus, for the ubiquitous

---

[25] Though he, perhaps, makes '*ressentiment*' do too much work in explaining slave morality, and does not do enough genealogy on the origin of *ressentiment* itself.

practice of punishment a single ultimate starting point is unlikely to exist, whereas for the, culturally more specific, conception of 'free will' it may. The institution of 'morality' itself, being made up of so many diverse elements, could almost certainly not be traced to a single starting point.[26])

In sum, though Nietzsche's genealogy leaves the origin of personal accountability vague, the 'debtor–creditor relationship' is, indeed, a fertile model for the phenomenology of guilt and enables us to see just how varied are the circumstances which can occasion it, in both moral *and* pre-moral ethics.

ENDNOTE: OUTLINE OF A MODEL FOR GUILT AND SHAME[27]

Guilt is an experience of reprehensible failure (not necessarily intentional) to respect ethical obligations which one recognizes as justified. More broadly conceived, it is the phenomenology of being inadequate to one's loyalties. This definition has four main features. First, guilt presupposes loyalty to the rules against which one has failed. Second, insofar as someone is presumed harmed by that failure, the experience of guilt generally involves the thought of a victim[28]—though that thought may turn out to be illusory, since breaking the relevant obligation may, in fact, hurt no one. Third, there must be a witness (or enforcer) to point out the failure and thereby to trigger the experience. This witness is *necessarily* internal—i.e. the inner censor who recognizes the obligations and their failure to be respected—but can, in addition, be external (though an external witness need not be the same as the victim, if there is one). Fourth—and least important by far—guilt is an experience of impotence. For once the debtor accepts that credits must be repaid (a precondition for his feeling guilt), it is only insufficient self-mastery or

---

[26] Raymond Geuss interestingly contrasts the 'seemingly unlimited and ramifying series of ancestors' traced by a typical genealogy to the singular point of origin that marks a pedigree. See his 'Nietzsche and Genealogy', *European Journal of Philosophy*, 2/3 (1994), 274–92, especially n. 8 and p. 276.

[27] This whole Endnote owes a great deal to Bernard Williams's discussion of guilt and shame in *Shame and Necessity*, though he might disagree with much of what I suggest here.

[28] That victim can, of course, be oneself as well as others—as in feelings of guilt towards oneself (e.g. for having wasted or 'betrayed' one's talents).

bad luck or inability to know the terms of the creditor or, in moralized guilt, the liability of an essentially flawed nature—all of them forms of powerlessness—that prevents a mutually agreed discharging of the debt.

If, as the whole thrust of this chapter has suggested, the only necessary condition for all guilt is failure to honour obligations to which the agent is loyal, then neither actual retribution, nor actual contracts, nor, therefore, actual victims, are invariably required to trigger it. Guilt could be triggered even if no one had reminded the agent of his failure by their anger, even if his commitment to the rule or code were entirely 'unilateral' (and, perhaps, unreasonable to those putatively hurt by its infringement!), and even if, therefore, he had manifestly harmed no one. Such a model may be useful in explaining, for example, the perplexing phenomenon of 'survivor guilt', where exactly these conditions obtain.

With shame, by contrast, the agent's concern is primarily with (perceived) impotence.[29] There are three key points here. First, what is decisive about one's failure to meet certain standards is not, as with guilt, that one has been disloyal to them or hurt a victim in the process, but simply that one has been insufficiently powerful to meet them. In other words, the standards matter primarily as indices of one's power rather than for any other reason. This means not that the standards *themselves* are devoid of ethical content and concern only power—on the contrary, they may be ethically extremely sophisticated—but, rather, that what matters about their infringement is that it shows up a lack of power: for example, of self-mastery. This need *not*, however, make shame a more selfish emotion than guilt, both because the power with which shame is concerned may be crucial precisely to the agent's social roles and responsibilities and because the standards in relation to which the agent has failed may, as just mentioned, embody an ethic that is concerned with far more than just power.

Second, failure to meet such standards must be *observed* (or be believed by the agent to be observed) by a witness. The witness may be either external or internalized and must matter to, or be respected by, the agent (for example, for his own power or for common membership of an ethical or familial community). But the role of the witness—whether external or internal—is quite different in shame and

[29] Cf. Williams, *Shame and Necessity*, e.g. 221.

in guilt. For one thing, in shame an internalized witness is not necessary—whereas an internal censor is essential to guilt. An external
witness, in whose eyes one wishes to appear powerful (or at least not
to lose power) will suffice; and, again unlike guilt, one need *not*
espouse the standards in relation to which an external witness judges
one's power in order to feel shame at falling short of them. In other
words, in shame the external witness is far more important than he
is in guilt (if he features at all in triggering the latter). For another
thing, the internal censor in guilt is committed to the relevant standards for more complex (or, at least, for different) ethical reasons
than is the case in shame—where, as just mentioned, the agent
observes standards mainly out of a need to feel (or be perceived as)
not impotent.

Third, this need to feel powerful is *not* necessarily connected to
social acceptance: the internalized witness need not be simply a
proxy for an external or social witness. Indeed, the less (in any given
ethical community) the individual's self-esteem is explicitly a function of his social acceptance, the more the need to feel powerful is
something one feels 'before oneself'.

These proposals suggest that shame and guilt are, indeed, quite
different. First, with shame, the standards against which the agent
fails either command his loyalty only as measures of power (though,
as mentioned, this does not preclude those standards from being
ethically sophisticated), or do not command his loyalty at all (i.e.
where his concern is purely with impotence in the eyes of an external witness whose respect he desires, but whose standards he may
not share); whereas with guilt, the agent is not only necessarily loyal
to the standards against which he has failed, but is loyal for reasons
that extend beyond a concern with power. Second, for shame, an
external witness can suffice, whereas for guilt an internalized censor
is essential. Third, in shame there is no necessary presumption of a
victim who is harmed by the failure; whereas for guilt there is always
such a presumption. Shame and guilt overlap *only* insofar as guilt is
experienced as impotence (though, as I have suggested, impotence is
the least significant feature of guilt). But there is clearly no sense in
which guilt is simply a special case of shame.

This is not, however, to subscribe to the view that shame and guilt
belong to different sorts of ethics, in that, say, shame is pre-moral
and guilt is moral. As has been argued in this chapter from a purely
theoretical point of view—i.e. without reference to the kind of

historical societies analysed by Williams—shame and guilt can both exist in pre-moral as well as in moral communities, since neither of them necessarily makes moral assumptions.

5

Asceticism in Life-Enhancement and Life-Denial

In this chapter I continue to explore the contrast between the traditional 'morality' that Nietzsche repudiates and the new ethic that he espouses by focusing on a concept that, in his view, crucially structures moral thinking, namely, the 'ascetic ideal'. In addition, I suggest that there is a broader ascetic conceptual form, of which the ascetic *ideal* itself is only an extreme (life-denying) version, and which is also capable of other, potentially life-enhancing, instantiations—notably in Nietzsche's own concepts of 'self-overcoming' and of the healthy 'soul'. This wider discussion hopefully enables me not simply to analyse the role of the ascetic ideal, according to Nietzsche, in Platonic-Christian 'morality' (as has been done well by other authors[1]), but also to show why, with this concept too, life-enhancing forms are possible. But first I must say what I mean by the 'ascetic conceptual form'.

5.1 THE 'ASCETIC CONCEPTUAL FORM': A DEFINITION

In general terms, ascetic thinking posits a domain of high value, towards which we strive, that is generally in conflict or competition with a domain of lesser or negative value, over which we seek mastery and which must therefore be suppressed, destroyed, or transcended. The polarity of superior and inferior value-domains structures, or contributes to structuring, an ethical 'world-view'—embracing, *inter alia*, conceptions of the functions, aims, and priorities of living, and

[1] See, for example: Maudemarie Clark, *Nietzsche on Truth and Philosophy* (Cambridge: Cambridge University Press, 1990), 159–203; and Henry Staten, *Nietzsche's Voice* (Ithaca, NY: Cornell University Press, 1990), chapter 2, esp. 48–64.

interpretations of suffering. This world-view is dominated by the idea that a worthwhile life is a 'striving' towards comprehending or becoming or expressing more fully the higher domain and, as a necessary corollary, taking a stand against the domain of lesser value.

The value-hierarchy of the ascetic conceptual form differs from ordinary rankings of values in two ways. First, the ascetic form structures one's *whole* world—ethical, religious, aesthetic, and so on—and is therefore the axis on which all other values must be situated. To that extent, the hierarchy is regarded as fixed and sometimes, as we will see, as unconditioned. Second, in ascetic thought, the lower value-domain is not simply a lesser or an opposed value, but is *the* thing to be overcome or repudiated if the higher value is to be attained. It is variously considered to be a danger or debtor to the higher—a danger in the sense that, say, dissipation or sin is taken to be a danger to accomplishment or good; a debtor in the sense that the lower domain receives truth, meaning, or 'being' from the higher.[2] In the limiting case—namely, the 'ascetic ideal' itself, which is, of course, Nietzsche's main target in *GM* III—the lower domain is 'the world' or 'life' *as such*, and is something to be overcome *in toto*. Here Man adopts the absurd pose of 'judge of the world who in the end places existence itself upon his scales and finds it wanting'.[3] (We can immediately see that the ascetic ideal structures *ressentiment*, which is directed at the world as such in just this way.) In other words, in the limiting case, the higher value is taken as a standard *extrinsic* to life, and thus to temporality and contingency as such, by which life as a whole is judged. Short of this limiting case, however, the ascetic form is capable of life-enhancing expressions— and common to all these is that the higher value is *intrinsic* to life. In section 5.7, I return to this crucial distinction between the extrinsic (life-denying) and intrinsic (potentially life-enhancing) expressions of the ascetic form.

Anything structured by the ascetic form—whether it is life-enhancing or life-denying—is, therefore, stretched across an inflexible gradient of value, one end of which the agent necessarily

---

[2] As, for example, in the relationship between Platonic *phainomena* and their 'Forms', or Christian 'souls' and their God.

[3] *GS*, 346 (cf. *TI*, II, 2 and *TI*, V, 5). This is, of course, exactly the sort of judgement made by Schopenhauer, when he proclaims that the world's 'non-existence would be preferable to its existence'. (Arthur Schopenhauer, *The World as Will and Representation*, trans. E. F. J. Payne (New York: Dover, 1969), vol. ii, chapter XLVI, p. 576; cf. vol. i, § 59.)

'devalues' and the other end of which he necessarily 'strives' towards (by comprehending, becoming, or expressing it). Thus, to consider chastity in terms of the ascetic conceptual form is not merely to see it as opposed to sensuality—which would be compatible with allowing the two to exist in an 'unstable equilibrium' (*GM*, III, 2)—but to take it as absolutely and invariably superior in value to sensuality, and, in the limiting case of the ascetic ideal, to regard the fact of sensuality as an argument against 'the world' as such (i.e. against the lower domain of which sensuality is taken to be a defining quality).

Let us note in passing that the value-hierarchy of the ascetic form can, in principle, accommodate various specific ontologies—from dualisms (such as 'real/apparent', uncontingent/contingent, ideal/phenomenal, or invariant/temporal) to monisms (such as an Aristotelian hierarchy of the functions of the 'soul'). Moreover, the position of 'higher value' is occupiable not only by the metaphysically real—such as God, Kant's 'thing-in-itself', or Plato's Forms—but also by Universals, or ideals, or other abstract items that are privileged in relation to the domain of lower value. In sum, the ascetic conceptual form is capable of considerable flexibility; and, short of the limiting case where life *in toto* is denied *in toto*, it is capable of life-enhancing expressions—among them the 'self-overcoming' that is so central to Nietzsche's ethic. Before discussing this limiting case—i.e. the ascetic ideal proper—I turn to the life-enhancing instances of ascetic thinking.

5.2 LIFE-ENHANCING EXPRESSIONS OF THE ASCETIC FORM

That the ascetic form is capable of strongly life-enhancing expressions, and that Nietzsche's ethic recognizes this, may be seen, in particular, in his enormous emphasis on discipline and, in general, in his conception of the healthy 'soul'.

Discipline is central to Nietzsche's ethic. Throughout his writings, he insists on the self-imposition of 'hardness', 'form', 'tyranny', and 'style' (e.g. *BGE*, 87 and 188; *GS*, 290; *GM*, II, 2 and *passim*)—so much so that he is even prepared to praise Christianity on account of the discipline that it demands (e.g. *BGE*, 188 and 263) or Platonism insofar as it induces mastery of one's senses (*BGE*, 14). Self-discipline is, for Nietzsche, so vital 'to the whole human animal, to *man*' that, without irony, he calls it 'the *moral* imperative of nature' (*BGE*, 188—my italics)—i.e. an imperative which one may justifiably universalize.[4] No achievement is possible, in his view, without eliminating distractions to one's primary ends, so as to focus on them all one's 'time, energy, love, and interest'; and such ruthlessness is exemplified by 'the lives of all the great, fruitful, inventive spirits', whose '*best* existence' and '*fairest* fruitfulness' it promotes (*GM*, III, 8). The philosopher, in particular, 'sees in it an optimum condition for the highest and boldest spirituality' in which his existence, far from being denied, is almost brutally affirmed (*GM*, III, 7). In short, it is axiomatic, for Nietzsche, that any creative passion presupposes great emotional order in the self, and the elimination of *laissez-aller* (such emotional order being, of course, enforced not necessarily by reason, as in Plato's model of the soul, but by other emotions or drives). Thus:

> The most spiritual men, as the *strongest*, find their happiness where others would find their destruction: in the labyrinth, in hardness against themselves and others, in experiments; their joy is self-conquest; asceticism becomes in them nature, need, and instinct. Difficult tasks are a privilege to them; to play with burdens that crush others, a recreation. Knowledge—a form of asceticism. They are the most venerable kind of man; that does not preclude their being the most cheerful and the kindliest. (*A*, 57)

Now self-discipline is not merely Nietzsche's (probably sole) 'moral imperative'; it is also central to a cluster of key interrelated concepts, among them 'sublimation', 'culture', 'autonomy', 'freedom', 'self-overcoming', and 'soul'. 'Sublimation', as we saw in Chapter 3.1.2, is the highly refined and distilled expression of basic drives which is impossible without the precise control of self-discipline. 'Higher culture' (including the attainment of knowledge) is, as we have also seen, 'a spiritualization of cruelty'—the turning-inwards of instincts of cruelty: for 'any insistence on profundity and thoroughness is a violation, a desire to hurt the basic will of the spirit which unceasingly strives for the apparent and superficial' (*BGE*, 229). 'Autonomy', as we saw in Chapter 4.2.4, depends upon 'breeding' the '*sovereign individual*', the one with sufficient self-control to earn

---

[4] Discipline is universalizable, for Nietzsche, because it is a prerequisite for achieving not simply his good but just about any good that has been recognized by one of the great ethical systems. Obviously, it is a 'hypothetical' imperative in that it is conditional upon subscribing to those goods.

the '*right* to make promises' (*GM*, II, 2). 'Freedom' is equated by Nietzsche with 'power over oneself' (*GM*, II, 2; cf. *GS*, 347). 'Self-overcoming', with which Zarathustra is so concerned, is the incorporation or repudiation or destruction of one state or emotion or achievement in order to attain one still 'higher' (i.e. still more life-enhancing)—which is why 'negating *and destroying* are conditions of saying Yes' (*EH*, IV, 4) and why *décadence* and what is bad, insofar as they constitute something to be overcome, can be conditions for life-enhancement. Finally, all of these concepts are exemplified in, and in some cases presuppose, Nietzsche's image of the healthy 'soul'[5] as a 'multiplicity' of often warring drives forged into a hierarchy precisely by the disciplining effect of a commanding drive, precisely by the overcoming of 'lower' (i.e. cruder, 'animal') or 'decadent' (i.e. life-denying, defeatist) drives.

The essential point about this picture of the healthy soul, and the reason why it is *ascetic* in form, is that attaining the good is conceived not simply in terms of aiming at a higher value or of forging a whole out of a 'multiplicity of drives' (essential though both those aims are), but also as active opposition to a lower value or state—which must be destroyed, transformed, or co-opted by the higher. This opposition is valuable, not just for the conventional reason that distractions to the higher value must be eliminated, but, above all, for creating a great expanding tension within the soul which enables it to be maximally alive. In other words, so the hypothesis goes, there is something life-enhancing about stretching a soul across a gradient of opposed values—opposed, that is, *not* in terms of the old dichotomies of real/apparent or eternal/temporal in which 'metaphysicians' have such 'faith' (*BGE*, 2), but rather in terms of the natural 'order of rank' into which the individual drives of the soul (or the people in a society) are, for Nietzsche, inescapably organized. And the steeper the gradient(s)—i.e. the more pronounced the opposition(s)—that an individual can tolerate, the more self-overcoming will be necessary, and the more fully and creatively he can live. This life-enhancing opposition of values within the soul is surely what Nietzsche has in mind when, in discussing bad conscience, he claims that the 'soul voluntarily at odds with itself', into which a 'contradiction' and 'a No' have been branded, is 'the womb of all ideal and

---

[5] Nietzsche uses the terms 'soul' and 'self' interchangeably. His picture of the healthy soul applies, *pari passu*, to the vital society. See, for example, *BGE*, 12; *WP*, 485, 488, 490, 966; *GM*, II, 16–18.

imaginative phenomena' (*GM*, II, 18). It is surely what leads him to suggest that the internalization of opposing (and inescapable, i.e. non-arbitrary) values, one of which *must* overcome the other, fosters new and fertile types of thinking—i.e. in terms of concepts embracing polar opposites (ibid.). And, one may conjecture, it is why he never advances the *Übermensch* as a clear ideal. For the *Übermensch*, who has conquered everything 'lower' in himself, who has, it seems, over-come, in turns, both the 'animal' in man and 'man' himself (i.e. his higher humanity),[6] *would have nothing left to overcome*. His soul would no longer be ascetically structured by an opposition of higher and lower values; he would, internally, be conflict-free and thus sterile.

Now to maintain and, indeed, intensify this crucial opposition of values requires a state of uncompromising vigilance directed at two objectives. The first is to *maximize* the 'distances' within the soul—which is a metaphor for embracing, as intensely as possible, the most diverse values and perspectives, which then strive to 'overcome' (i.e. to co-opt, transform, or destroy) each other, just as 'master' and 'slave' drives attempt to do. The second objective is to *sustain* these distances and tensions in the face of the laziness, indifference, or 'egalitarian' instincts that would happily see them collapse or that are ignorant of their importance—vices, we should note, to which the superior orders within the soul (or society) may be every bit as sus-ceptible as are the lower orders. Nietzsche's name for this uncom-promising vigilance is the '*pathos of distance*'. From the pathos of distance, he says, arises 'the craving for an ever-new widening of dis-tances within the soul itself, the development of ever higher, rarer, more remote, further-stretching, more comprehensive states . . . the continual "self-overcoming of man"' (*BGE*, 257; cf. *A*, 57). Thus, it sustains and enhances the life-enhancing polarizations between higher and lower valuations within the soul (or, indeed, society)—polarizations that are not arbitrary but reflect 'the ingrained differ-ence between strata' (ibid.), a natural hierarchy of valuations between different types of drives (in the soul) or people (in a society). And it is because Christians, anti-clerical revolutionaries, and moral rela-tivists are united in their egalitarianism—however otherwise opposed

---

[6] This interpretation of the *Übermensch* seems justified by statements such as: '*I teach you the Übermensch*. Man is something that will be overcome'; and 'Man is a rope, tied between animal and *Übermensch*' (*Z*, Prologue, 3–4, my translation). For Rosen the image of the 'rope' shows the extreme difficulty and danger of attempting to overcome 'man' or the 'flesh' in us. (Stanley Rosen, *The Mask of Enlightenment: Nietzsche's Zarathustra* (Cambridge: Cambridge University Press, 1995), 40–56.)

they claim to be—that Nietzsche regards them all as undermining the very possibility of a healthy soul (or society). In short, the 'pathos of distance' is the backbone of the Nietzschean soul (and society): only it can prevent the essential distinctions and oppositions between the soul's constituent values (or the drives that express those values) from collapsing into 'decadent' uniformity; only it sustains the ascetic structure of a healthy soul or society.

This crucial importance of opposing, destroying, sublimating, or otherwise 'overcoming', lower values or states is missed by those who see Nietzsche as advocating a total yea-saying, a sort of Woodstock of the psychic or social economy. Thus, Charles Taylor's claim that Nietzsche 'tried to break out of the whole form of thought he defined as "moral", i.e., all forms which involve the rejection of the supposedly "lower" in us, of our will to power, and to come to a more total self-affirmation, a yea-saying to what one is',[7] apart from inadequately defining the conception of morality which Nietzsche rejects, loses the centrality and *severity* of self-overcoming in Nietzsche's ethic. Indeed, insofar as Nietzsche's key concepts remain thoroughly structured by the ascetic form, he does *not*, I suggest, try to 'break out of' the moral—or, indeed, Platonic—form of thought. For example, his conception of the healthy soul obviously retains more than a passing resemblance of Plato's—in its analogy to a healthy society, in the idea of domination of 'lower' parts by 'higher', and in diagnosing sickness as a fading of demarcations between the strata.[8] But Nietzsche does not remain bound by traditional thinking: he also provides us with materials for an alternative ethic—one that, for example, eschews systematic universalization of standards and rules, unconditioned valuations, and notions parasitic on metaphysical dualism like 'freedom of the will', essential guilt, egalitarianism, or 'world'-denying asceticism. This enables him to 'break out of' those aspects of traditional morality which he finds life-denying without jettisoning concepts or values that are also susceptible of life-enhancing functions; and we have seen in previous chapters how this leads him to retain an important role

---

[7] Charles Taylor, *Sources of the Self: The Making of the Modern Identity* (Cambridge: Cambridge University Press, 1989), 70.

[8] For a discussion of resemblances between classical thought and Nietzsche's emphasis on harmonious hierarchy within the soul—on, for example, the need to 'become master of the chaos one is' (*WP*, 842)—see Luc Ferry, *Homo Aestheticus: The Invention of Taste in the Democratic Age*, trans. Robert de Loaiza (Chicago: University of Chicago Press, 1993).

for such concepts and values as bad conscience and pity, or guilt and altruism. In this section we have shown that for two further traditional concepts—namely 'soul' and the 'ascetic' form—life-enhancing functions are not only possible, by Nietzsche's own standards, but are an inextricable part of his new ethic.

5.3 LIFE-DENYING EXPRESSIONS: THE ASCETIC IDEAL'S STRUCTURE AND MOTIVES

In its extreme form, the 'ascetic ideal', by contrast to the life-enhancing asceticism that we have just been discussing, reflects man's '*will* to erect an ideal . . . and in the face of it to feel the palpable certainty of his own absolute unworthiness' (*GM*, II, 22). Here the higher valuation denotes a realm of the absolute and the timeless, and the lower valuation embraces 'the human, . . . the animal, . . . the material, . . . the senses, . . . reason itself, . . .' and other features of ordinary life. This valuation is driven by a '*will to nothingness*, an aversion to life . . .' (*GM*, III, 28)—and is catalysed by that omnipresent type, the 'priest'. Thus, the 'idea at issue here is the [low] *valuation* the ascetic priest places on our life' (*GM*, III, 11), which he opposes outright to a higher mode of existence, to which this life is at best a means and then only through its own denial. To justify this valuation, such a will 'look[s] for error precisely where the instinct of life [i.e. for the real and the actual] most unconditionally posits truth' (*GM*, III, 12)—i.e. it posits as illusory exactly what one naturally regards as real, and as real what is illusory.

Now an interpretation, for Nietzsche, always serves the urge for power: 'all events in the organic world are a subduing, a *becoming master*, and all subduing and becoming master involves a fresh interpretation' (*GM*, II, 12). Interpretation is, in turn, the attaching of a specific meaning to an enduring 'thing' or 'drama' (to take up the distinction between actions and their meanings proposed in *GM*, II, 12–13). It follows, by hypothesis, that an interpretation that devalues life/the phenomenal world/temporality must have the function, not of destroying it *per se*, but of mastery over it—i.e. of making life liveable. And this is precisely what Nietzsche means by saying that 'the ascetic ideal is an artifice for the *preservation* of life', while that 'denier', the ascetic priest, 'is among the greatest *conserving* and yes-creating forces of life' (*GM*, III, 13).

Striking though this conclusion is, it is actually uninformative, given Nietzsche's characterization of all organic events as 'a *becoming master*', his explanation of all actions and events in terms of power. Given this premiss, it is necessarily true that the ascetic ideal is life-preserving (as, on Nietzsche's conception of a value, any 'higher' value or strategy except, presumably, premeditated suicide, would be—i.e. any value or strategy that is a product of deep instinct or distilled thinking as opposed to being an impulsive palliative or an un-'ruminated' thought). This means that we must look for a more specific account of what motivates the ascetic ideal.

And Nietzsche provides us with such an account. In *GM* III, we find that the 'weak' and the 'strong' each have motives for embracing the ascetic ideal: the weak out of vengefulness—against the strong, against themselves, and against life as such; the strong out of nausea at, and pity for, the weak.

The weak can tolerate their helplessness only by casting blame— i.e. by finding or imagining 'a *guilty* agent who is susceptible to suffering' (*GM*, III, 15). Blame anaesthetizes despair by conjuring up the even more savage emotion of hatred which, as it were, distracts the sufferer from his pain. It has three targets: first the fortunate, whose confidence the weak attempt to subvert with the 'Problem of Suffering'; second, the sufferer's own self, which the priest encourages him to see as the cause of his misfortune, thus redirecting *ressentiment* inwards; and third, life itself for being the domain of suffering. The priest, I take Nietzsche to be claiming, favours blame over cruder forms of violence or sensuality, because blame can be more subtly manipulated—for example, by influencing the choice of target, by relating it to higher ethical aims whose betrayal occasions the suffering, and, as Nietzsche points out, by directing it inwards. This inward-direction of blame not only protects society from the vengeful (*GM*, III, 16), but is also crucial to the priest's power: for self-abnegation makes the agent submissive and, by causing distress, induces him to turn to the priest for further help. And, of course, the priest finds fertile soil for this self-blame in the suffering of 'bad conscience', where, as discussed in the previous chapter (4.2.2), the individual becomes a liability to himself.

The strong, for their part, overwhelmed by the suffering of the sick majority, and persuaded by it of the disgrace of their good fortune in the face of such universal misery, turn their back in despair on the world, terminally infected by the contagions of '*great nausea at man'* and *'great pity for man'*. The union of pity and nausea begets the 'will to nothingness', the defining will of life-denying asceticism and 'the "last will" of man' (*GM*, III, 14).

Now there are, in general, three antidotes through which both weak and strong find release from their respective suffering—the weak from the appalling pessimism of universal blameworthiness, the strong from their great nausea and pity. The first such antidote Nietzsche terms *'hibernation'*—in which willing, desiring, and thinking are maximally suppressed and quietened. The ethical correlate of hibernation is 'selflessness', while its metaphysical correlate is union with 'the one', a state of 'redemption' from life which demands not world-engaging virtues, but detachment (*GM*, III, 17). The second antidote might be termed *'distraction'*—in which either mechanical activity, such as work, punctiliousness, and the treadmill of regular duties, or petty pleasures of altruism and community, divert consciousness from suffering and even from self as such (*GM*, III, 18). And the third, and most far-reaching, antidote to suffering is the 'ascetic ideal' itself—which both denigrates life as the guilty domain and promises release from it. Here the 'priest' complements his exploitation of guilt—his directing inwards of *ressentiment*, his insistence that suffering is explained as punishment for guilt—with a story of transcendence, of the 'sinner' redeemed. He therefore achieves release from pain in two ways: through a sheer 'orgy of [guilty] feeling'—the latter expressing the terror and rapture of guilt and redemption, sin and punishment; and through the promise of a 'beyond' free of suffering. Hence the ascetic ideal turns out to be an analgesic against one type of pain—that of the basic guilt and 'bad conscience' of socialized man and, in general, of impotence and inferiority—by unleashing other, more complex, types of pain— namely those created by seeing man as guilty as such, as sinful, as punished by suffering, as suffering for god, as redeemable from sin, and so on (*GM*, III, 20). The result is a 'shattered nervous system', a destroyed 'psychical health', and a ruined artistic taste (valuing, for example, the petty piety and rococo vehemence of the ascetic New Testament over the Old Testament and the literature of ancient Greece—*GM*, III, 21–2). These are consequences which lead Nietzsche to describe the ascetic ideal as *'the true calamity* in the history of European health' (*GM*, III, 21), though the 'slave' still considers his loyalty to it a mark of innate superiority. But all three of these antidotes alleviate, at best, only the danger and distress of *ressentiment*, not its cause—and, in particular, not the *'physiological inhibition'* whose impotence fuels such bitterness and anger (*GM*, III, 17).

'Surely', we moderns say, 'we are beyond these sorts of antidotes: they became ineffective with the "death of God". Their utility depended upon belief in sin, essential guilt, divine redemption, and the like. Science—shorthand for the methodical, empirical, truthfulness of all *Wissenschaft*—has released us from such illusory analgesics.' To which Nietzsche, of course, replies: Nonsense! Science may be employed as an antidote to suffering in precisely these three ways. Science, too, enables us to hibernate—from our own wider conscious and unconscious life. Science, too, provides distraction—in the treadmill of research and the meanderings of anaemic curiosity. Third, science, too, expresses the (conceptual form of the) ascetic ideal. For insofar as science's unstated and unjustified presupposition is that truth is unconditionally valuable—i.e. that seeking or knowing truth is a supreme and absolute value in relation to which everything else in life is less valuable and for the sake of which everything else in life must, if necessary, be sacrificed and transcended—science rests on *'faith in the ascetic ideal itself'* (*GM*, III, 24). Science, that is, expresses 'faith in a *metaphysical* value, the absolute value of *truth*, sanctioned and guaranteed by [the ascetic] ideal alone (it stands or falls with this ideal)' (ibid.). This will 'to truth at any price', regardless of its prudential value, is the will not to deceive *anyone*, including oneself—and, as Nietzsche memorably puts it, with such a will *'we stand on moral ground'* (*GS*, 344). This is why he says, in two brilliantly concise statements of his thesis, that 'the religious instinct is . . . in the process of growing powerfully [e.g. with the 'will to truth' of science and of atheism]—but the theistic satisfaction it refuses with deep suspicion' (*BGE*, 53); and that '[m]odern philosophy, being an epistemological skepticism, is . . . *anti-Christian*', though 'by no means anti-religious' (*BGE*, 54).

Nietzsche, let us note, much respects the audacity of this 'ultimate . . . faith in science'. Unlike the use of science for hibernation and distraction (*GM*, III, 23), or of 'modern historiography' in its 'nihilistic' and 'hedonistic' forms (*GM*, III, 26), which are all possible *without* the possession of any real scientific conscience, faith in 'the absolute value of truth still inspires passion, love, ardor, and *suffering*' (*GM*, III, 23). Science—and atheism—are *'the latest and noblest form'* of the ascetic ideal (ibid.) only, says Nietzsche in a crucial caveat, among these 'rarer cases, . . . the last idealists left among philosophers and scholars' (*GM*, III, 24). The rest are too weary for science or atheism *as matters of conscience*: theirs is the weak faith of the pedant, not the passionate faith of the idealist.

Yet this residual faith in 'the absolute value of *truth*' (*GM*, III, 24) will eventually repudiate as untruthful (or unverifiable) the very idea of the absolute and the unconditioned, and will, therefore, reject the concepts (especially those stemming from Christian dogma) and the values (notably unconditional truthfulness itself) that are parasitic on that idea. 'Faith in truth' will cause us to see that we live in a world where everything is conditioned and cannot be otherwise intelligibly conceived, and that this includes the value of truth itself (for life has abundant need of untruth). As a result, Nietzsche says: 'After Christian truthfulness has drawn one inference after another [against Christianity as a dogma], it must end by drawing its *most striking inference*, its inference *against* itself; this will happen . . . when it poses the question "*what is the meaning of all will to truth?*"' (*GM*, III, 27.)

5.4 FORCING TRUTH TO BE A CONDITIONED VALUE

This startling and original argument adds up, I suggest, to a profound challenge to the idea of an unconditioned value—that is, to the metaphysical idea that values can be self-justifying, rather than derivative from, or dependent upon, other values or needs. In particular, it casts fatal doubt on the idea that truth itself—whether or not it is conceived as metaphysically real: 'as being, as God' (*GM*, III, 24)—is unconditionally valuable.[9] Instead, it forces us to justify the value of truth—to which the West, as the descendent of the Platonic and Judaeo-Christian traditions, is still, to a great degree, committed—in terms of its *internal* necessity to other goods or forms of life, which must themselves be justified without, if possible, appealing circularly to the value of truth. Though Nietzsche himself does not lay out the form of such a justification, it would, I suggest,

---

[9] Yet the further idea that only the unconditional value of truth has grounded the value of science itself—in the sense of accounting for its prestige and motivating or justifying its pursuit—is one which I argue against in Chapter 9, where I suggest that there can be (and have been) other motives and justifications for being deeply committed to science than valuing truth *per se*.

proceed along the lines of a transcendental argument: namely, and very schematically, that truth is a constitutive value internal to an activity, such as science, or to a social requirement, such as effective communication, or to certain acts of consciousness (such as believing, which must, arguably, be regarded as aiming at the truth of what is believed), or, indeed, to a type of person, such as Nietzsche's 'nobles' who are defined, in part, by their self-perception as truthful—in the sense that seeking or knowing or telling truths, at least to a particular degree of accuracy and over a particular range of truths, is—or, in some cases, must be believed to be—indispensable to the success of such practices or forms of life. And insofar as the value of truth can thus be justified as internal to certain practices or as presupposed by specific forms of life, it is independent of a metaphysical grounding.

Clearly, however, this form of justification does not commit us to the further assumptions that truth-seeking or -knowing or -telling:

(1) is the value which justifies or motivates or explains the actual historical development of these practices;

(2) must, internally to these practices, range over all relevant truths or aim for absolute accuracy (ambitions which might be not only unnecessary but even damaging to the enterprise of truth-seeking or truth-telling: thus, to aim for omniscience within his domain would be as absurd for a scientist as telling every truth in one's possession would be pointless for the purpose of social communication);

(3) is, external to these practices, always more valuable than its opposite (viz. truth more valuable than falsity, or sincerity more valuable than lying);

(4) is, external to these practices, the highest of all values.

One or more of these assumptions has, historically, often been integral to the unconditional valuation of truth that Nietzsche attacks. However, on a transcendental justification of the value of truth— which seems the most suitable form of justification after the 'death of God' (i.e. of metaphysical justifications)—none of these assumptions need, or should, be made.

I recognize, however, that, despite the power of Nietzsche's critique of the value of truth, the latter is *still*, in practice, widely regarded as intrinsically, rather than merely instrumentally, valuable. In that sense, it does, willy-nilly, persist in functioning as the external justification, or at least as *a* major external justification, of the very forms of life to which, I have suggested, it is internal. This persistence begs one of the hardest questions of all: namely, why it is that even after the demolition of its metaphysical scaffolding by Nietzsche and his followers, the value of truth retains an authority under both sceptical attack on its real value (to 'life') and attempts to demonstrate the purely historical contingency of that authority, that, for example, God manifestly does not.[10] An answer to this baffling question—i.e. of why reverence for truth remains despite the blatant irreverence inherent in even the possibility of such attacks— might employ two sorts of argument: first, a psychological argument that to regard truth as intrinsically, rather than merely instrumentally, valuable somehow ethically orients or roots us more successfully than does either the idea of God or other traditional ethical baggage; second, a historical argument that if, indeed, truth retains its status as an intrinsic value, it does so because buttressed by the massive force of the Platonic and Judaeo-Christian traditions—both of which regard truth as unconditionally valuable, but only one of which posits the 'dead' monotheistic God. Any such attempt to answer the question about why those traditions could come to the aid of truth but not, say, of God would, of course, require a detailed account of how truth became an intrinsic value in the first place— an account that Nietzsche himself does not provide and that I will not attempt, but that his genealogical method might offer us the resources to (at least hypothetically) reconstruct.

5.5 IS THE ASCETIC IDEAL NECESSARILY LIFE-DENYING?

There is another large question about Nietzsche's critique of the ascetic ideal to which we must now turn: namely, whether he is justified in claiming that it is *necessarily* life-denying, especially when its superior value is conceived metaphysically as God or Truth and the inferior embodies worldliness, temporality, and the like—i.e. why '*all* that willing which has taken its direction from the ascetic ideal' should be motivated by 'a will to nothingness' (*GM*, III, 28—my

---

[10] It was, perhaps, precisely because Nietzsche himself felt the power of this resilience that he demanded only that the value of truth 'be *experimentally* called into question' (*GM*, III, 24—my italics).

italics). To ask this question is the same as to ask why metaphysical dualism should necessarily be life-denying.

I suggest, on the contrary, that though the belief that the 'world'— and all its predicates such as temporality—are to be transcended for the sake of something eternal, divine, and true can clearly be employed by a will to negate life, by terminal pessimism, despair, and indifference, such a belief can also have a life-enhancing function. This is so not only because such religious belief has a residual value in imposing discipline (which Nietzsche himself recognizes), but for three further and more important considerations, two theoretical and one 'empirical':

1. First, the Judaeo-Christian conceit that man participates in, and so must try to perfect his 'imitation', or expression, of the divine essence and, moreover, is God's viceroy of nature, may be highly empowering beliefs, inducing men and women to feats of imagination and effort for which they might otherwise lack the courage—or even the conception. It is in this sense that, for example, the concept of 'free will' may be life-enhancing, notwithstanding such life-denying uses as those outlined in the previous chapter (4.3).

2. Second, the idea that life 'on earth' is merely a means to approaching the divine can also be interpreted to make life-enhancement, in just Nietzsche's sense, a *duty* to God, a way of honouring and knowing his creation. (Faith in the divine or transcendent would then be life-denying only insofar as it explicitly prohibits, or removes purpose from, living fully in 'this world'.)

3. As a matter of historical fact, the very European civilization that Nietzsche considers to be dedicated to the ascetic ideal and so to a '*will to nothingness*' has been culturally one of the richest in world history—a simple fact with which his account of the calamity and ubiquity of the ascetic ideal appears inconsistent.

Nietzsche's avoidance of these basic points (which will be discussed more fully in Chapter 9.4), is reflected in his assertion that a great life-enhancer, like Raphael, even if he professes Christianity, cannot *really* be a Christian and, by the same token, that *Parsifal*, a work suffused with Christian motifs, must be the product of *décadence*. Thus he claims that 'Raphael said Yes, Raphael *did* Yes; consequently, Raphael was no Christian' (*TI*, IX, 9); and belittles what is among the most innovative and profound of all Wagner's music, principally on account of *Parsifal*'s ostensibly Christian libretto (*GM*, III, 2–4).

Nietzsche, it seems to me, makes two erroneous assumptions here. The first is that 'life-enhancement' presupposes an attitude of acceptance, and even love, of the world in all its inescapable elements— i.e. the attitude underlying *amor fati* and affirmation of the 'Eternal Return' (see, for example, *BGE*, 56). This assumption, as I argued in Chapter 2.3, exhibits a conflation of fact and value: i.e. a stipulation that because the world is thus and so in its basic nature, our values must, in some sense, 'affirm' those features. Whereas such comprehensive affirmation or love may be irrelevant to great creativity. (Too many artists have been religious in just the sense decried by Nietzsche not to suggest this rival hypothesis.)

The second assumption is that to be a 'Christian' is necessarily to embrace the extreme asceticism which denies *in toto* the world *in toto*, out of just the hatred and despair that Nietzsche's conception of *ressentiment* so well portrays. Only on this assumption can we make sense of his claim about Raphael or, indeed, of his whole attack on the ascetic ideal in its Christian manifestation. But this extreme asceticism[11] cannot, I suggest, be taken to embrace, *either theoretically or historically*, all the variants of 'Judaeo-Christianity', let alone all 'willing which has taken its direction from the ascetic ideal'.

5.6 WHY THE 'TRANSCENDENT' NEED NOT PRESUPPOSE THE ASCETIC IDEAL

I have just suggested that belief in god (or the transcendent in general) which is structured by the ascetic ideal (short of its extreme expression) need not be life-denying. Less controversial, for Nietzsche, is the further proposition that belief in god(s) or the transcendent need not be structured by the ascetic ideal *at all*. In other words, such belief need not see the divine as a goal which one must strive to attain or 'imitate' or 'become' and, hence, which entails transcending 'this world'. On the contrary, man is seen as capable of living only in his domain—and conceives his god(s) as celebrating his nature and attainments, and as inspiring him to either virtue *or* folly. On this picture of man's relationship to god(s) the divine may still be honoured incomparably higher than the worldly; and it may still legitimate man's values and purposes. But man's relationship to it is

---

[11] Which is vividly summarized in the last paragraph of *GM*, III, 28.

not structured by the ascetic ideal so long as life is not seen as something to be *overcome* for the sake of god. Instead, the point of seeking the gods' assistance or approval, or of fathoming their intentions, is only to find honour and fortune and virtue in this world, and to celebrate one's own qualities and achievements.

This is, roughly, how Nietzsche conceives of the Greeks' relationship to their gods (e.g. *GM*, II, 23) or of ancient Israel's relationship to its Yahweh (*A*, 25; cf. *A*, 16, first paragraph). He suggests that the Greek gods affirmed human life, first, by embodying and thus endorsing the 'animal' in man, and, second, by allowing mortals to foist upon them guilt (and not, like Christianity, punishment) for the world's evil—thus enabling humans to rejoice in their 'freedom of soul':

. . . the *Greek gods*, those reflections of noble and autocratic men, in whom *the animal* in man felt deified and did *not* lacerate itself, did *not* rage against itself!

. . . 'foolishness', 'folly', a little 'disturbance in the head', this much even the Greeks of the strongest, bravest age conceded of themselves as the reason of much that was bad and calamitous . . . Even this disturbance in the head, however, presented a problem . . . 'He must have been deluded by a *god*', they concluded finally . . . In this way the gods served in those days to justify man to a certain extent even in his wickedness, they served as the originators of evil . . . they took upon themselves, not the punishment but, what is *nobler*, the guilt. (*GM*, II, 23)

Whether or not these particular conjectures are sound—and it is questionable, for example, whether Homer's gods really claimed the guilt for worldly evil[12]—they are not needed to make our main point: namely that there is nothing *inherently* life-denying about worshipping gods, doing things for the sake of gods, seeing them as legislating or embodying the highest values and purposes, attributing to them overriding power, or even considering the perfection, and thus in a sense the value, of ordinary human life as inferior by comparison. None of these attitudes of respect is structured by the ascetic

---

[12] E. V. Rieu, for example, without citing Nietzsche, says that 'Christian apologists of a later age made a mistake when they suggested that the pagans had invented the gods and their iniquities as an excuse for themselves. Homer never censures a god nor lets a mortal use a god's misdeeds as a pretext for his own.' Rieu does corroborate Nietzsche, however, in claiming that, whereas the Christian God makes man in his image, 'Homer regards his gods, though immortal, as made in the image and likeness of man' and sees them as 'there to administer, [though] not necessarily to obey, man's moral code' (Homer, *The Odyssey*, trans. E. V. Rieu (London: Penguin, 1985), introduction, 15).

ideal. And all of them—which are, indeed, evinced by such a para-digmatic life-enhancer as Homer's Odysseus—are actually life-enhancing where they inspire and cajole men to live virtuously and fully. They become life-denying only where men see respect for gods as *entailing* a life of comprehensive repudiation, in which all higher talents and possibilities seem worthless or even evil in relation to the divine yardstick.

But if, on Nietzsche's own admission, conceptions of the tran-scendent can exist which are free of such life-denying entailments—notably, conceptions of gods which project onto them man's 'animal' nature or which otherwise see them as endorsing one's power—then why seek to 'complete our de-deification' of nature, as he suggests we should (*GS*, 109)? Nietzsche both contradicts that admission and ignores man's inevitable need for certain anthropomorphisms (such as the constants of logic) by supposing that to 'begin to "*naturalize*" humanity in terms of a pure, newly discovered, newly redeemed nature' will necessarily enhance life; and that 'shadows of God'—notably imputing to the world anthropomorphic qualities such as beauty or order or the features of an organism—necessarily 'darken our minds' (*GS*, 109, *passim*). Though he foresaw, brilliantly, that the attempt to de-deify the world totally, and so to pursue the mod-ernist project to its bitter, postmodernist, end, would happen *any-way*—under pressure of not just the reasons but also the 'taste' of the modern sceptical mind—to assume, as he does,[13] that any incre-mental destruction of theistic or anthropomorphic conceptions of the universe is, *ipso facto*, life-enhancing is, it seems to me, to remain trapped in that uncritical atheistic spirit, that Voltairean blind enthu-siasm for demystification, at which Nietzsche himself pokes fun. Indeed, as he suggests elsewhere, it may be that if we abolish our reverences, we will finally abolish ourselves (*GS*, 346).[14]

In sum: my point is that 'life-enhancement' demands not that rev-erence for god(s) be wholly supplanted by reverence for man, or that conceptions of the universe employing supra-natural or anthropo-morphic categories give way entirely to those employing 'naturalis-

---

[13] At least in this passage (*GS*, 109).

[14] Even if Nietzsche's point is that we are trapped in the anthropomorphisms of our Platonic-Christian heritage, and that specifically *these* are life-denying and must be finally abolished, I do not think that he provides a cogent case. However, in *GS*, 109, he makes a general assault on 'thinking that the world is a living being' and demands, instead, that we conceive its 'total character' as 'chaos'—a demand whose unintelligibility and undesir-ability I consider in Chapter 10.2.1.

tic' categories, but that reverence for the divine is not conceived as *entailing* repudiation of 'the world'—i.e. is not structured by the ascetic ideal in its most extreme form.

5.7 IN WHAT SENSE IS THE ASCETIC IDEAL MAN'S ONLY MEANING 'SO FAR'?

Finally, let us turn to the intriguing—and, I will suggest, philosophically very significant—claim with which Nietzsche concludes his essay on the ascetic ideal: that '[a]part from the ascetic ideal, man, the human *animal*, had no meaning so far' (*GM*, III, 28). Nietzsche cannot possibly be proposing here that *all* meanings ascribed 'so far' in history to human actions and events are structured by the ascetic ideal—and so express the '*will to nothingness*' by which, he says, 'all that willing which has taken its direction from the ascetic ideal' is motivated (ibid.). For such a proposal would commit him to the view either that, down the ages, life-enhancers have *never* sought meanings for actions and events, or that they have actively willed 'nothingness'. The first of these alternatives is extremely improbable (indeed, impossible, if all our actions and perceptions involve 'interpretations'); while the second would entail that willing 'nothingness' is consistent with life-enhancement, which Nietzsche obviously does not accept.

What Nietzsche is proposing, I suggest, is not that *all* questions about the meaning of human actions and events, or even about the value or 'justification' of one's life as a whole, are answered in terms of the ascetic ideal, but rather that only questions about the meaning of man *qua* animal or about 'why man *at all*?' (ibid.—my italics) get answered in this way. Such questions, we should note, themselves presuppose that it is intelligible, first, to distinguish between man *qua* 'human *animal*' and man *qua* something categorically different, and, second, to assume that a perspective is possible from which man *qua* 'human *animal*' can be evaluated and an alternative to it envisaged. But to make such a presupposition is *already* to espouse the essential dualism of the ascetic ideal: namely, the positing of two discontinuous realms, the one being, in this case, of the 'human animal', and the other being of something radically distinct from the latter—such as 'Spirit', or 'Mind', or 'Will', or 'God'— with, putatively, an absolutely separate and superior meaning (or value). In other words, the ascetic ideal is not merely the *answer* to the question about the meaning of man *qua* animal or about 'why man *at all*?', but also *structures* it. The question itself, that is, pre-supposes the ascetic idealism (and hence morality) that marks its answer.[15]

My proposal is, therefore, that, for a non-moral culture, the 'animal' in man—or, indeed, 'man' or 'life' conceived in these dual-istic terms—is not even identified as a *candidate* for ascriptions of meaning or value. What is philosophically remarkable is not, there-fore, that such questions about the meaning or value of 'man, the human *animal*' get answered in terms of the ascetic ideal, but that they get asked in the first place—that, phenomenologically, the agent stands 'extrinsically' over against man or life as such. Indeed, it is when 'man' or 'life' or suffering[16] *as such* becomes a candidate for the extrinsic ascription of meaning or value—i.e. for evaluation from a perspective purportedly independent of man *qua* 'human animal'— and a phenomenon to which the possibility of an alternative is regarded as intelligible, that the seeds of the moral revolution are sown. If so, even to raise such questions is a symptom of '*a will to nothingness*'.

If, however, the ascetic ideal is the only meaning ascribed[17] so far to 'man, the human *animal*', and if 'all that willing which has taken its direction from the ascetic ideal' expresses '*a will to nothingness*', does this mean that life-enhancers have never willed the ascetic ideal or never sought a meaning for 'man, the human *animal*'? Nietzsche's answer to this question is clearest for artists: though some indeed espouse the ascetic ideal, they do not genuinely *will* it, but rather employ it superficially, opportunistically, and imitatively, as 'a prop'

[15] For an ethic structured by the ascetic ideal, the 'animal' in man is his unfreedom, and freedom is attainable only by transcending it; whereas, for Nietzsche, the 'animal' is all the individual can intelligibly be conceived as being, and freedom is the result of 'breeding' it to bear the 'right to make promises' (*GM*, II, 2).

[16] Nietzsche notes time and again how intensely sensitive the Christian West is to suf-fering, and suggests that the ascetic ideal is an interpretation aimed at making suffering more bearable (though it may end up exacerbating it by, for example, ascribing it to man's sinfulness). However, in line with my argument that 'global' questions, such as 'why suf-fering *at all*?', are, when extrinsically posed, not just answered by the ascetic ideal but themselves structured by it, we may suggest that this inordinate sensitivity to suffering does not just promote ascetically ideal thinking but also results from it, and especially from the idea that there is an *alternative* to suffering or to what is held to be the subject of suf-fering (i.e. 'man, the human *animal*').

[17] And, perhaps, *ascribable*, in the sense that a question structured by the ascetic ideal must, one surmises, receive an answer that is similarly structured.

or 'an established authority', to justify and glorify their work (*GM*, III, 5). In general, Nietzsche claims, artists'[18] allegiance to values and philosophies is superficial and tactical; unlike the genuine philosopher they lack the courageous independence and self-knowledge and cold eye for reality to create (i.e. 'will') their own values and philosophy. They are 'to all eternity separated from the "real", the actual' (*GM*, III, 4); they 'do not stand nearly independently enough in the world and *against* the world for their changing valuations to deserve attention *in themselves*' (*GM*, III, 5). This is, however, no indictment of artists: their spirit is necessarily too fluid, too mercurial, too responsive to the complexity of life, to accommodate itself naturally to a rigid, single value-hierarchy like one structured by the ascetic form. Were they to achieve the detachment and consistency of viewpoint required to pursue philosophical questions (let alone to ask 'extrinsic' questions about the meaning of man *qua* animal), their artistic prowess would vanish. For 'to lay hold of actuality, for once actually to *be*' is 'what is most forbidden' the artist (*GM*, III, 4). In short: the life-enhancer, at least insofar as he is an artist, possesses neither the necessary detachment to ask the (ascetically structured) question about the meaning of 'man, the human *animal*' nor sufficient commitment to the (ascetically structured) answer for the latter to count as expressing a *will* to 'nothingness'. The artist may employ the ascetic ideal as a way of dignifying or embellishing his work, but his commitment to it is (usually) insufficient to become seriously life-denying.

This account prompts at least two questions: first, is it true of artists (as a type) that 'standing alone is contrary to their deepest instincts' (*GM*, III, 5)? And, second, even if it is true, does it preclude their genuine commitment to ideals structured by the ascetic form, at least when the latter is not used to justify total resignation or world-denial? I have neither competence nor space to address these questions properly, but three comments are in order. First, Nietzsche's conception of an artist is perhaps excessively homogeneous. There are those artists whose profession of values seems strikingly independent and consistent: Dostoevsky, Zola, or Beethoven, for example, cannot be said to employ philosophical views merely to 'justify' or decorate their works; nor can their commitment to values

---

[18] As I suggested in Chapter 3.1.3, by 'artist' Nietzsche means the 'artist'-type—which can coexist in one individual with the 'philosopher'-type (or with the 'master' and 'slave' types).

be easily ascribed to themselves *qua* philosopher-types rather than *qua* artists (a distinction that might provide one way of defending Nietzsche's statement about artists' lack of independence). Second, artists are surely capable of genuine allegiance to ascetic forms, in just the sort of life-enhancing way that I suggested earlier—i.e. as a 'striving' towards comprehending or becoming or expressing more fully the higher domain in a bipolar value-hierarchy. There is a sense in which this is so for Beethoven or Wagner (and not just in the latter's final period, as Nietzsche suggests in *GM*, III, 2–4), and which seems crucially to inform some of their greatest music—for example, Beethoven's Ninth Symphony or Wagner's *Tristan*. Third, in general, a genuine commitment to a philosophical system does not require either the courage or the detachment that Nietzsche suggests. Indeed, Nietzsche's own theory that allegiances to values are driven by deep emotional needs—and that values are 'conditions' for an individual's enhancement—suggests that an artist is every bit as capable of commitment to a philosophy as is a thinker, though, perhaps in a less structured or reasoned or informed way.

5.8 CONCLUSION

We may, then, draw the following conclusions from our critique of Nietzsche's conception of the ascetic ideal:

1. There is a general ascetic conceptual form, of which both life-enhancing and life-denying expressions are possible. It ultimately structures *both* the ideal of traditional 'morality'—i.e. to transcend everything changing, 'becoming', and ephemeral for the sake of what is conceived as permanent, fixed, and in 'being'—*and* core concepts of Nietzsche's new ethic, such as 'self-overcoming', 'autonomy', and the healthy 'soul'.

2. In essence, for Nietzsche, life-enhancing expressions of the ascetic form assume a viewpoint or standard 'intrinsic' to 'the world' and human practices: both the 'lower' value that they seek to overcome and the 'higher' value for which they strive are within 'life'. The possibility of an evaluative standpoint external to life itself—or to its predicates such as temporality, animality, contingency, suffering, the corporeal, and the like—is not assumed.

3. By contrast, for Nietzsche, life-denying expressions of the ascetic form presuppose the possibility of exactly such an external

standpoint from which questions about the meaning or value of life *as such* (or of its putative defining predicates, such as 'man, the human *animal*') may be asked. In the limiting case, the answer to such questions involves a complete transcendence, or denial, of 'life' or 'world' itself. Here, suffering is perceived to be such a problem that it places in question the value of life and existence as a whole. Though the ascetic ideal is the only answer given to such a question, it is also, I suggested, presupposed by that question.

4. Though Nietzsche is surely right that the limiting case, where the world *in toto* is devalued *in toto*, is life-denying (for such a valuation tends to make living pointless or even perverse), we must question his pervasive assumption that if concepts and values devalue temporality, flux, and becoming—and hence 'the world' insofar as the latter is identified with these features—and, correspondingly, strive for some value-domain conceived as 'transcendent', they *necessarily* inhibit human flourishing. Epistemologically (or logically), Nietzsche may be right that such concepts, and the extrinsic standpoint they assume, are vacuous: for example, that notions of 'the beyond' or the 'thing-in-itself' are incoherent; or that no warrant exists for conceiving what is in flux as less 'real' than what is (conceived as) unchanging. But psychologically, he has not convincingly shown, either by theoretical argument or by genealogical investigation, that dualism, with its emphasis on devaluing worldly predicates such as temporality or flux or the 'animal' in man and on actualizing the corresponding divine predicates, necessarily impedes life-enhancement. As I have repeatedly suggested, the tremendous cultural richness of 'ascetic' cultures, such as those of Christendom or Buddhism, places such an assumption in particular need of justification—a justification that is not provided simply by pronouncing every individual or epoch of genius to be, at bottom, pagan, as Nietzsche does, for example, with Raphael and the Renaissance.

5. Finally, if, as I have argued, the ascetic conceptual form structures both the old morality that Nietzsche attacks *and* key concepts in the new ethic that he espouses, then it plays a literally pivotal role in his philosophy. In the old morality, asceticism, in the shape of the ascetic ideal, was an end in itself. In the new ethic, however, asceticism, in the shape of concepts like 'self-overcoming', is only a means to an end. That end is the new ideal embodied by Nietzsche's philosophy—the substitute for the old ascetic ideal—which, I shall now suggest, is 'to become what one is'.

6

The New Ideal: 'To become what one is'

The aims of this concluding chapter of Part I are threefold: first, to summarize the conception of morality that Nietzsche repudiates; second, to propose that, of the various candidates for his new ideal, the one that is most consistent with his standard of 'life-enhancement' is to 'become what one is'; and, third, to suggest that Nietzsche regards both his critique of morality and the new ethic he advances in its place as, in key respects, based on *facts* about what promotes or hinders ('higher') human flourishing—with the result that those who engage with Nietzsche's philosophy cannot selectively ignore, without attempting to refute, certain elements that they may find distasteful, such as his conception of justice. In all three cases, I attempt to gather together the threads of previous chapters—in the first case, by highlighting the principal features of 'morality' that we have encountered in each chapter hitherto; in the second case, by reminding ourselves that any new Nietzschean ideal must be compatible with his three criteria of life-enhancement—a demand not met, I suggest, by either his doctrine of 'Eternal Return' or his conception of the 'sovereign individual' (or, indeed, of the '*Übermensch*'); and, in the third case, by recalling the sense in which Nietzsche conceives of values as 'objective', and then tracing some disturbing consequences of a central Nietzschean hypothesis which we encountered in Chapter 3.1.2—namely, that creativity presupposes cruelty.

6.1 THE CONCEPTION OF MORALITY REJECTED BY NIETZSCHE: A SUMMARY

I propose that the overall conception of morality rejected by Nietzsche encompasses six principal ideas:[1]

---

[1] Maudemarie Clark (in Schacht (ed.), *Nietzsche, Genealogy, Morality*, 15–34) rightly observes that Nietzsche scholars tend to assess his attack on 'morality' against their own

1. The idea that the good necessarily embodies certain values (notably altruism, equality, and pity) or traits of character (notably benevolence and sympathy)—e.g. *TI*, IX, 35–7; *BGE*, 33; *GM*, I, 2–3; *GS*, 377; *A*, 7.[2]

2. The idea that these values are unconditionally valid—that they, as it were, vindicate themselves (e.g. *TI*, V, 6; *GS*, 335; *BGE*, 221 and 272).

3. A particular attitude which motivates them—namely '*ressentiment*' (e.g. *GM*, I, 10–11, 13–14; II, 11 and 17; III, 14–16)—expressed by the 'reactive' manner of valuing, whose very broad scope we surveyed in Chapter 3.5. *Ressentiment* owes its great power, first, to its comprehensiveness—i.e. its being directed not merely against particular events, or values, or people, but against existence, time, or the world, as such; second, to the imaginary satisfactions that its insatiability forces it to seek and that are harder than more tangible forms of revenge for the 'masters' to identify or resist (these satisfactions are principally the metaphysical fictions underlying morality); and, third, to the great development of intellect, prudence, and self-control which it fosters (*GM*, I, 10).

4. The linked concepts of 'guilt' and 'bad conscience'—both taken in their extreme, 'moral', form (e.g. *GM*, II, 21–3; *GM*, III, 15). 'Guilt'—along with 'free will' and the 'ascetic ideal' (see (5) and (6) below)—is the principal means of enforcing 'slave' morality. These means are needed because in a world of slave values—such as meekness and pity—enforcement and punishment, at least as inflicted by humans rather than by God, cannot become too overtly violent. Thus, the offender must, ideally, enforce his *own* obedience to these values through the operation of moralized guilt—i.e. through the conviction not merely that the act was bad, but that its badness both expresses intrinsic evil and is ineliminable (except by divine forgiveness). Thus, in non-moral societies, badness and blame are reserved only for the act, and, where mercy is not countenanced, punishment consists in some retributive justice to 'repay' the debt incurred by

conceptions of morality, rather than against his own conception. To this one might add that many authors tend to see Nietzsche's conception of 'morality' as turning on only two or three elements, such as universal duties, essential guilt, or radically free will, rather than on the range indicated here.

[2] For a good summary of values (or the attitudes behind them) that are normative for the 'morality' rejected by Nietzsche, see Brian Leiter, 'Morality in the Pejorative Sense: On the Logic of Nietzsche's Critique of Morality', *British Journal for the History of Philosophy*, 3/1 (1995), 113–45, esp. 134–5.

the offender to his victim; whereas in a moral society, badness and blame attach to the offender in his 'essence'. This notion of 'essential' guilt is given additional weight by:

5. The concept of radical 'free will' (e.g. *BGE*, 19, 21, and 32; *TI*, VI, 7) in which a subject or its will, conceived metaphysically, is distinguished from its actions, thus enabling blame to be assigned separately to an action and to the subject, or intention, behind it. This, in turn, enables the subject to be deemed (i) guilty independently of his actions—and hence guilty in his 'essence' (here we find the role of original sin and baptism), (ii) absolutely responsible for his actions, and thus absolutely guilty for his failings (e.g. *TI*, VI, 7), (iii) maximally interesting to god(s) (*GM*, II, 7)—hence always observed, and, as a result, incapable of spontaneity in the 'noble' fashion, and (iv) uniquely capable of changing the sense of his will—e.g. by repudiating 'masterly' traits in favour of slavishness, or even denying his will altogether (Schopenhauer). (i) to (iii) persuade the agent that he *must* change his will, or at least continually attend to the possible need to change it; while (iv) persuades him that he *can* change his will (a fiction with many possible applications, such as that masters are free to be weak, and that slaves are meek by choice). In other words, with 'free will', guilt can become extraordinarily intense and wide-ranging. But what structures the essential, hence ineliminable, guilt of man is:

6. The 'ascetic ideal', by which contingency, flux, the 'animal' in man, and other such predicates of life are extrinsically judged to be less valuable or perfect than a domain purified of them (e.g. *GM*, III, 11–13). Slave values, such as meekness and self-denial, belong to this picture of man, because they both recognize his imperfection and relate him to idealized perfection. We may note that by devaluing the world of flux in relation to a domain of transcendent value, the ascetic ideal accommodates all the key psychological drives that characterize *ressentiment:* it allows the resentment to have a general object (i.e. the 'phenomenal' world); it provides a powerful 'effigy' of that object (i.e. as 'phenomenon', 'impermanence', intrinsically guilty, and so on—all of which are part of an ' "inverted world" ': *GM*, III, 14); and, finally, it permits imaginary revenge against that object (i.e. the satisfaction of damning it as 'unreal', 'evil', and 'punished by God'). The ascetic ideal, by assuming standards that are purportedly extrinsic to the 'phenomena' and practices of life that they judge or justify, therefore structures a powerful philosophical ethics that both embodies *ressentiment* and justifies its imaginary revenge.

Only by taking these six ideas *together* can we appreciate, first, the sheer scope that the old morality has for Nietzsche; second, why that morality has sufficient power to overwhelm the 'masters'; and, third, what his 'immoralism' actually denotes. The first point reminds us that when Nietzsche sometimes designates only one or other of these six ideas as characteristic of the 'moral phase' of mankind (e.g. the separation of intention and action associated with the concept of 'free will': *BGE*, 32), this does not exhaust his conception of 'morality'. The second point helps solve the puzzle, about which the secondary literature seems surprisingly unexercised, of *why* Nietzsche's self-assured 'masters' should succumb so decisively to the moral blandishments of an angry bunch of mediocrities, by suggesting that the enormous historical success of morality (which is a fact, even if Nietzsche's particular genealogical account of its victories is fictional) owes much to the *collective* force of these six ideas. And the third point indicates that Nietzsche's 'immoralism' denotes his rejection of any morality (or ethic) embracing these six particular ideas—though, clearly, not of any ethic at all. In short: *only* insofar as 'morality' has traditionally incorporated those six ideas may Nietzsche be said to reject 'morality' as such.[3]

6.2 A LIFE-ENHANCING IDEAL: 'TO BECOME WHAT ONE IS'

The 'positive' ethic that Nietzsche advances in place of morality is denoted by 'life-enhancement', the three criteria for which we

[3] In other words, when Nietzsche calls himself an 'immoralist', he is rejecting only the '*moral* in the narrower sense', or 'morality in the traditional sense, the morality of intentions'—an ethic which followed the '*pre-moral*' and is on the threshold of being superseded by the '*extra-moral*' in a process that he calls the 'overcoming of morality' (all quotes from *BGE*, 32). It is clear from this passage that Nietzsche occasionally employs the term 'morality' both as type (i.e. any form of moral code, or what is better called 'ethic') and as token (i.e. traditional 'slave' morality), and that his attack is restricted to the latter—that is, to any ethic embracing all or most of the six features just summarized. Thus, when he sometimes talks of 'morality' in an approving sense or in the plural—as in his reference to 'noble morality' or '*higher*' moralities (e.g. *BGE*, 202)—he is referring either to morality as type or to tokens distinct from traditional morality. The two quotes below illustrate this use of 'morality' as both type and token. In the first quote, 'morality' is used in both senses, while in the second it denotes only the (traditional) token: '*Morality in Europe today is herd animal morality*—in other words, as we understand it, merely *one* type of human morality beside which, before which, and after which many other types, above all *higher* moralities, are, or ought to be, possible' (*BGE*, 202); 'belief in morality, in all morality, falters . . . we need a *critique* of moral values, *the value of these values must first be called into question*' (*GM*, P, 6).

reconstructed in Chapter 3.1.[4] In the course of his works, Nietzsche seems to search for the '*opposing ideal*' to that of ascetic life-denial (e.g. *GM*, III, 23 and 25; cf. *GM*, II, 24)—an ideal that will be embraced by the most life-enhancing person and so take the place of the old ascetic ideal.[5] The candidates for this ideal that he most conspicuously entertains are to 'become what one is' (e.g. *EH*, subtitle and II, 9; *GS*, 270 and 335; *Z*, IV, 1), to attain 'the sovereign individual' (e.g. *GM*, II, 2), and to affirm 'Eternal Return' or '*amor fati*' (e.g. *GS*, 341; *Z*, III, 2 and 13; *TI*, X, 5; *BGE*, 56; *EH*, II, 10). My proposal here is that, of these three candidates, the ideal that best embodies Nietzsche's new ethic—and that most effectively picks out the genuine life-enhancer—is 'to become what one is'.[6] By contrast, the perfectly 'sovereign individual' (who, I will argue, *is* the *Übermensch*) is both unattainable and undesirable; while affirming 'Eternal Return' is neither necessary nor unique to 'life-enhancement', and is, therefore, not a reliable test of the latter.

6.2.1 Definition

> *What does your conscience say?*—'You shall become the person you are.' (*GS*, 270)

> We . . . *want to become those we are*—human beings who are new, unique, incomparable, who give themselves laws, who create themselves. (*GS*, 335)

To become 'what one is' is, I suggest, for an individual to actualize his or her highest possibilities—i.e. to find the most life-enhancing way(s) in which someone with his or her particular endowments of nature, nurture, and life-circumstances (and hence particular historical inheritance) could live. This actualizing of an individual's potential is not, however, Aristotelian, for two reasons. First, for Aristotle

---

[4] These three criteria, we recall, are: (i) power (as a gross measure); (ii) refinement or sublimation—which makes possible the co-option, rather than the extirpation, of all powerful drives, including those, such as unchecked cruelty, that in their 'raw' state could be excessively destructive to the individual or community; and (iii) 'form-creation' that invites love of world and life—i.e. sublimated power as expressed in the three types of creativity most valued by Nietzsche: 'genuine' philosophy, great art, and giving 'style' to an autonomous character.

[5] An ideal, for Nietzsche, is not, of course, an abstract Platonic archetype distinguished from its instances, but simply a way to 'bring out the main features' (*TI*, IX, 8)—in this case of Nietzsche's conception of the most life-enhancing person.

[6] This wording is taken from the second paragraph of *EH*, II, 9; and also appears, slightly modified, in the previous paragraph and in the subtitle of *Ecce Homo*: 'How One Becomes What One Is.'

the class over which 'potentiality' ranges is the human species, or at least a particular social stratum of human male, whereas for Nietzsche it is the individual. (The distinction is not, in fact, absolute because, for Nietzsche, there are aspects of potentiality, such as one's capacity to understand certain higher problems, which range over 'spiritual' strata or 'types' of human beings—e.g. *BGE*, 213.) Second, and more interestingly, for Nietzsche, unlike for Aristotle, the perfect and final actualization of a clear and fixed potential is neither possible, nor knowable, nor should be sought.

It is not *possible* because the attainment of 'life-enhancement', for any given individual, is not the simple unfolding of a single, unchangeable potentiality latent in him or her. As I argued in Chapter 2.4, a Nietzschean *telos* has the following features: (*a*) it consists of a number of possible *telē* consistent with an individual's nature, nurture, and life-circumstances, or, to put the matter another way, a range of possible values that will 'preserve and enhance' the particular person he or she is; (*b*) it is fluid insofar as the nurture and life-circumstances that shape it are themselves constantly evolving, and insofar as it can, at any point in time, be actualized in several different possible ways; hence (*c*) it has not *even a theoretical* single terminus of perfect fulfilment or maximum good.

Moreover, such a terminus could not be *known*, even if it were theoretically possible, because of the extreme opacity of the drives, emotions, and needs that constitute the heterogeneous Nietzschean 'self', combined with the unfathomable complexity of the nature, nurture, and circumstances that shape us. Nietzsche may be referring to this unspecifiability of the maximum good for an individual when he says that we do not and cannot know '[w]hat is best in us' (*BGE*, 249). We shall trace some of the ethical consequences of this point in a moment—especially, the difficulty of judging the value of our individual actions.

But, most interestingly of all, a terminus should not even be *sought* or defined—at least before the time is ripe. To attempt to discover, before one has lived and tested oneself sufficiently, 'what one is'— i.e. the 'organizing "idea"' (*EH*, II, 9)[7] or dominating 'drives' (*BGE*, 6) around which one's whole life will take shape—can prevent one

---

[7] Nietzsche employs various approximately equivalent terms for 'organizing "idea"': e.g., 'personal providence' (*GS*, 277); 'single taste' (*GS*, 290); 'granite of spiritual *fatum*' (*BGE*, 231); and the '*one* will, *one* health, *one* soil, *one* sun', from which 'our ideas, our values' grow with such 'necessity' (*GM*, P, 2).

becoming what one is; for, as just mentioned, 'what one is' evolves only under the pressure of lived experience. Indeed, to become one-self one must often take 'wrong roads' (*EH*, II, 9) and even 'fight for a time on the side of our opponents' (*GS*, 323). Perhaps this is why Nietzsche quotes Goethe as saying that 'Truly high respect one can have only for those who do not *seek* themselves' (*BGE*, 266)—and why Nietzsche himself says so bluntly: 'To become what one is, one must not have the faintest notion *what* one is' (*EH*, II, 9). The motto for 'becoming what you are' therefore seems to be: 'seek and ye shall not find'. In Chapter 10.4.2, I return to this point, which the sec-ondary literature tends to overlook or underrate.

6.2.2 Nietzschean 'authenticity'

These considerations suggest that we should refrain from attributing to Nietzsche a simple ideal of 'authenticity'—one that presupposes that one has a maximum good or potential (i.e. one's ultimate end), which can and should be discovered, and which then constitutes a yardstick against which to evaluate one's specific actions. As to the end, we have already said that each individual might be capable of enhancing his life in a variety of alternative ways,[8] that one cannot know the maximum good for oneself, and that one should not seek to discover (prematurely) what one is. As to the means to an overall end, the real value to us of our individual actions is, as we will shortly discuss, opaque; and, anyway, truthfulness to an overall con-ception of the good can at any time be undermined by the overrid-ing need for self-respect, which often requires self-delusion and artistic falsification (*GS*, 290). Moreover, insofar as any self-knowledge is needed in order to become what we are (and if we are an 'artist' this may be minimal), it is limited to four main tasks.[9] First, we must eliminate falsehoods that are life-denying—notably those perpetrated by conventional morality (these will be further dis-

---

[8] Golomb sees Nietzsche's conception of authenticity as an amalgam between two mod-els of authenticity: one based on the biological metaphor of actualizing an innate poten-tial; the other, and more prominent in Nietzsche's thought, based on the artistic metaphor of freely shaping oneself as a work of art (Jacob Golomb, *In Search of Authenticity: From Kierkegaard to Camus* (London: Routledge, 1995), 69).

[9] This limitation on the value of self-knowledge is frequently overlooked in the sec-ondary literature—for example, by Thiele, who claims that, for Nietzsche, the 'task of ordering souls *above all* requires self-knowledge' (my italics). See Leslie Paul Thiele, *Friedrich Nietzsche and the Politics of the Soul: A Study of Heroic Individualism* (Princeton: Princeton University Press, 1990), 207.

cussed in Chapter 10.1.1 and 10.2.1). Second, we must know our strengths and weaknesses in order to create out of ourselves a character with 'style'. Third, we must take responsibility for our 'highest' values: in other words, *really* understand what it is uncompromisingly to 'become' them, to follow through their demands on us to the bitter end, and to 'promise' ourselves in respect of them. (What this requires of us in the case of our valuation of *truth* will be considered in Part II.) And, fourth, we must 'purify' our values to ensure that we are always pursuing more rather than less life-enhancing options. I will now explicate this fourth point, because it interestingly indicates the limits—but also the possibilities—for something resembling practical reasoning in Nietzsche's ethic.

6.2.3 'Purifying' our values

To become what we are, we (if we can) must 'live dangerously', testing the highways and byways of experience, and strengthening ourselves through great suffering and exposure to terrible truths. Meanwhile, we must keep our consciousness 'clear of all great imperatives' (*EH*, II, 9). At the same time, however, 'we must become the best learners and discoverers of everything that is lawful and necessary in the world' (*GS*, 335). And in the light of this experience and learning we must evaluate what is life-denying and what is life-enhancing for us, by examining the functions of our values and practices.

Now how we perform this evaluation provides one of the most striking illustrations of the contrast between the old morality and the new Nietzschean ethic. In the old morality, one had particular standards which were applied to individual actions or their intentions. The latter were, quite simply, deemed good or bad when measured against those standards.[10] In the Nietzschean ethic, by contrast, the 'unit of evaluation' is not an individual action but a lived life; and the 'evaluator' is not a single standard but a cluster of standards forming an individual's conception of the good (such as Nietzsche's own three criteria of life-enhancement). This claim is worth teasing out a little further.

[10] Even when the context or circumstances of actions or their intentions are very precisely specified, as in the casuistic tradition, the basic unit of evaluation in conventional morality, I take Nietzsche to be saying, is always the individual action (or intention) or type of action (or intention).

6.2.3.1 *The opacity of our actions*

The starting point of Nietzsche's argument is the impossibility of knowing more than superficially either the *causes* (ethical[11] or otherwise) or the *consequences* (ethical[12] or otherwise) of particular actions. Both are too complex to describe precisely. Thus, every action, says Nietzsche, is utterly 'unique and irretrievable' (*GS*, 335), 'open to many interpretations', 'unfathomable' (*BGE*, 287), and, at least in more complex cases like artistic creation, subject to 'thousandfold laws' that 'defy all formulation through concepts' (*BGE*, 188).[13] The total value of an agent's actions in promoting his or her good—as measured, say, by the standard of 'life-enhancement'—cannot, therefore, be judged either by their immediate consequences or by single moral rules or standards that pick out only particular causes (motives, intentions) or effects of them. Nor, conversely, can the outcomes of individual actions count as arguments for or against particular values or rules ('our opinions about "good" and "noble" and "great" can never be *proved true* by our actions because every action is unknowable'—*GS*, 335). Hence we should stop being obsessed by 'the "moral value of our actions" '—i.e. judging individual actions by universal standards—and, instead, get on with the 'purification of our . . . valuations' and the '*creation of our own new tables of what is good*' (*GS*, 335)—i.e. of our own individual values.

This unknowability of our individual actions, and of their causes and consequences, points to four conclusions:

---

[11] i.e. as motivated by adherence to certain values, rules, or standards.

[12] i.e. as evaluated by certain values, rules, or standards.

[13] This idea that our actions follow laws that cannot be conceptualized seems to contain two thoughts: first, something like a Wittgensteinian 'private language argument', that concepts can refer only to what is publicly shared and hence to nothing that is strictly individual, and, second, the supposition that empirical concepts, being shared and therefore general, pick out predicates of a level of generality and ambiguity several notches cruder than the finely grained events and mechanisms that underlie our every action. This, at any rate, is the interpretation I give to, respectively, the following two passages: '*consciousness has developed only under the pressure of the need for communication* . . . conscious thinking *takes the form of words* . . . given the best will in the world to understand ourselves as individually as possible, to "know ourselves", each of us will always succeed in becoming aware only of what is not individual but "average". Our thoughts themselves are continually governed by the character of consciousness' (*GS*, 354); 'how strictly and subtly [the artist] obeys thousandfold laws precisely [in the moment of creative inspiration], laws that precisely on account of their hardness and determination defy all formulation through concepts (even the firmest concept is, compared with them, not free of fluctuation, multiplicity, and ambiguity)' (*BGE*, 188).

First, individual actions, whether judged by their causes or consequences or both, are not the right 'unit' of ethical evaluation, at
any rate as measured by Nietzsche's criteria of life-enhancement.
That is, neither the good achieved by an act nor the value of an
agent's values can be judged by that single act—let alone by a single
'intention' (or consequence, or type of consequence) of a single act—
but can only be broadly gauged over a longer period of 'lived life'.
That they can only be broadly gauged, rather than precisely determined, is crucial, because Nietzsche's thoroughgoing determinism—
his idea that everything is ultimately linked to everything
else—means that even a complete summation of the actions of an
individual's life would still constitute an incomplete, and arbitrary,
unit of evaluation, since those actions would be related to countless
others outside the conventional boundaries of that single life. Strictly
speaking, the only complete unit of evaluation would include every
event that has ever occurred—and it is, of course, precisely this totality that Nietzsche says 'Yes' to in affirming the 'Eternal Return'. (To
put this point in Quinean language: our actions must face the tribunal of our ethical judgements collectively and not singly—and,
ideally, the unit of ethical significance will be every interrelated event
and so constitute a sample of infinite size.)

Second, if an action has such a complex causal history, then its
'intention' would simply be a certain phenomenon or epiphenom-
enon which fashion or vanity or resentment or our ethical rules pick
out from the hugely detailed psychology (conscious and unconscious)
of that action. And even if intentions in some sense are, or denote,
genuine 'causes' of actions—rather than simply correlates of the urge
to interpose a pure willing subject between the causes and effects of
actions—one may wonder how important they really are in the total
causal history of an action, and how we could ever answer that question with sufficient certainty to *judge* actions, let alone agents, by
their intentions. (In place of 'intentions', but quite unlike them in
that it is not, it seems, parasitic on a classical concept of a controlling 'will', Nietzsche substitutes the notion of an 'organizing "idea"'
or 'taste', which denotes an individual's dominating drive and discipline—and which may be seen as the spokesman rather than the
author of our actions. We will return to this notion in 6.2.4 below
and in Chapters 8.6 and 10.4.2.)

Third, evaluations of our individual *values* are themselves merely
rough and revisable estimates—(i) because outcomes, even over a

longer stretch of time than that of single actions, can only be broadly rather than comprehensively assessed, (ii) because it may be impossible to trace the effects of just one value or, conversely, to be sure of ascribing certain effects to the operation of a single value, and (iii) because values, as we have repeatedly stated, can be judged only in the context of a precise specification of their functions, which are themselves influenced by other values. Indeed, to judge the value of one value may actually be, willy–nilly, to judge the effect of a collection of values operating in the life of a particular individual or society or epoch. Thus, it may be that our *values* similarly face the tribunal of 'life-enhancement' collectively, as an 'ethic', rather than individually. Perhaps it is such considerations that lead Nietzsche to infer from his discussion of the unknowability of both individual actions and the effect of particular values in motivating them that we should '*limit* ourselves to the purification of our opinions and valuations' (*GS*, 335).

Fourth, the obstacles to accurate introspection must crucially limit the value of one of morality's key values: namely *pity*. For pity assumes the possibility of accurate knowledge of the inner state and suffering of another; and, to the extent that such knowledge is unavailable, the value of pity will be circumscribed. This, indeed, is precisely one of Nietzsche's main arguments against pity—which, he says, 'strips away from the suffering of others whatever is distinctively personal' and refuses to recognize that 'one simply knows nothing of the whole inner sequence and intricacies that are distress for *me* or for *you*' (*GS*, 338). Only those who share the *same* suffering as another can, Nietzsche suggests, begin to understand the latter's inner state.

In sum: in seeking the *truth* about the nature or value of (i) our actions, (ii) our 'intentions', and (iii) our values, the best that we can do may be to study all three in their aggregate—i.e. as, respectively, (i) a lived life, (ii) an 'organizing "idea"', and (iii) a set of values, about whose value in enhancing or diminishing our life we should endeavour to purify or refine our generalizations. Contrary to some traditional claims, such truth-seeking cannot enable us to know either what is best in us and for us, or to evaluate the intentions or consequences of our individual actions. These conclusions are, I suggest, among Nietzsche's most interesting contributions to ethics.[14]

---

[14] It is noteworthy that even Kant doubted whether we could disentangle the causes of our actions, and thus whether we could ever know that we had done the right thing out

6.2.4 The master drive

Nietzsche's determinism suggests that one either possesses the dominant drive(s) that moulds one into a whole personality and that enables one to 'become what one is', or one lacks it. His opposition both to the notion of 'free will' as *causa prima* and to conferring primacy on consciousness means that this dominant drive cannot be summoned in a conventional voluntaristic fashion[15]—for the 'will to overcome an affect is ultimately only the will of another, or of several other, affects' (*BGE*, 117)—though it can be strengthened by a life of discipline, 'hardness', and risk. It may be there all along, as part of one's inherited rank order of drives (*A*, 57), or it may emerge as a victor from the ongoing battles within the self (*BGE*, 19). These battles are largely unconscious: for consciousness—and concepts—are assigned an essentially passive role by Nietzsche, as spokesmen, or consequences, of the truces, victories, and defeats in the wars being fought subconsciously. The master drive that emerges from, or determines, their outcome is manifested in what Nietzsche variously calls our innate 'organizing "idea"' (*EH*, II, 9), 'single taste' (*GS*, 290), and 'personal providence' (*GS*, 277).

Yet reason and knowledge can decisively influence the outcome of these emotional conflicts—and can play a central role in the 'purification' of our values to which, as we have just seen, Nietzsche urges us. This must be so, or he could not insist that '[l]earning changes' all but one's 'granite' core of spiritual *fatum* (*BGE*, 231), or that his genealogies will, by appealing to our commitment to truth, eventually destroy the old morality. But for reason and knowledge to have this power, for them to be capable of, as it were, emboldening or subduing particular drives, we must be receptive to them in three ways already outlined in Chapter 2.4: first, by sufficiently valuing

of the right motive (i.e. the thought of one's duty to the moral law): '[W]e can never, even by the most strenuous self-examination, get to the bottom of our secret impulsions [*Triebfedern*]', as Kant says in the *Grundlagen* (Immanuel Kant, *Groundwork of the Metaphysic of Morals*, trans. H. J. Paton (New York: Harper & Row, 1964), chapter 2, 75). However, this empirical problem obviously in no way prevented Kant from grounding his ethics in a conception of pure agency.

[15] Nietzsche's rejection of certain metaphysical conceptions of 'free will', as of related notions such as God, subject, and substance, has, we recall, both epistemological and ethical grounds—the former (and *less* decisive for Nietzsche) being the unverifiability of these notions, the latter being their life-denying consequences, especially the destruction of 'the innocence of becoming' through inflated ascriptions of responsibility and guilt (e.g. *TI*, VI, 7).

truthfulness—ultimately in virtue of our Platonic-Christian ethical inheritance; second, by receptiveness to just the kind of ('internal') reasons for action which we encounter, say, in Nietzsche's genealogies; and, third, by possessing sufficiently strong controlling drives to bring about new practices and to overcome the old habits which obstruct them. These three types of receptivity are, of course, entirely compatible with Nietzsche's non-metaphysical theory of willing.

Once again, then, we are confronted by that peculiar mixture of the passive and the active that characterizes the 'master'. In order to permit the emergence of a dominant drive which will forge out of us a unified personality, we must be passive in that we avoid seeking or willing or defining that drive directly or prematurely. But we must be active by engaging in the boldest, broadest, and most rigorous exercise of our various talents: i.e. under strong mental *and* physical discipline, thorough education, reverence for oneself and reality, and negating nothing except weaknesses. Not introspection but '[d]anger alone acquaints us with our own resources, our virtues, . . . our *spirit*' (*TI*, IX, 38). Indeed, the hardships which have to be endured to experience, to risk, and to discipline oneself so comprehensively, are a *measure* of the freedom thus attained (*TI*, IX, 38). And because these hardships have enabled the whole to be created they are 'redeemed and affirmed in the whole' (*TI*, IX, 49).

In sum, 'becoming what one is' is, above all, a *process* of steadily increasing life-enhancement, that demands bold living, strict discipline, and, in the light of prolonged experience, 'purification' of one's values. But it lacks both an optimum end that can be defined theoretically or known practically *and* the possibility of judging the value of our individual actions as means towards such an end.

6.3 THE 'SOVEREIGN INDIVIDUAL'

Now one might suppose from Nietzsche's praise of the '*sovereign individual*'—the one who has achieved perfect self-mastery and hence genuine freedom (*GM*, II, 2)—that he or she embodies the new ideal. After all, Nietzsche regards this individual as the solution to the 'real problem regarding man', which is to 'breed an animal *with the right to make promises*' (*GM*, II, 1), and as 'the end of this tremendous process' (*GM*, II, 2). But, I suggest, from Nietzsche's *own point of view*, the final achievement of this individual is both unattainable and undesirable, and so cannot be his ideal.

He is *unattainable* because in order to achieve perfect mastery over himself and circumstances (and thus perfect 'free will' in Nietzsche's sense of the term), he would need to be *infallible* in controlling the myriad drives and dependencies created by his nature, nurture, and life-circumstances. In other words, he would need to be a man-god, invested with precisely the absolute autonomy of the 'dead' God. But this man-god is, I suggest, as elusive as the old deity for which he might be regarded as substituting: absolute independence of circumstances and perfect self-legislation are beyond even 'higher' men. Indeed, to aim at such 'autonomy' would arguably be yet another symptom of the urge to be insulated from contingency, which Nietzsche so powerfully decries in its metaphysical or religious manifestation. As Berkowitz's sensitive reading of *Zarathustra* suggests, the latter's own efforts to attain just such godlike mastery appear to end in failure;[16] and, if this reading is justified, it may reflect Nietzsche's intent to show us, through his account of Zarathustra's life, that any such ambition is doomed.[17]

Moreover, such perfect autonomy is bound to be *undesirable* because if, as Zarathustra puts it, life is *'that which must always overcome itself'* (*Z*, II, 12), when overcoming comes to an end so too does a worthwhile life. This, indeed, reflects the paradoxical nature of the *Übermensch*, who has lived life to the full by taking 'overcoming' to its limit, but, in doing so, has ultimately destroyed the point of living—a perfect illustration of Nietzsche's law that *all* great things—which, as the *Übermensch* shows, include life itself—'bring about their own destruction through an act of self-overcoming' (*GM*, III, 27). And the absolutely sovereign individual is, I suggest, none other than the *Übermensch:* for in mastering every obstacle to promising himself, he, like the *Übermensch*, has *nothing left* to overcome (see Chapter 5.2).[18]

[16] Berkowitz, *Nietzsche*, chapters 7 and 8, *passim*, esp. 207–13.

[17] Berdyaev, in his magnificent study of Dostoevsky, argues (and portrays Dostoevsky as arguing) that attempts to be a 'man-god' necessarily 'collapse into a state of pitiable weakness and futility', and that the Nietzschean *Übermensch* 'kills true manhood' (Nicholas Berdyaev, *Dostoevsky*, trans. Donald Attwater (Cleveland: The World Publishing Company, 1957), 98–9, and chapters 2 and 3, *passim*).

[18] Stanley Rosen gives a subtle and fascinating account of the *Übermensch*, which differs in key respects from mine, in *The Mask of Enlightenment*, esp. 49–52, 70–2, and 141–3. Robert Pippin interestingly discusses Zarathustra's changing attitude to the *Übermensch* in 'Irony and Affirmation in Nietzsche's *Thus Spoke Zarathustra*', in M. A. Gillespie and

Now there are four further reasons, though these are not Nietzsche's, why the perfectly sovereign individual is undesirable as an ideal. First, such hermetic sovereignty would isolate the 'higher man' from all nourishment of love and friendship and other human relationships—nourishment which may, as a straightforward fact about human nature, be essential to his finding the vision and the courage for his difficult path. Nietzsche's radical individualism not only largely ignores such needs,[19] but treats all demanding human entanglements, such as friendship or marriage, as at best distractions and at worst crippling (e.g. for the philosopher—*GM*, III, 7).[20] Second, there are clearly other, more basic, human needs, such as for food, shelter, and health which, if unsatisfied, can preclude any higher ambitions; and these, too, are not considered by Nietzsche. Third, even if he waived all these 'lower' needs aside, as not pertinent to his philosophical aims, his general insistence that 'higher men' have particularly 'complicated conditions of life' (*BGE*, 62), many of which presumably involve external dependence of some kind, such as the right cultural environment, suggests that autonomy will only be secured at the price of starving the individual of whatever Nietzsche regards as these life-giving conditions.[21] Finally, his refusal of adequate normative constraints on the individual's freedom risks making the 'higher' man at least as vulnerable to the 'mob' as he is, according to Nietzsche, under 'morality'. I will return to this last point in section 6.5.2 below.

T. B. Strong (eds.), *Nietzsche's New Seas: Explorations in Philosophy, Aesthetics, and Politics* (Chicago: University of Chicago Press, 1988), 50 ff.

[19] Zarathustra even calls 'the cessation of all need . . . the origin of . . . virtue' (*Z*, I, 22, 1).

[20] Thus a suggestion, such as Lester Hunt's, for 'revising Nietzsche's conception of virtue, so that it is not merely a certain integration of the self but, in addition, a certain integration of the self into the community around one' makes communitarian (and, possibly, egalitarian) assumptions that Nietzsche fights tooth and nail, as Hunt himself recognizes. (See Lester H. Hunt, *Nietzsche and the Origin of Virtue* (London: Routledge, 1991), 179 and chapter 9, *passim*.)

[21] For example, the discovery of one's own highest values may itself depend crucially and intricately upon one's social relationships. Indeed, if one goes so far as to hold, with Alasdair MacIntyre, that goods can be discovered *only* by entering into social relationships 'whose central bond is a shared vision of . . . goods', then to be isolated from such relationships 'will be to debar oneself from finding any good outside of oneself' (MacIntyre, *After Virtue*, 258).

6.4 'ETERNAL RETURN'

The third candidate for Nietzsche's new ideal that I shall consider, and perhaps the most popular in the secondary literature, is the affirmation of 'Eternal Return'—i.e. of the idea that all events recur infinitely in an identical manner and order (see, for example: *GS*, 341; *Z*, III, 2 and 13). Clark, for example, calls it Nietzsche's 'counterideal' to the ascetic ideal;[22] Lampert claims that it provides 'a new grounding of normative thinking';[23] and Thiele describes it as the 'ultimate test of the order of rank' and '*the* defining characteristic of a higher man'.[24] Unlike these authors, however, I argue that the ability to affirm 'Eternal Return' is, as Nietzsche presents it, neither necessary nor unique to the life-enhancer and cannot, therefore, be a useful 'counterideal' for his ethic of life-enhancement.[25]

First, it is a straightforward fact that a capacity for life-enhancement—i.e. for creating forms that express sublimated power and that invite love of life—does not require a predisposition on the part of the creator to affirm everything about his life and the world, a fact evidenced by the frequent association of depression and genius.

[22] Clark, *Nietzsche on Truth and Philosophy*, chapter 8, 253 and *passim*.

[23] Laurence Lampert, *Nietzsche's Teaching: An Interpretation of* Thus Spoke Zarathustra (New Haven: Yale University Press, 1986), 274.

[24] Thiele, *Friedrich Nietzsche and the Politics of the Soul*, 197.

[25] A large secondary literature exists on the possible interpretations of Nietzsche's presentation of the 'Eternal Return', on their role in his cosmology and ethics, and on their logical coherence—or lack of it. (See, for example: Clark, *Nietzsche on Truth and Philosophy*, chapter 8; Arthur C. Danto, *Nietzsche as Philosopher* (New York: Macmillan, 1965), 201–13; Heidegger, *Nietzsche*, i. 18–24; ii, part 1; and iii. 209–15; Karl Löwith, *Nietzsche's Philosophy of the Eternal Recurrence of the Same*, trans. J. Harvey Lomax (Berkeley and Los Angeles: University of California Press, 1997); Bernd Magnus, *Nietzsche's Existential Imperative* (Bloomington, Ind.: Indiana University Press, 1978), chapters 5 and 6; Nehamas, *Nietzsche: Life as Literature*, chapter 5; and Rosen, *The Mask of Enlightenment*, 169–71, 177–89, and 201–2.) I am sceptical about 'Eternal Return' as a 'cosmological' hypothesis, in part because there is no reason why probability should lead us to expect that, given infinite time, all possible events will occur even once, let alone that they will recur in an identical form and order. I will not, however, venture here into this complex subject—or the more general theme of closed time—on which discussion goes back to antiquity. (See, for example, Richard Sorabji's books *Matter, Space, and Motion: Theories in Antiquity and their Sequel* (London: Duckworth, 1988), 163–83; and *Time, Creation, and the Continuum: Theories in Antiquity and the Early Middle Ages* (London: Duckworth, 1983), 182–90.) For purposes of the present discussion, it is best to pass over the question of whether Nietzsche provides grounds for conceiving of existence as eternally recurring, and to focus entirely on what it would mean, ethically and psychologically, to affirm such a hypothesis, whether or not the latter is justified or justifiable, and whether or not Nietzsche even intended to promulgate it.

Life-enhancement and life-affirmation (or world-affirmation) are *not* identical, though easily conflated. Nietzsche's assumption that it takes a life-enhancer to affirm 'Eternal Return' (or that *amor fati* is a 'formula for greatness'—*EH*, II, 10) may therefore be another instance of his error that to be creative involves, or presupposes, affirming the world in all those features, such as the temporal and the phenomenal, that the ascetic ideal longs to 'overcome'. Nietzsche asks: 'how well disposed would you have to become to yourself and to life *to crave nothing more fervently* than this ultimate eternal confirmation and seal [i.e. of affirming 'Eternal Return']?' (*GS*, 341). But many life-enhancers are not 'well-disposed' either to themselves or to much of life—indeed, their dissatisfaction may be crucial to their creativity. If so, a capacity for life-enhancement and a capacity for willing the 'Eternal Return' may conflict,[26] which does not make such willing a suitable ideal for an ethic of life-enhancement.

Second, genuinely to affirm the 'Eternal Return' would require one to look at reality, including the reality of one's own nature, with maximum clarity and truthfulness—else the terrible facts that make of such affirmation a 'test' could simply be ignored. But this truthfulness, we recall, is precisely what real artists—Nietzsche's paradigmatic life-enhancers—are constitutionally incapable of, and *must* be incapable of if they are to remain creative (cf. *GM*, III, 4). If '[w]hoever is completely and wholly an artist is to all eternity separated from the "real", the actual' and, moreover, is 'forbidden', above all, to 'lay hold of actuality' (ibid.), then the 'Eternal Return' is not genuinely affirmable by them and so cannot be even a necessary condition of being a life-enhancer.

Third, the capacity to affirm 'Eternal Return' not only fails to pick out all life-enhancers, but may be possessed by certain life-deniers—insofar as it can be affirmed out of weak motives, such as fear of losing the past or of final death. For affirming 'Eternal Return' or *amor*

---

[26] It will not work to suggest, as a counter-argument, that such life-enhancers can, in fact, will the 'Eternal Return' by affirming, along with everything else, the fact of their being badly disposed to their life and its recurrence—i.e. by willing the recurrence of their repudiations. First, such an argument would generate the *reductio ad absurdum* that one could comprehensively repudiate oneself and life and yet pass the test of 'Eternal Return' simply by affirming the recurrence of those repudiations (out of fear, for example, of the still worse alternative of final death). Second, to affirm 'Eternal Return' is to will the recurrence not simply of one's acts of repudiation, but of *what* they repudiate. Otherwise, one would not be affirming everything about one's life, and it would be hard to make sense of Nietzsche's suggestion, just cited, that one needs to be well disposed to oneself *and* to 'life' in order to crave the 'Eternal Return'.

fati—'that one wants nothing to be different . . . in all eternity' (*EH*, II, 10)—is a test of strength only if it involves affirming what we most dread. If, like Zarathustra, what we most dread includes the recurrence of the 'small man' (*Z*, III, 13, 2), then affirming 'Eternal Return' is indeed such a test. But if what an individual most fears is not the 'small man' or the recurrence of horrors, but, say, the irrecoverable losses entailed by linear time (e.g. the finality of death)—just the sorts of fears that, according to Nietzsche, helped generate the life-denying metaphysics of transcendence—then affirming 'Eternal Return' will be far easier for him than affirming a single non-recurring life. Indeed, the test of strength for such an individual would be to affirm a *finite* existence—and it is strange that Nietzsche does not make *this* his test of strength since so many of the concepts whose functions in traditional metaphysics, theology, morality, and epistemology he opposes are, as he presents them, motivated precisely by fear of death and the craving for eternity.

Fourth, Nietzsche's assumption that maximally to love life is to '*crave*' (*GS*, 341) a future that is *identical* to the past—including a life-denying past—is extremely dubious as a psychological proposition. For one thing, identical recurrence would necessarily be inexperienceable, whether or not we have grounds for accepting it as a cosmological doctrine, simply because absolutely identical cycles could not be distinguished from one another. And whether a state of affairs which one *knows* cannot be experienced would really be one's 'greatest weight' is open to question. For another thing, and more importantly, it surely makes at least equal, if not greater, sense to suggest that someone who loves life and is capable of 'form-creation' that invites love of life would will (and not merely prefer) an *increase* in their life-enhancement with each cycle of existence. To be sure, Nietzsche's deterministic premiss of the causal interrelatedness of all events entails that to reprehend one event is to reprehend the whole world, including one's own life;[27] but to this purely logical inference (as, perhaps, to many others points of logic or fact) *love* of life, with its overriding urge to 'enhance' life, will, it seems to me, be impervious. Finally, though in a cosmos of identical recurrence love of life

---

[27] Nietzsche suggests that, if everything is causally linked to everything else, then to affirm one event in our lives is to affirm the whole universe. Thus: 'Have you ever said Yes to a single joy? O my friends, then you said Yes too to *all* woe. All things are entangled . . . if ever you wanted one thing twice, . . . then you wanted *all* back' (*Z*, IV, 19, 10). Or: 'If we affirm one single moment, we thus affirm . . . all existence' (*WP*, 1032).

would be blatantly deceiving itself by believing that it can successfully will greater life-enhancement in each successive cycle of existence and, moreover, that it can consistently accept some events
while repudiating others, Nietzsche fails to argue that *just such* a
deception would be life-denying. (Indeed, this might be exactly the
kind of deception that is life-enhancing—especially if it is free both
of resentment at its inevitable failure and of the metaphysical illusion that what it reprehends is ultimately overcomeable in an other-
worldly realm.)[28]

Since, for all these reasons, the affirmation of 'Eternal Return' is
neither necessary nor unique to the life-enhancer, it is not, I suggest,
the supremely rigorous test either of life-enhancement or of courageous *amor fati* that Nietzsche seems to think it is. Nonetheless, it
may have a more restricted, but still crucial, role as the only response
consistent with life-enhancement to a very particular sort of question
which the inheritors of the Platonic-Christian tradition are especially
prone to ask: namely about the value of existence taken *as a whole*—
including, and despite, its terrible features (a question which, as
Bernard Williams points out, is the classic question of theodicy[29]).
As I argued in Chapter 5.7, this is precisely the question which,
when asked in a particular way—i.e. in a dualist way, about the
meaning of 'man, the human *animal*'—only the ascetic ideal has 'so
far' answered. My contention here is that when that same kind of
question is asked in a manner that makes *no* dualist presuppositions,
affirming the 'Eternal Return' is, for Nietzsche, the only answer
which a life-enhancer could give.

Of course, even within the Platonic-Christian tradition, some
people, in virtue of their 'type', will not be inclined to ask that universal question—and they, importantly, include many life-enhancers
who, like 'artists', may be incapable of the detachment needed to do

---

[28] By the same token, Nietzsche fails to justify Zarathustra's assertion that 'to re-
create all "it was" into a "thus I willed it"—that alone should I call redemption' (*Z*, II,
20). For the individual sovereignly to will what is 'necessary', for his free willing to be a
law-giving that is aligned with the deep necessity of the world, has a recognizably Kantian
form, and again reflects the degree to which Nietzsche is, in part, a typically 'modern'
thinker. But whether such willing (i.e. in this case, of an inescapable past) is *either* a necessary mark of the life-enhancer *or* unique to life-enhancers is quite another matter.

[29] See Bernard Williams, '*The Women of Trachis*: Fictions, Pessimism, Ethics', in R. B.
Louden and P. Schollmeier (eds.), *The Greeks and Us: Essays in Honor of Arthur W. H.
Adkins* (Chicago: University of Chicago Press, 1996), 43–53, esp. 46–7. My discussion of
the relationship of affirming 'Eternal Return' to the traditional question of theodicy is
heavily indebted to Williams's article.

so, or who live in the realm of the 'superficial' and are oblivious to universal questions about the value or nature of reality as such. Indeed, not to feel the urge even to raise the question may reflect a still more life-enhancing state than to respond to it by affirming 'Eternal Return': for raising the question is already a sign that the horrors of the world have become a burden that, without a satisfactory response, threatens to crush; and answering it with an affirmation of 'Eternal Return' may turn out, as Nietzsche suggests, to be one's 'greatest weight' (*GS*, 341), and so to be inimical to the light-footedness of spirit to which he so consistently aspires. In any event, if the question of theodicy is the question to which, once raised, affirming 'Eternal Return' is the life-enhancer's response, then the class of potential affirmers must be limited to those who are capable of 'laying hold of reality', such as scientists, philosophers, and other truth-seekers and, still more specifically, to those in this class who are prone to asking that very question.

Construed, following Williams, as Nietzsche's response to the old question of theodicy, the affirmation of 'Eternal Return', as Nietzsche presents it (for example, in *GS*, 341), has three very particular features. First, as Williams points out, by being an affirmation, it takes the form of an attitude or an act, rather than, as in traditional theodicies, of a justification or a calculation (i.e. of the overall value of life or existence).[30] Second, this means that it transcends any reasoned calculus of welfare—for example, of costs versus benefits (as, say, Leibniz proposes) or of some ultimate end that vindicates or necessitates the means (as, say, Hegel or Christianity advocates). Such cosmic calculations, when they are not unintelligible, are inevitably open to subsequent doubts—if only about how diverse sorts of good and bad, of achievement and horror, can be commensurable—and so are incapable of grounding the kind of unqualified yea-saying which Nietzsche seeks in affirming 'Eternal Return'.[31] This, as we have

[30] Williams, '*The Women of Trachis*', 47. I am grateful to Professor Williams for reminding me of the moment in Goethe's *Faust*, part I, when, Faust, in the second episode in his study, where he is being disturbed by the 'poodle', himself insists on the primacy of action over assertion, by expressing dissatisfaction with the phrase 'In the beginning was the Word' (*das Wort*), then rejecting two alternatives to 'Word' in this phrase, namely 'Thought' or 'Idea' (*der Sinn*) and 'Power' (*die Kraft*), and finally plumping for 'Deed' (*die Tat*) as, roughly, what ultimately creates and governs the main features of our lives. See J. W. Goethe, *Faust I*, 'Studierzimmer', in *Goethes Werke*, iii, 6th edn., ed. Erich Trunz (Hamburg: Christian Wegner Verlag, 1962), 44, lines 1224–37.

[31] It is true that Nietzsche sometimes marshals arguments that seem to assume the possibility of just such calculations: in particular, when he speculates that what we find

seen, does not deter Nietzsche's Zarathustra from proclaiming that 'redemption' of the world is indeed possible—i.e. by retrospectively willing the necessity of the past (*Z*, II, 20); but one knows this possibility for oneself only by undertaking such an *act* and not by successfully *understanding* a traditional form of justification. Third, this act of affirmation is free of a standpoint or standard of evaluation that purports to be extrinsic to what is being judged—which means that it is free not only of an extrinsic judgement about 'the worldly' but also of world- or history-transcending concepts, notably those intrinsic to dualism. Indeed, I suggest that Nietzsche's conception of 'Eternal Return' embodies, or serves as a metaphor for, the diametrically different ontology to which he subscribes: namely, one of inextricable union between 'being' and 'becoming', or eternity and flux, or permanence and temporality—pairs that in the metaphysical tradition, as he construes it, are regarded as embracing precisely the 'opposite valuations' or discontinuous realms[32] which are presupposed by all such extrinsic valuations.

Given these three elements of a response to the question of theodicy, affirming 'Eternal Return' is, indeed, an excellent 'test' of one's immunity to a traditional, ascetically ideal, response to that question: for to affirm it is necessarily to affirm the union of being and becoming and, conversely, to repudiate the kind of 'other-worldly' consolations that the ascetic ideal structures, especially the idea that we can ultimately escape 'the world' and all its predicates, such as fate, suffering, imperfection, the 'small man', and time. Moreover, if to affirm 'Eternal Return' is to hold that nothing can be either ultimately transcended or, by contrast, lost in the past (because it will infinitely recur) and, indeed, that everything is linked together in continuous causal chains (so that to affirm one moment is to affirm every moment), then this doctrine confers inescapable significance

repulsive or fearsome about existence may be necessary to its greatest accomplishments—either *instrumentally*, in, say, the sense that (what we deem) good can, in a series of causally related events, arise only out of (what we deem) bad, or *constitutively*, in the sense that what we find bad or frightening is part of, rather than simply a means to, what we value—e.g. in the way that he takes art to be a sublimation of cruelty. But, in his presentation of affirming the 'Eternal Return', these arguments, it would seem, simply have no role to play.

[32] Thus, Nietzsche says: 'To impose upon becoming the character of being—that is the supreme will to power . . . That *everything recurs* is the closest *approximation of a world of becoming to a world of being*' (*WP*, 617). Nietzsche calls this latter thought the 'high point of the meditation' (ibid.), suggesting that it, indeed, points to the real significance of 'Eternal Return'.

and *presence* on everything in life, down to the smallest detail. It manœuvres us into an encounter with all that exists—i.e. has existed and will continue to exist in virtue of its 'return'—and so restores, in principle, that relatedness with all being from which a metaphysics of transcendence purportedly removed or protected us. In that sense, it is thoroughly opposed to the old ascetic ideal, reason enough for Nietzsche to call it 'the fundamental conception' of *Thus Spoke Zarathustra* (*EH*, *Z*, 1)—even though its failure to pick out the entire class of life-enhancers means, as I have said, that it cannot be a counter-*ideal* for his ethic of life-enhancement.

Yet does not affirming 'Eternal Return' still presuppose the very universalism of the metaphysical tradition that it putatively overcomes, namely, first, in its concern with the *value* of existence as a whole and, second, in its essentialist (even if hypothetical) *conception* of existence—i.e. of all existence *as* eternally recurring and therefore as both being and becoming? My answer is that, though affirming 'Eternal Return' indeed resembles traditional metaphysics in its universal scope, it is unencumbered by precisely those aspects of the tradition to which Nietzsche is most severely opposed, notably dualism and the 'atomistic need' that, we recall, lies at its heart. Hence, as I have argued, Nietzsche's overall *evaluation* of existence does not claim a point of view that is supposedly extrinsic, or superior in value, or absolute, in relation to what it judges; while his *conception* of all existence as eternally recurring in no way appeals to essential as distinct from incidental properties, or to the idea that the permanent and the changing inhabit discontinuous domains, or to the presupposition that there are aspects of reality which can be metaphysically sheltered from whatever it is that we, as individuals, dread—be it torture and suffering, or time and contingency. Indeed, the whole point of 'Eternal Return', both as an affirmation and as a conception, is that it is free of exactly such categories.

I do *not*, however, believe that affirming 'Eternal Return', even in this more limited sense as the answer to a specific sort of question (of theodicy) asked only by certain types of people, is *either* unique *or* necessary to life-enhancers because, respectively, the third and fourth of my earlier objections would still stand—i.e. fear of final death would still constitute a sufficient motive for affirming it and love of life might still crave greater life-enhancement from one cosmic cycle to the next. My proposal, instead, is that, ethically, affirming the 'Eternal Return' constitutes a foolproof test only of desire for 'this' life and of indifference to traditional forms of response to the question of theodicy, be they based on cosmic cost-benefit summations or structured by the ascetic ideal; while, conceptually, 'Eternal Return' is best seen as a metaphor for Nietzsche's repudiation of any supposed discontinuity between being and becoming—a metaphor for a world in which everything is in flux but is also, in the sense of its eternal recurrence, permanent. Yet, because 'Eternal Return' cannot be genuinely affirmed by one major class of life-enhancers, namely 'artists', and, conversely, could be successfully affirmed by those with 'weak' motives, such as fear of death, it is not an infallible mark of life-enhancers, and is thus unfit to be the new *ideal* for Nietzsche's ethic of life-enhancement.[33]

6.5 GENERAL CLAIMS IN NIETZSCHE'S ETHICS: THE CASE OF CRUELTY

Finally, we must turn to a question that reading Nietzsche insistently provokes: namely, to what extent, in his critique of morality and in his new ethic, he is making claims to which he invites general agreement (at least among those of the same 'rank' or 'type'), rather than opinions which are, in some sense, advanced simply as 'his own'. It is tempting to answer this question by asserting that Nietzsche is at most seeking general agreement on a methodology or procedure by which individuals would re-examine the functions of their highest values in the light of their own standards of flourishing, but that his specific arguments against morality or for his new ethic are based purely on standards or perspectives that he has no grounds for expecting others to share. On this view, if Nietzsche 'imposes' anything it is only a maxim opposing the universalization of values, thus releasing us from any need to consider seriously views he expresses that we may find distasteful—notably those concerning cruelty and justice.

This position is, however, altogether too comfortable. Though, in keeping with his general repudiation of universal prescriptions,

---

[33] Nietzsche's early theodicy is clearly that the world can be justified only as an aesthetic phenomenon (*BT*, 5 and 24); and it would be interesting to investigate the philosophical relations between this assertion and his late theodicy of 'Eternal Return', and, in particular, whether the capacity to affirm the former better picks out the class of life-enhancers.

Nietzsche clearly does not invite everyone to assent to a specific set of ethical standards in place of morality, he *does* advance as true, and to that extent makes it impossible for his readers to side-step consideration of, two types of proposition. The first is that 'morality' employs a host of unverifiable fictions—notably metaphysically laden concepts such as 'free will', 'essential guilt', or others discussed in previous chapters. The second is that morality is inimical to flourishing in most of those respects, notably artistic vigour, that Nietzsche himself values; indeed, that such vigour is fostered precisely by conditions that morality opposes, such as overt cruelty, the 'rights of the few', and the *'order of castes'*—which latter Nietzsche calls 'the sanction of a *natural order*, a natural lawfulness of the first rank' (*A*, 57).

Both types of proposition are regarded by Nietzsche as straightforwardly factual—in the sense that they are discoverable by simply 'reading' the world as it is and so by anyone with sufficiently perceptive senses, sufficient strength for and commitment to truth, and sufficient mastery over *ressentiment* and its fictionalizing perspectives. Though, for Nietzsche, such qualities are confined to a select audience of 'higher' people, who are the 'types' to whom he primarily addresses himself, this does not make the claims themselves any less factual. In other words, that a fact is true only for a particular person (in the sense that she has what it takes to perceive or understand it) clearly does not mean that she has *made* it true.[34]

Now Nietzsche's theoretical ground for expecting such agreement, even from those who share none of his values (except, of course, truthfulness), is, as we have often noted, that he sees a value as a *condition* for the preservation of a certain 'type' of person. Thus, if cruelty is, in a certain sense, a condition for the success of an artist, then that is a fact which, providing one is not blinded by the fictions of morality, one would accept, however one values art. And that he *does* expect wide agreement on the two types of proposition just mentioned is evident from his prediction that just such agreement, the result of 'supreme self-examination on the part of humanity', will drive the 'revaluation of all values' (*EH*, IV, 1).

---

[34] Empirical truths on which agreement is to be expected are not incompatible with 'perspectivism' (see Chapter 7.3) and, indeed, are presupposed by Nietzsche's whole genealogical method, which claims to describe accurately the functions of various values (see Chapter 7.5).

For these reasons, we cannot whitewash Nietzsche's ethics by insisting that his radical individualism commits him to propounding his less savoury values and claims as 'merely' his own opinion; and we must, therefore, peer a little further into his very troubling conceptions of justice and of the value of cruelty.

6.5.1 A world safe for cruelty

Human values, for all their heterogeneity, are broadly lined up by Nietzsche on two sides of a sharp ethical divide between the '"supreme rights of the few"' and the '"supreme rights of the majority"'—the former being championed by the Renaissance and pre-Christian Rome, and the latter by 'Judaea' and its ethical descendants, such as the French Revolution (*GM*, I, 16). To be committed to the former battalion is, he clearly suggests, to endorse statements such as the following:

. . . a good and healthy aristocracy . . . accepts with a good conscience the sacrifice of untold human beings who, *for its sake*, must be reduced and lowered to incomplete human beings, to slaves, to instruments. (*BGE*, 258)

. . . egoism belongs to the nature of a noble soul—I mean that unshakable faith that to a being such as 'we are' other beings must be subordinate by nature and have to sacrifice themselves. The noble soul accepts this fact of its egoism without any question mark, . . . rather as something that may be founded in the primordial law of things: if it sought a name for this fact it would say, 'it is justice itself'. (*BGE*, 265)

The weak and the failures shall perish: first principle of *our* love of man. And they shall even be given every possible assistance. (*A*, 2)

For Nietzsche, 'mercy' is merely tolerance towards the ineluctably inferior, and is either, as in the first quote that follows, purely discretionary or, as in the second, motivated by the utility of the mediocre:

[Mercy is] the privilege of the most powerful man, or better, his—beyond the law. (*GM*, II, 10)

. . . a high culture depends on [the mediocre]. When the exceptional human being treats the mediocre more tenderly than himself and his peers, this is not mere politeness of the heart—it is simply his *duty*. (*A*, 57)

'Justice' is endorsed only as the honouring, or enforcing, or compensating for the breach, *either* of contractual agreements between approximately equal powers (e.g. *GM*, P, 4; II, 4; II, 8) *or* of laws imposed by the noble upon the rabble (e.g. *GM*, II, 11). These agreements and laws, it should be noted, are occasional conveniences, not universal necessities, let alone 'rights':

from the highest biological standpoint, legal conditions can never be other than *exceptional conditions*, since they constitute a partial restriction of the will of life, which is bent upon power . . . A legal order thought of as sovereign and universal, not as a means in the struggle between power-complexes but as a means of *preventing* all struggle in general . . . would be a principle *hostile to life*, . . . an attempt to assassinate the future of man, a sign of weariness, a secret path to nothingness. (*GM*, II, 11)

Here we have an example of just the sort of 'condition' for the promotion of 'higher' men that, by being advanced as empirically rooted, Nietzsche intends us not to dodge. Such a conception of justice recognizes equal rights only for peers—i.e. those of the same 'rank'—and explicitly repudiates the notion of universal rights to basic types of protection or empowerment. Lower ranks have either unequal rights—determined not by humane considerations but simply by which of their needs must be respected if they are efficiently to support the elite (e.g. *A*, 57)—or else no rights at all.[35] Automatic protection of minorities against majorities or equal opportunity for advancement, whether intellectual, social, or political, eliminates, on this view, both the struggle and the respect for the natural 'order of rank' which are conditions for the flourishing of the highest types. If such conditions include cruel exploitation or even the 'sacrifice of untold human beings', then such acts are not necessary injustices but, in their accordance with the 'highest biological standpoint', deeply just. In its form, this concept of justice bears striking resemblance to Heraclitus' *dikē*: i.e. faithfulness to a *logos*, an account of how life essentially is, deviation from which brings inevitable disaster even to gods—a resemblance that is perhaps no coincidence, given Nietzsche's admiration for that thinker.

---

[35] For example: 'one has duties only to one's peers', i.e. to those who are similar in strength and value standards. '[A]gainst beings of a lower rank, against everything alien, one may behave as one pleases' (*BGE*, 260; cf. 259). This kind of passage is alarming, though Kaufmann, in his footnote, attempts to sanitize it. Indeed, surprisingly few authors tackle head-on Nietzsche's appalling conception of justice. One who does so is Ofelia Schutte, in *Beyond Nihilism: Nietzsche without Masks* (Chicago: Chicago University Press, 1984), esp. 157–9, 169–72, and 184–5. Another is John Andrew Bernstein in *Nietzsche's Moral Philosophy* (Rutherford, NJ: Fairleigh Dickinson University Press, 1987)—though, in places, his account is merely an undiscriminating polemic against Nietzsche.

6.5.2 *The tension between creative and destructive cruelty*

Now such formulations display a deep tension between the life-enhancing and life-denying consequences of the uninhibited cruelty seemingly licensed by Nietzsche's 'immoralism'.

On the one hand, we have his claim that great 'creativity' is, as a simple matter of fact about human nature, nourished by cruelty. This claim couples two basic, and to the liberal mind revolutionary, propositions: first, that great people flourish under conditions of immoral justice (e.g. *BGE*, 44); second, that culture is itself the 'spiritualization' of cruelty (*BGE*, 229). The first proposition means that overt cruelty and danger are essential stimulants of the powers needed to flourish; while the second means that flourishing itself involves the refined deployment of cruel and destructive impulses. Both propositions are, we recall, exemplified by the 'slave', whose impotence fosters the development of intellectual and artistic powers *and* spiritualizes his urge for revenge, which is unable to discharge itself directly (*GM*, I, 7 and 11).[36]

On the other hand, Nietzsche's immoral order threatens to destroy just the person whose creativity it supposedly nourishes. For in that order the 'rabble' would, in principle, be free to accomplish by force the very suppression of the 'noble' that, Nietzsche claims, they once achieved by universal morality. Though, in his later thought in particular, he entertains the idea of a self-regulating 'order of castes' where the 'mediocre' majority confine themselves contentedly to the lowest caste, in order to allow the 'most spiritual' to get on peacefully with life-enhancing creation (e.g. *A*, 57), his immoralism is actually far too modern, far too radically individualist, far too predicated on self-legislation, to countenance or leave room for the absolute authorities, such as God, Nature, History, or Tradition, that would be indispensable to enforcing such rigid social roles and so to protecting the creative elite from the destructive 'rabble'. And though community *is* possible in a Nietzschean order—at least between peers 'similar in strength and value standards' (*BGE*, 259)—it never overrides the individual's search for 'life-enhancement' and

---

[36] Nietzsche also employs this theory to propose that the criminal, precisely because of his destructive urges, is the potentially life-enhancing type whose social ostracization has caused him to go wrong—the 'strong human being under unfavorable circumstances' (*TI*, IX, 45). Indeed, he proposes that 'almost all forms of existence which we consider distinguished' once belonged to this type, be it 'the scientific character, the artist, the genius', or other 'innovators of the spirit' (*TI*, IX, 45, *passim*).

its obligations never extend to those of different 'rank'.[37] (This conflict between, on the one hand, Nietzsche's conception of a healthy society based on castes that recognize innate differences between types of human beings and hence types of human destiny, and, on the other hand, his extreme espousal of modern notions of autonomous self-legislation, reflects the ineliminable tension between 'ancient' and 'modern' in his thought, to which we will return in Chapter 10.1.1.) Indeed, if we take seriously, as we should, Nietzsche's concept of *ressentiment*, with its general scope and its impossibility of finding final satisfaction, then the rabble's urge to suppress the exceptional will persist even if the latter are no longer politically or socially dominant—or perhaps *especially* if those inhibiting constraints no longer exist. For it is not just the 'noble soul', as Nietzsche holds, but the ignoble, too, who believes that 'to a being such as "we are" other beings must be subordinate by nature and have to sacrifice themselves' (*BGE*, 265). This is the creed of every petty dictator, as well as of the Napoleons and Wagners, whom Nietzsche so admires. Though Nietzsche knows that egoism can be 'unworthy and contemptible' in the wrong hands (*TI*, IX, 33), his explicit repudiation of universally prescribed safeguards against arbitrary power ultimately threatens his own principal objective: namely, the creation of conditions favouring the 'highest type' of man.[38] In other words, Nietzsche's philosophy, in lacking a politics that could support his own conception of life-enhancement, relies on a romantic hope that the highest man must be possible, and that his asphyxiation by the vulgar is not inevitable.[39]

[37] This absence of rules that would override the individual's search for life-enhancement is a feature even of those rare passages where Nietzsche seems to argue for a more cohesive form of society—for example, at *GS*, 55, where he suggests that rules which bind the majority should be *respected* by the noble minority—indeed, that such respect by the elite may be 'the ultimate form and refinement in which noblemindedness reveals itself on earth'. Whatever we are to make of such passages, they are very much the exception in Nietzsche's works—and, like the other passages cited above, they provide no reasons why *the majority* should respect, or support, or allow themselves to be exploited by, Nietzsche's rarefied elites. Interestingly, Richard Rorty questions the *possibility* of a coherent Nietzschean politics by remarking that the 'sort of autonomy which self-creating ironists like Nietzsche . . . seek is not the sort of thing that *could* ever be embodied in social institutions' (Rorty, *Contingency, Irony, and Solidarity*, 65).

[38] Alain Boyer rightly suggests that Nietzsche's 'obsession' with hierarchy is not really based on a thorough critique of equality in the first place (Alain Boyer, 'Hierarchy and Truth', in L. Ferry and A. Renaut (eds.), *Why We Are Not Nietzscheans*, trans. Robert de Loaiza (Chicago: University of Chicago Press, 1997), 2).

[39] For considerations of Nietzsche's thoughts on politics, see, for example: Schutte, *Beyond Nihilism*, 161–88; Tracy B. Strong, *Friedrich Nietzsche and the Politics of*

An apologist for Nietzsche might suggest that his ethic is not alone in effectively legitimizing inhumanity. He might argue, for example, that some forms of utilitarianism could not prevent millions being sacrificed if greater numbers could thereby be saved; or that heinous maxims could be consistently universalized by Kant's Categorical Imperative—maxims against which Kant's injunction to treat all human beings as ends in themselves would afford no reliable protection, both because its conception of 'humanity' is vague and because it would be overridden by our *duty*, as rational agents, to respect just such universalized maxims. To this apologist one would reply that with Nietzsche there is not even an attempt to produce a systematic safety net against cruelty, especially if one judges oneself to be a 'higher' type of person with life-enhancing pursuits—and, to this extent, his philosophy licenses the atrocities of a Hitler even though, by his personal table of values, he excoriates anti-Semitism and virulent nationalism. Indeed, to that extent it is *irrelevant* whether or not Nietzsche himself advocates violence and bloodshed or whether he is the gentle person described by his contemporaries. The reality is that the supreme value he places on individual life-enhancement and self-legislation leaves room for, and in some cases explicitly justifies, unfettered brutality.

In sum: the point here is *not* to rebut Nietzsche's claim that 'everything evil, terrible, tyrannical in man' serves his enhancement '*as much as* its opposite does' (*BGE*, 44—my emphasis)—for such a rebuttal would be a major ethical undertaking in its own right. It is rather to suggest that the necessary *balance* between danger and safety which Nietzsche himself regards as a condition for flourishing (for example, in this quote from *BGE*, 44) is not vouchsafed by his extreme individualism. Indeed, such individualism seems not only self-defeating, but also quite unnecessary: for safeguards against those who have pretensions to sovereignty but lack nobility *could* be accepted on Nietzsche's theory of value as just another 'condition for the preservation' of 'higher' types. Since the overriding aim of his attack on morality is to liberate people from the repressiveness of the 'herd' instinct, this unrelieved potential danger to the 'higher' indi-

Transfiguration (expanded edn., Berkeley and Los Angeles: University of California Press, 1988), especially chapter 7, *passim*; Bruce Detwiler, *Nietzsche and the Politics of Aristocratic Radicalism* (Chicago: University of Chicago Press, 1990); Mark T. Warren, *Nietzsche and Political Thought* (Cambridge, Mass.: MIT Press, 1988); and David Owen, *Nietzsche, Politics and Modernity: A Critique of Liberal Reason* (London: SAGE Publications, 1995). The latter two authors see in Nietzsche the basis for a progressive politics.

vidual must count decisively against the success—and the *possibility* of success—of his project.

6.5.3 *The sublimation of cruelty*

Nonetheless, the general idea that culture is nourished by cruelty— i.e. that individual creativity is both fostered by danger and also *itself* a sublimation of cruelty and violence (so that the connection between creativity and danger is both social and psychic)—is unquestionably one of Nietzsche's most interesting, though deeply disturbing, proposals. If true—and this is a big 'if', because Nietzsche nowhere satisfactorily justifies it[40]—the implication is that culture is not so much a barrier to barbaric instincts as dependent on them and perhaps even nurturing of them. And though it is principally their sublimated form upon which culture is dependent, the possibility of de-sublimation into crude forms of violence presumably lurks. But if this is so, then two further hypotheses suggest themselves. The first is that, for Nietzsche, the constraints of civilization[41] not only foster culture, through the self-control and thus self-cruelty that they demand (from which flows the 'bad conscience'), but also conflict crucially with the needs of the life-enhancer, for whom social mores are something to be 'overcome'. And the second, and more interesting, hypothesis is that the richer a culture the *more* it may be predisposed to violence—through the de-sublimation of accumulated cruelty. If this were so, then it would become less mysterious that Nazism was perpetrated by a nation of unsurpassed culture. And one 'lesson' which is habitually drawn from that terrible event—namely that culture is no reliable barrier to barbaric instincts—becomes less surprising if culture is essentially *dependent* on them. Finally, if those instincts both underpin culture *and* threaten to destroy it, then we may have one reason for the intense vulnerability of all 'higher' attainments (and individuals) that Nietzsche repeatedly laments. To put the matter in terms of power and sublimation, two of Nietzsche's three criteria of life-enhancement, we may say that power is both a measure of life-enhancement and yet may also endanger it; and that

---

[40] Even for classical Greece—the one historical case of great creativity that Nietzsche does probe—he neglects to argue that a particular conception of justice was really essential to cultural achievement. In the case of the cultural accomplishments of the Christian West, the connection with immoral justice is even less well established by him.

[41] 'Civilization' conceived as systems of social development that place constraints upon barbaric instincts.

the power that is sublimated into all higher creations (notably of art, values, and one's own character), may also be re-released in raw, destructive form. These are, of course, merely conjectures; but they may have a powerful bearing on the most baffling of all the horrors perpetrated by the twentieth century.

6.6 CONCLUSION

This brings to a close Part I, in which I have attempted to give an overall picture of the morality rejected by Nietzsche, of the ethic that he puts in its place, and, in this chapter, of why we are not free simply to ignore some of his more disturbing claims. In Part II, we will endeavour to refine, expand, and justify all three elements of this picture by focusing on a single value which is central to both the old morality and Nietzsche's new ethic, and which excellently exemplifies the contrast between them. Indeed, this value is not only a paradigm of how Nietzsche goes about revaluing the old values; it is also, he believes, the principal force behind the wider 'revaluation of all values'. I am referring, of course, to the valuation of truth.

PART II

*From Old to New: Nietzsche's Revaluation of
the Value of Truth—a Case Study*

7

Scope of the Case Study

7.1 WHY CHOOSE THE VALUE OF TRUTH?

The purpose of this second part of the book is to examine in detail Nietzsche's critique of the value of truth—that is, of the truth that we possess in propositional, conscious knowledge[1]—in order more fully to understand how, employing his standard of 'life-enhancement', he goes about evaluating a value to which traditionally such supreme importance has been attached and, hence, how he 'revalues' it. Since Nietzsche attacks not values as such, but only their employment for life-denial, this suggests that, unless a value is not susceptible of *any* life-enhancing function, he seeks not its demise, but, on the contrary, how it can, by his standard, be *better* valued. This is so, at any rate, for our 'highest' values—for, in defining our identity as individuals or as an ethical community, these are values which reflect 'what we are' and which, when maximally employed in the service of 'life-enhancement', are therefore crucial to 'becoming what we are'.

Nietzsche's critique of the value of truth excellently exemplifies this approach: he wishes to be *more* truthful about the value of truth (to life-enhancement) than is the tradition that claims to value it unconditionally—i.e. that claims to see truth and truth-seeking[2] not merely as necessarily more valuable than falsity or falsehood-creating,[3] but as always more valuable than any other practice. His aim, in other words, is to respect *better* this 'highest' value by undermining traditional life-denying ways of conceiving and employing it—ways that, as he might put it, love not truth but permanence, and despise not falsity but flux. For, as he insists, 'what one has forbidden so far as a matter of principle has always been—truth alone' (*EH*, P, 3). And his motive for being more truthful about the value

---

[1] Which, in Zarathustra's vivid phrase, is what makes 'being thinkable' (Z, II, 12).

[2] At least over a certain range of subject-matter and to a certain accuracy.

[3] Art being, for Nietzsche, the highest of the falsehood-creating activities.

of truth is supplied, first, by his being, self-confessedly, a scion of the Platonic-Christian devotion to truth, and, second, by his vocation as a philosopher, a type to whose success that devotion is (in a qualified way) internal.

Of the various 'highest' values scrutinized by Nietzsche, none is better suited to our case study than the value of truth for at least three reasons:

1. No other value is so clearly central both to the old morality that Nietzsche attacks and to his own ethic.

2. There is a genuine puzzle why our occidental cultures should prize so highly truth and, consequently, accurate investigation and sincere expression.

3. According to Nietzsche, dedication to truth plays the starring role in destroying the old Platonic-Christian ethic and so in making way for 'immoralism'. It does so by discrediting any claim that the traditional functions of values, including the unconditional valuation of truth itself, enhance life; by casting fatal doubt on the supposed reality of their metaphysical groundings, such as God; by thus propelling the search for new, life-enhancing ethics; and, finally, by drawing the terrible 'inference *against* itself' insofar as it is regarded as an unconditioned value. Thus, it illustrates Nietzsche's 'law of life': that '[a]ll great things bring about their own destruction through an act of self-overcoming' (*GM*, III, 27).[4]

---

[4] Nietzsche's fascinating argument that Christian morality ultimately 'overcomes' itself by supplying the values for its own destruction may be put, still more broadly, as follows: that, since those who live within an ethical system cannot escape its hold over them, if they are to reform that system they can do so only by employing the conceptual and axiological commitments internal to it. The question, however, is whether, of all Christian morality's highest values, it is really its commitment to *truthfulness* that is primarily responsible for its 'self-overcoming'. It may be, I tentatively suggest, that Christianity's conception and valuation of *free will* is at least as important in its demise as is the value it places on truthfulness. For the Christian conception of 'free will' as a manifestation of the divine spark in man and as carrying the moral obligation that it be used is a cornerstone of modern ideas of autonomy and self-realization that, when pressed sufficiently far, simply conflict with the regimentation of a divine order, not to speak of any presupposition that man owes his every achievement to God. In other words, the idea that man possesses a divine spark which gives him the power to create independently—and, potentially, even in defiance—of God may be at least as subversive of the old metaphysical order as is a commitment to truth. This conjecture does not, however, affect the essential task of this part of the book: namely, to understand Nietzsche's arguments against *unconditionally* valuing truth and to see how he himself values truth.

7.2 STRATEGY FOR THE CASE STUDY

My strategy will be, first, to show the many-sidedness of Nietzsche's critique of the unconditioned valuation of truth (Chapter 8). I will then argue that uncompromising truthfulness can receive world-affirming justifications, in addition to the world-denying moral justification identified by Nietzsche (Chapter 9). Finally, in the concluding chapter I will attempt a summary of the value which Nietzsche still accords truth and truth-seeking after this sceptical onslaught (Chapter 10). I will argue that, for him, truth is valuable principally—but by no means exclusively—as our ultimate defence against the very moral and metaphysical fictions that make of it an unconditioned value; and that—contrary to what one might think—truth is *not* valuable, in Nietzsche's view, or is at least of highly restricted value, in helping us to discover 'what we are' and so in guiding strategies for individual 'self-realization'.

Before embarking on this task, it is necessary, on two counts, to summarize what I take Nietzsche's (explicit or implicit) *conception* of truth to be. First, we should try to be clear about *what it is* whose value he is questioning, particularly as his interpreters differ so much on this point. Second, there is much more at stake in this questioning of the value of truth if 'truth' itself still has for Nietzsche the hard empirical quality of unyielding fact, as I will argue it does, rather than being determined by, say, inter-subjective convention or 'pragmatic' success. For example, if Nietzsche's claim that, by his standard of life-enhancement, the dominant values and concepts of traditional morality have life-denying functions is taken as a 'fact' which we ignore at our peril (much as mountains in the flight path of an airplane are perils that pilots ignore at their peril), it is altogether more significant than if it is taken, say, purely as a conclusion internal to some local 'discourse' by which some people just happen to be culturally or politically 'conditioned'.

7.3 NIETZSCHE'S CONCEPTION OF TRUTH

Nietzsche, of course, rejects a conception of truth as correspondence to a metaphysical 'thing-in-itself'. He does so, first, for the epistemological reason that the putative thing-in-itself is not only unknowable but also unintelligible insofar as it presupposes a stand-point beyond flux and temporality; and, second, on the ethical grounds that to value such a standpoint is to value what is conceived as 'transcending' (phenomenal) life and so to 'deny' life. I will not, however, elaborate on Nietzsche's rejection of truth as correspon-dence to the 'thing-in-itself', as this would add nothing to the existing literature, which covers it extensively.[5] It is only worth underlining that once a metaphysical conception of truth as 'divine' (*GS*, 344) is abandoned, the question of its *nature* and the question of its *value* become distinct, as, of course, they are for Nietzsche.

Nietzsche's own conception of truth can, I suggest, be character-ized as an 'empirical perspectivism' in which objects or events are described as effects. Though his conception of truth is, to put it mildly, extremely sketchy and question-begging, I shall attempt to summarize the two main components of this formula: 'empirical per-spectivism' and 'objects or events as effects'.

7.3.1 *'Empirical perspectivism'*

A true utterance, on this conception, is a necessarily perspectival proposition—i.e. one inescapably impregnated with a partial, inter-pretative, viewpoint, but still claiming to 'read' a reality conceived as subject-independent. Perspectivism is, for Nietzsche, unavoidable for three kinds of reasons. First, the *speaker's* truth-claims cannot but be couched in terms of (*a*) his values and interpretations—themselves influenced by his interests and experiences both of a gen-eral sort (i.e. determined by his nature, nurture, and other life-circumstances) and pertaining to the specific object viewed or theme discussed, and (*b*) social or 'inter-subjective' conventions of a lin-guistic and conceptual kind.[6] Second, human consciousness is unable to grasp the world except in a very simplified way, as 'a surface- and sign-world': indeed, Nietzsche says, this is 'the essence of phenom-

---

[5] See, in particular, Clark's analysis of Nietzsche's attack on metaphysical realism, in chapters 2–7 of *Nietzsche on Truth and Philosophy*. Other good discussions of Nietzsche's conception of the nature of truth are in Schacht, *Nietzsche*, 52–117 and John T. Wilcox, *Truth and Value in Nietzsche: A Study of his Metaethics and Epistemology* (Ann Arbor: University of Michigan Press, 1974).

[6] These values, and the standpoints they presuppose, are, as argued in Chapter 2.1 and 2.6, not arbitrary, and certainly cannot be selected—or abandoned in favour of rival per-spectives—at whim.

enalism and perspectivism as I understand them' (*GS*, 354).[7]
Third—and an equally important reason for perspectivism—the
observed cannot but be seen partially since everything in the world,
according to Nietzsche, is ultimately 'bound to and conditioned by'
everything else (*WP*, 584)[8]—a crucial premiss, we recall, of his conception of 'Eternal Return'. Thus even one thing could never be
known completely except by knowing, as it were, all its interconnections with everything else in the world, which means understanding the whole history of those interconnections—which means,
at the limit, knowing the entire history of the world from every possible point of view. Since we can pick out only a small part of the
total relatedness of phenomena to each other, '[t]here are no isolated
judgements! An isolated judgement is never "true", never knowledge; only in the connection and relation of many judgements is
there any surety' (*WP*, 530)—an idea that resonates strikingly with
Quine's famous claim that 'the unit of empirical significance is the
whole of science' and that 'our statements about the external world
face the tribunal of sense experience not individually but only as a
corporate body'.[9]

The key point here, then, is that there is no inherent incompat-
ibility between a statement's being empirically warranted and its
being ineluctably a partial viewpoint, which is not necessarily more
'correct' than certain other viewpoints and is itself motivated by
interests of preservation or power.[10] Moreover, because an object (or
situation) is, in principle, viewable from an indefinite number of perspectives and in the context of an indefinite number of interpretations of 'the world',[11] motivated by diverse interests and values,

---

[7] Nietzsche's belief that we have very limited (conscious) access to reality is one
reason why he holds that our truth-claims are generally wildly under-determined by any
possible empirical evidence for them—and that they are thoroughly anaemic representa-
tions of the richness of states of affairs.

[8] Nehamas, in *Nietzsche: Life as Literature*, 103–4, has persuasively argued that the
inescapable indeterminacy of the borders of a family—of what constitutes its unity and
identity—infects, in Nietzsche's view, every single object in the world. Since the effects
of something are so extensively interrelated, its unity is to be found 'in the genealogical
account that connects one set of phenomena to another'. That is: 'the thing itself is to be
found in its genealogy'.

[9] W. V. O. Quine, 'Two Dogmas of Empiricism', in *From a Logical Point of View* (2nd
edn., New York: Harper & Row (Harper Torchbooks), 1963), 41–3.

[10] Brian Leiter makes a similar point in his 'Perspectivism in Nietzsche's *Genealogy of
Morals*', in Schacht (ed.), *Nietzsche, Genealogy, Morality*, 334–57.

[11] Nietzsche, in fact, refers to the possibility that the world may include infinite interpretations as '*Our new "infinite"*' (*GS*, 374).

there is no fully 'objective' view of it, in the sense of a total or an impartial view which every agent with the requisite cognitive capacities would necessarily agree upon. Such objectivity is unavailable because it would require an agent to view it from *every possible* perspective and under *every possible* interpretation, which is clearly impossible since an agent's perspectives and interpretations are always limited by his individuality, however rich and many-sided it is. But what is possible is to *multiply* our perspectives on something; and this multiplicity is, famously, exactly what Nietzsche's conception of 'objectivity' is (*GM*, III, 12).

7.3.2 *Objects as effects: Nietzsche's conception of the empirical*

Nietzsche holds, as we have seen, that there are not doers and their deeds, or things and their effects, or subjects and their predicates, or substances and their qualities, but that, in all these pairs, there is only the second, while the first is a fictional manifestation of the 'atomistic need' (*BGE*, 12). In the *Nachlass*, he summarizes this idea by saying that 'a "thing" is the sum of its effects' (*WP*, 551)—i.e. it is not known *by* its effects; rather it *is* its effects. Thus, he says: 'If I remove all the relationships, all the "properties", all the "activities" of a thing, the thing does not remain over; because thingness has only been invented by us owing to the requirements of logic . . . ' (*WP*, 558).

Nietzsche's charge, in other words, is that we have traditionally mistaken what is merely the grammatical subject for a real 'something' which is an underlying agent of deeds, effects, predicates, and qualities—and, moreover, that this 'something', which is variously called 'free will', 'subject', 'substance', 'soul', 'self', and 'atoms', is in all these diverse cases not an accidental error but an expression of a strong psychological need (the 'atomistic need'), namely for a continuant or cause to 'stand fast', to remain fixed, and to be the ultimate locus of agency (e.g. *GM*, I, 13; *BGE*, 21; *TI*, VI, 3).[12] Of course, this charge raises major questions, which Nietzsche does not really address, about how things are to be individuated and identified; or, in regard to the banished 'self', about what it is to be an agent who recognizes himself as a distinct individual and as the 'owner' of his actions. But what is so original and valuable about this

---

[12] This sceptical element in Nietzsche's thought is illuminatingly discussed by Peter Poellner in *Nietzsche and Metaphysics* (Oxford: Clarendon Press, 1995), esp. chapter 2.

thesis is not, in fact, the idea that objects or persons are no more than bundles of properties or effects, a claim which other philosophers have addressed more rigorously, but, first, the *connection* Nietzsche makes between all these seemingly unrelated ways of distinguishing between effects *and* their supposed agency, cause, or ground, and, second, his tracing these ways to a common metaphysical and moral root—i.e. a metaphysics of permanence (of the enduring thing-in-itself) and a morality of universal values and equality (which, as mentioned in concluding Chapter 3.2, is just what the quality-less subject connives in).

By abolishing this hidden locus of agency, our conception of an object becomes a description of a certain bundle of effects, as experienced by us, and the 'truth' about it is some empirical verification of that conception. This is remarkably similar to Peirce's classic 'pragmatic maxim':

Consider what effects, that might conceivably have practical bearing, we conceive the object of our conception to have. Then our conception of these effects is the whole of our conception of the object.[13]

Yet, Nietzsche's conception of objects as effects in no way commits him to the very different 'pragmatist' theory of truth attributed to him by, for example, Danto—i.e. that something is true if it 'works' for me.[14] Danto's theory cannot be right as an interpretation of Nietzsche for at least two reasons. First, it is belied by Nietzsche's whole investigation of the *value* of truth, which presupposes and explicitly states that something can be true, and recognized as such, while being useless or even harmful to my life-enhancement, and conversely that something can be false and nonetheless extremely valuable to me (e.g. *GS*, 344; *BGE*, 39). As we will see in the next three chapters, one of Nietzsche's most original contributions is to advance all sorts of ways in which untruth can be of value or truth of disvalue—i.e. in which the truth or falsity of statements cannot be simply reduced to their (perceived) utility or value to an agent; and

---

[13] Cited in Hilary Putnam, 'Pragmatism', *Proceedings of the Aristotelian Society*, 95 (1995), 291.

[14] Danto, *Nietzsche as Philosopher*, 72 (cf. Rosen's claim that, for Nietzsche, 'there is no truth about the world, other than the truth of practical necessity' in Stanley Rosen, *The Question of Being: A Reversal of Heidegger* (New Haven: Yale University Press, 1993), 174; or Grimm's argument that for Nietzsche something is 'true' if it increases my power or my experience of power—in Rüdiger H. Grimm, *Nietzsche's Theory of Knowledge* (Berlin: Walter de Gruyter, 1977)). Nahamas also counters Danto on this point, in *Nietzsche: Life as Literature*, 52–5.

it seems to me that his investigation into the value of truth counts as prima-facie evidence against Danto's attribution to him of a 'pragmatist' theory of truth.

Second, Danto is directly contradicted by Nietzsche's insistence that a principal cause of *error* is to regard as true whatever gives one strength or pleasure—this error being nothing other than Danto's pragmatist theory of truth! The psychological explanation, says Nietzsche, for the '*error of imaginary causes*'—such as the causes of painful mental and emotional states—is that we make the 'proof of pleasure ("of strength") . . . a criterion of truth' (*TI*, VI, 4–5, *passim*; cf. *A*, 50). Many other errors, such as beliefs in substance and identity, were held to be true because they 'proved to be useful'— and it 'was only very late that such propositions were denied and doubted; . . . that truth emerged' (*GS*, 110).[15] Finally, we should recall the passage where Nietzsche explicitly states that value to life is 'no argument' for the *truth* of a belief:

We have arranged for ourselves a world in which we can live—by positing bodies, lines planes . . . But that does not prove them. Life is no argument. The conditions of life might include error. (*GS*, 121; cf. *BGE*, 4 and *GS*, 111–16).

The few times when Nietzsche presents a seemingly Danto-esque view—for example, that '[t]he criterion of truth resides in the enhancement of the feeling of power' (*WP*, 534)—not only occur principally in the unpublished *Nachlass*, but can, I suggest, be interpreted as referring to what has often been *claimed* as 'true', rather than what we have warrant to call 'true'—a distinction that, as I have already insisted, Nietzsche is committed to making despite his rejection of Platonic or Kantian metaphysics. This interpretation is confirmed by inspecting key passages near the one just cited.[16]

Truth and falsity are, therefore, not mere functions of what we *deem* useful—let alone of what is *actually* useful. What warrants our truth-claims, for Nietzsche, is, indeed, something like an empirical

---

[15] Note that Nietzsche's references to 'truth', 'error', 'imaginary' causes, and 'real' causes are nowhere in these passages placed between inverted commas. He clearly separates what is true from what is imagined by us to be true; indeed, the extracts from *TI* appear under the heading: 'The Four Great Errors'.

[16] For example: 'Everything simple is merely imaginary, is not "true". But whatever is real, whatever is true, is neither one nor even reducible to one' (*WP*, 536). 'In the formation of reason, logic, the categories, it was *need* that was authoritative: the need, not to "know", but to subsume, to schematize, for the purpose of intelligibility and calculation' (*WP*, 515).

determination supplied by subject-independent reality (whatever that would precisely be).

This conclusion is supported both by Nietzsche's actual statements on the nature of truth (see section 7.4) and, rather more decisively, by the very nature of his philosophical project—where he clearly sees himself as advancing empirically founded truths in, above all, his investigation of the functions of values (see section 7.5).

7.4 NIETZSCHE'S STATEMENTS ON THE NATURE OF TRUTH

Nietzsche makes many short and often ambiguous statements on the nature of truth and the true—though these cannot be said to amount to a 'theory' of truth. In line with the conception of truth that I attribute to him—i.e. one that has an empirical determination—he makes statements like the following:

[Our] estimates might be . . . mere foreground estimates . . . Supposing, that is, that not just man is the 'measure of things' (*BGE*, 3)

. . . we must become the best learners and discoverers of everything that is lawful and necessary in the world (*GS*, 335)

The *lie* of the ideal has so far been the curse on reality (*EH*, P, 2)

. . . the *strength* of knowledge does not depend on its degree of truth but on its age . . ., on its character as a condition of life. (*GS*, 110)

. . . all evidence of truth come[s] only from the senses. (*BGE*, 134)

. . . what one has forbidden so far as a matter of principle has always been— truth alone. (*EH*, P, 3)

On the other hand, he sometimes seems to construe truths as 'illusions':

Truths are illusions which we have forgotten are illusions . . . (*TL*, 84)

. . . facts is precisely what there is not, only interpretations. (*WP*, 481)

The world with which we are concerned is false, i.e., is not a fact but a fable and approximation on the basis of a meagre sum of observations; it is 'in flux', as something in a state of becoming, as a falsehood always changing but never getting near the truth: for—there is no 'truth'. (*WP*, 616)

There are many kinds of eyes . . . and consequently there are many kinds of 'truths', and consequently there is no truth. (*WP*, 540)

Truth is the kind of error without which a certain species of life could not live. The value for *life* is ultimately decisive. (*WP*, 493)

I suggest that the 'truth' which Nietzsche here says is an illusion or error (for example, in the first and fifth citations) again refers to claims that unrevisably true, non-perspectival propositions—i.e. views from either nowhere or everywhere—are possible, or simply to nostrums that, through convention or utility, get to be regarded as truths. For if this is what we have hitherto called 'true', and if we now reject it, then we are bound to see it as illusion or even to deny that there is any such thing as 'truth'. This reading is also consistent with what he says immediately before the first citation—'What then is truth? A moveable host of metaphors . . . which, after long usage, seem to a people to be fixed, canonical, and binding'—and immediately following the second: 'We cannot establish any fact "in itself"; perhaps it is folly to want to do such a thing.' What Nietzsche is, arguably, saying in these two sentences is not that all 'truths'—or metaphors[17]—are simply figural formulations hallowed by convention, but (in the first sentence) that long usage makes us forget the partiality and revisability and even complete falsity of many claims that, because they generally 'work' and are accepted, we have come to see as true; and (in the second sentence) that an impartial knowledge of a metaphysical reality is both impossible and incoherent. None of this, however, commits Nietzsche to opposing the possibility of an empirical check on our interpretations by a world existing independently of perceivers.

In short, the problem, Nietzsche seems to suggest, with what has been called 'truth' is that we have often looked for the wrong thing (e.g. metaphysical reality; impartial propositions about an invariant reality) with the wrong methods (e.g. the 'immediate certainties' of Descartes), and the wrong attitude (looking for what will comfort, and thus away from reality—which terrifies). At the same time, we have underrated the extent to which prejudice, partiality of perspective, and valuation are impregnated in all thought (e.g. of the philosophers—*BGE*, 2–6) or the error inherent in at least all sortal concepts—namely 'to treat as equal what is merely similar' (*GS*, 111).

---

[17] Clark, following Davidson, rightly reminds us that if Nietzsche really did believe that metaphors are never literally true, he was quite simply wrong: *Nietzsche on Truth and Philosophy*, 69 n. 3. However, Clark questions this whole interpretation of Nietzsche—and, more generally, the view (held, for example, by Paul de Man) that he saw all language as figural and hence as incapable of expressing 'literal truth'. (See Maudemarie Clark, 'Language and Deconstruction: Nietzsche, de Man, and Postmodernism', in Clayton Koelb (ed.), *Nietzsche as Postmodernist: Essays Pro and Contra* (Albany, NY: State University of New York Press, 1990), 75–90.)

This impatience for unrevisable knowledge may have been necessary: scrupulous beings would perish, though 'their ways might have been truer' (ibid.). But impatience will no more reveal something as elusive and infinitely complex as a 'true' conception of reality than it can win a woman: hence, I suggest, Nietzsche's recurring metaphor of truth as a woman (e.g. *BGE*, P; *GS*, P, 4)—and even of life as a woman (*GS*, 339).

Ultimately, however, Nietzsche's empirically laden conception of truth emerges most clearly, not from his fuzzy and disjointed musings on the subject, but from his claims to describe accurately how things are in the world—examples of which we will now consider.[18]

7.5 THE EMPIRICAL NATURE OF NIETZSCHE'S TRUTH-CLAIMS

These claims are, basically, of two types: ontological and ethical.

'Ontological' here denotes what sorts of things are, for Nietzsche, most fundamental to correct explanations of human (ethical) life— for example, the 'rank order' of human beings (*A*, 57; *BGE*, 221; *GS*, 373), the 'eternal basic text of *homo natura*' (*BGE*, 230), the 'primeval law' that those of insufficient rank are repulsed 'mercilessly' by problems that they are not 'predestined' to solve (*BGE*, 213), and the existence 'in real life . . . of *strong* and *weak* wills' (*BGE*, 21). These facts are presented as read off from the world, and the claims they replace or oppose as inversions of reality (e.g. *BGE*, 12; *GS*, 110).[19]

Ethical claims fall, in general, into two categories: first, 'naturalistic' explanations of the function, in life-enhancement or life-denial, of values, such as the ascetic ideal or pity, and practices, such as punishment or discipline; and, second, how those values and practices correlate to 'types' or 'ranks' of person and the 'conditions' for their

---

[18] Schacht, too, takes Nietzsche to be making claims about the nature of the world, and makes an excellent case to this end in *Nietzsche*, chapters 2 and 4, *passim*, esp. 95–117 and 188–205.

[19] Nietzsche's demand that 'the basic text of *homo natura* must again be recognized' beneath the 'overly enthusiastic interpretations and connotations that have so far been scrawled and painted over' it (*BGE*, 230) suggests that it is not adequate to interpret him as saying that 'coming to know oneself . . . is identical with the process of inventing a new language—that is, of thinking up some new metaphors', as Richard Rorty claims (Rorty, *Contingency, Irony, and Solidarity*, 27).

flourishing. It is precisely such claims to truth that Nietzsche wishes to advance by looking systematically into the history of values, customs, and concepts, at 'what is documented, what can actually be *confirmed* and has *actually* existed' (my italics), rather than merely 'gazing around haphazardly in the blue' (*GM*, P, 7). And it is precisely through the discovery of such truths that Nietzsche believes 'morality' will be overcome. Indeed, his note to *GM*, I, 17 reads like a potted research proposal for this very purpose: '*All* the sciences have from now on to prepare the way for the future task of the philosophers . . . the solution of the *problem of value*, the determination of the *order of rank among values*'. The problem with the 'science of morality' hitherto has been *too little* truth seeking, too little honest 'description'. These remarks make sense, I suggest, only if Nietzsche regards analysis of the origin and function of values as capable of yielding something like empirically warranted interpretations.

To the extent, therefore, that Nietzsche talks of '*our* truths' (e.g. *BGE*, 202) or '*my* truths' (e.g. *BGE*, 231), or emphasizes the rhetorical and aesthetic dimensions of language or the metaphorical content of concepts or the impregnation of discourse with valuation and 'prejudice', he is suggesting not that the true is simply whatever commands agreement at any given time and place, but two quite different things: first, that the perspectivist input into truth-claims inevitably reflects such conventions and vocabularies, and, second, that only certain types of people are receptive to certain truths about how things actually are in the world. Even if, for him, the truth-value of propositions and beliefs is often indeterminable, he clearly holds that true and false statements can be made at least about their life-value and about what kind of people tend to espouse them.[20]

---

[20] An entirely different approach to Nietzsche's conception of truth is advanced by Heidegger. He suggests that Nietzsche's conception of truth is related to his (Heraclitean) conception of justice—though, Heidegger adds, this linkage is not acknowledged by Nietzsche himself! The link between these conceptions of truth and justice is, Heidegger suggests, supplied by the Greek word *homoiōsis*, an attunement or harmony of one thing (say a proposition or an act) with another (say, the underlying lawfulness of the cosmos). Thus Nietzsche implicitly 'fixat[es] the essence of truth as *homoiōsis*, and interpret[s] the latter as justice' (p. 141)—justice being taken in something like the Heraclitean sense of *dikē*, the compulsion for all things to be in accordance or harmony with *logos* (Fr. D.1/I), deviation from which will result in inevitable retribution, both for the inanimate (e.g. the sun—D. 94/XLIV) and for the animate (e.g. men—D. 28B/LXXXVII: '*Dikē* will catch up with those who invent lies'). Of course, for Heidegger this conception of truth as justice is part of his historicist vision of Nietzsche as the culmination of Western metaphysics: 'the abolition of the metaphysical distinction between a true and an apparent world forces us back into the traditional metaphysical essential determination of truth as *homoiōsis*, and

7.6 NIETZSCHE'S TALK OF FALSEHOOD

A critic of my suggestion that Nietzsche espouses empirical per-spectivism might observe that when he talks of truth, he occasion-ally places that word between inverted commas, so that all along he may be referring to something entirely unempirical. What is, how-ever, unremarked is the fact that he never, to my knowledge, places his talk of 'falsehood' or 'lies' or 'errors' between inverted commas. Thus, concepts like 'free will' (*BGE*, 18 and 21) or 'materialistic atomism' (*BGE*, 12) or 'Plato's invention of the pure spirit and the good as such' (*BGE*, P) are baldly referred to as thoroughly 'refuted' or as straightforward 'errors'; a certain kind of 'piety' is described as 'the most consistent of all falsifications' (*BGE*, 59). Elsewhere he dis-tinguishes, in traditional empirical fashion, between ' "finding" and "inventing" ' (*'finden' und 'erfinden'*)—mocking the young German Idealists for their innocence of the difference (*BGE*, 11).

But if Nietzsche believes in the possibility of false statements, then, by definition, he must believe in the possibility of true ones. Indeed, if anything, Nietzsche *ought* to have used inverted commas in speaking of his principal category of 'lies'—those of metaphysics—since this type of proposition is unfalsifiable. For example, the 'lie involved in the belief in God' is impossible to demonstrate: for nei-ther can God be shown to be 'dead'—even if promises of divine intervention made on his behalf turn out to be hollow—nor can the metaphysical presuppositions of his existence be shown to be false.

7.7 CONCLUSION

In conclusion, the best evidence that Nietzsche espouses 'empirical perspectivism' is not that he himself puts forward a theory of truth to this effect but rather that it is presupposed by one of his

at the same time into the interpretation of truth as "justice" ' (p. 138). Justice is 'the way in which the essence of truth must be understood at the end of Western metaphysics' (p. 141). Whatever one thinks of Heidegger's self-serving determination to make Nietzsche the 'last metaphysician', this posited relation between justice, *homoiōsis*, and Nietzsche's conception of truth is deeply thought-provoking. (Quotes from Heidegger are from his *Nietzsche*, vol. iii, trans. Joan Stambaugh, David Farrell Krell, and Frank Capuzzi, part 1, chapter 21. References to Heraclitus are from Charles H. Kahn, *The Art and Thought of Heraclitus* (Cambridge: Cambridge University Press, 1979).)

principal philosophical aims, namely to understand the value to life-enhancement of traditional values. That he sees the discourse in which truth-claims are couched as constructed of metaphors, impregnated with valuations, or embedded in specific cultures and practices, does not mean that, for him, truth is synonymous with, or reducible to, such figural, 'local', or 'inter-subjective' conventions. Nietzsche's seeming denials of the possibility of empirical truth—that have given many of his analytic readers so much anguish and his postmodernist ones such poetic licence—are interpretable as denials only insofar as the true is conceived, as Nietzsche surely held it had traditionally been, in terms of statements that are (i) incorrigible, (ii) non-vague, (iii) made from no particular perspective—be it social, historical, affective, or practical, and (iv) about a putative metaphysical 'reality'. At least after *The Birth of Tragedy*, and perhaps even implicitly there, Nietzsche simply repudiates these four conditions—and, indeed, regards not only our general conception of the true but also many of our particular 'truths', especially those proclaimed by Western morality and religion, as having failed even the simplest tests of empirical rigour. Above all, Nietzsche holds that we have been *insufficiently* truthful to the facts about what enhances life—and, indeed, that our exorbitant valuation of truth is itself a direct result of this lack of truthfulness. We now turn to why this should be so.

8

The Unconditional Value of Truth: Nietzsche's Pioneering Critique

Nietzsche's critique of the value of truth—of the truth possessed in propositional, conscious knowledge—is, in the first instance, directed against the idea that it could be unconditioned: i.e. that its value is not dependent upon other valuations or needs. At the limit, this idea incorporates four axioms:

(1) Truth is always more valuable than falsity.

(2) Truth-seeking is always more valuable than any other activity.

(3) Truth-telling is always more valuable than deception (whether of myself or of others).

(4) Other activities are valuable (i.e. themselves justified) only insofar as they enhance truth-knowing, -seeking, or -telling. Hence, whatever activities are taken as affording privileged access to truth—be they religious, scientific, or artistic—will be ascribed supreme value.

These axioms of the 'will to truth'—i.e. the will 'to *make* all being thinkable' (*Z*, II, 12)—are motivated by the 'generalization "I do not want to deceive"', which includes 'the special case "I do not want to deceive myself"' (*GS*, 344). They are *moral* axioms because, Nietzsche convincingly argues, no calculus of utility could possibly establish them. Moreover, he advances a variety of reasons why they deny life—indeed, why they can subserve a 'will to death' (*GS*, 344). These reasons provide us, I suggest, with useful materials for probing the value of truth *even* when it is not regarded as unconditioned. They fall under six headings:

- The value of untruth
- The nihilism of the unconditional
- The poverty of some truths
- The elusiveness of truth about the 'deep' structure of reality; and the lost riches of the 'superficial'

- The paralysing effects of reflective self-consciousness
- The danger of premature self-knowledge.

Though all these headings concern the value of *possessing* truth, the last three, in particular, also concern the value, or rather disvalue, of the process of *seeking* truth. In other words, under all these headings, the guiding question is: 'here we have, or can have access to, certain truths; what is their value to life-enhancement?' By contrast, under the last three the additional question is: 'whatever the value of certain truths to life-enhancement would be, is the activity of *seeking* them itself inimical to life-enhancement?'—for example, because it causes us to neglect more life-enhancing pursuits (such as living in the 'superficial') or because the state of consciousness associated with this enormous emphasis on truth is, in some sense, paralysing.

8.1 THE VALUE OF UNTRUTH

Nietzsche advances both a general argument why unconditionally valuing truth is life-denying and a list of specific reasons why untruth may be valuable.[1]

8.1.1 General argument

1. It is empirically the case that truth is sometimes dangerous and falsity life-preserving (*GS*, 344)—that untruth is a 'condition of life' (*BGE*, 4). *Any* unconditional valuation therefore:

---

[1] Nietzsche's famously misogynistic statements, for example, that 'woman' embodies untruth, 'does not *want* truth', and has 'the lie' as 'her great art' and 'mere appearance and beauty' as her 'highest concern' (*BGE*, 232), though deeply distasteful in tone, should, perhaps, also be seen in the light of his valuing untruth, art, beauty, and the 'superficial'. In other words, to the extent that these supposed features of 'woman' are integral to Nietzsche's conception of a healthy ethics and psychic economy (and, indeed, of life itself: for 'life is a woman'—*GS*, 339), his misogyny may be less crude than it at first appears. Derrida vividly exposes this ambivalence, seeing 'woman' as crucial to Nietzsche's attack on both the substance and the style of the philosophical tradition. Thus, she stands opposed not only, for example, to that tradition's conception and valuation of reason and truth (in virtue of her allegedly untruthful, irrational, elusive nature), but also to its literal, serious, exact, systematic tone (in virtue of her seductive, subversive wiles, her indefinability, and her inclination to the ornate and the imprecise). See Jacques Derrida, *Spurs: Nietzsche's Styles*, trans. Barbara Harlow (Chicago: University of Chicago Press, 1979), esp. 55–101. For another defence of the subtlety of Nietzsche's views on women (and on love between the sexes), based principally on *GS*, 361–3, see Laurence Lampert's *Nietzsche and Modern Times: A Study of Bacon, Descartes and Nietzsche* (New Haven: Yale University Press, 1993), 368–87.

(a) is false to the nature and needs of life (*GS*, 344);
(b) ignores the diversity of human types (e.g. 'What serves the higher type of men as nourishment or delectation must almost be poison for a very different and inferior type'—*BGE*, 30; cf. *BGE*, 198–9; *A*, 11);
(c) ignores the changing needs of the individual—whose convictions may turn out to be 'only . . . steps to self-knowledge, signposts to the problem *we are* . . . ' (*BGE*, 231).

2. In addition, there is no a priori reason, nothing one can 'know in advance of the character of existence', to warrant the faith that '*[n]othing* is needed *more* than truth' (*GS*, 344).

3. But if, empirically, untruth is a condition of life and, a priori, there is no reason to value truth unconditionally, then faith in such unconditionality—faith that knowledge has 'absolute utility' (*GS*, 37)—cannot be prudential and must be moral (*GS*, 344).

4. Hence, anything, like 'science'[2] or the absolute refusal to deceive oneself or others, that presupposes the unconditional value of truth, affirms a 'world' other than this one.[3]

8.1.2 Specific reasons for the value of untruth

'Untruth' (encompassing, in much of Nietzsche's usage, not only what is known to be false but also what is unverifiable or unfalsifiable) may be 'a condition of life' in six specific senses, most of which we have encountered in previous chapters:

First, falsification is integral to the creation of beauty, which is, in turn, embodied in two broad ways: the work of art (in which 'the *lie* is sanctified'—*GM*, III, 25); and giving 'style' to our character (*GS*, 290) or becoming 'poets of our life' (*GS*, 299).

Second, untruth is necessary for being a certain type of person—notably the 'artist', for whom 'to lay hold of actuality', at least that of his or her own nature, is 'most forbidden' (*GM*, III, 4). As discussed in Chapter 3.1.3, I take 'artist', like 'slave', 'master', and 'philosopher', to denote a type which can be admixed with others in

---

[2] Again, 'science' is to be taken in the broadest sense of the disciplines encompassed by *Wissenschaft*.

[3] Nietzsche does not, however, unconditionally reject the unconditional, though he considers it 'the worst of tastes' (*BGE*, 31); for he leaves room for it, first, as itself one of the fictions without which 'man could not live' (e.g. *BGE*, 4) and, second, as indispensable to the 'herd morality' to which the majority are suited, and which enables the latter effectively to support the elite (e.g. *WP*, 132, 287, 894; cf. *A*, 57).

the whole economy of a 'soul', and hence assume that this prohibition extends beyond those who are artists by occupation. Moreover, the essential idea here may have a wider application: namely, in the possibility that *deceiving, or refusing the truth about,* oneself is essential precisely to preserving *truthfulness* to 'what one is'—i.e. that the dominant drives or 'organizing "idea"' which crucially define what one is must be protected from all possible agents of distraction or destruction, including shame-causing witnesses, be they others or oneself. Such protection is achieved by befuddling these witnesses with 'masks'—and the need for such masks is dictated not only by the power of the *observer* but also by the sensitivity to scrutiny, or the 'conscience' or truthfulness, of the *observed*. (It is obvious that since shame requires an observer *and* an observed, its intensity depends not only on the censure of the observer—whether he be another person or an internalized witness—but also on the scrupulousness of the observed in relation to the rules whose disrespect occasions shame.)

Third, 'fictions', such as the concepts and conventions of logic and grammar, are necessary for structuring thought and cognition (e.g. *GS*, 111–12; *BGE*, 21).

Fourth, our ethics, too, may be structured by 'fictions'—such as the ascetic ideal, god, or the unconditioned—which, like all the concepts he attacks, Nietzsche allows can be life-enhancing if used to endorse what is strongest and noblest in us (see Chapters 3–5 above, *passim*; cf. *BGE*, 4).

Fifth, untruth is necessary for psychic defence—against overloading the emotions or the intellect: hence the need for 'stupidity' and for limiting oneself to the manageable, for simplifying the manifold, and for refusing whatever is totally 'contradictory'; against intrusion: hence the need for 'masks' and for deception of others; and against one's own memory: hence the need for self-deception and forgetfulness (e.g. *BGE*, 230, *passim*; *BGE*, 40; *GM*, II, 1). Such simplification and deception are needed if we are to gain mastery of ourselves and circumstances.

Sixth, if we value truth, we must also value untruth insofar as the former arises out of the latter—insofar as falsehood may be a springboard to truth, as Nietzsche, in one of his most teasing paradoxes, suggests is the case. Exactly how truth *could* 'originate out of error, . . . or the will to truth out of the will to deception' (*BGE*, 2) is considered in section 8.7 below, but one principal way is that both our conception and our valuation of truth have 'hitherto' been structured and justified by the errors of Platonic metaphysics—i.e. by one of the four types of 'nihilism' to which we now turn.

8.2 THE NIHILISM OF THE UNCONDITIONAL

Nietzsche, as I read him, identifies four broad types of destructive nihilism—i.e. the passionate embracing of 'nothingness' and so of certain values, notably unconditional truthfulness, that both presuppose and enhance this condition. (In contrast, he also identifies a weak-blooded nihilism which is marked by *indifference* towards those—and other—'highest' values or towards their decline.[4]) These four types of destructive nihilism constitute its successive historical stages—and each is related quite specifically to the unconditional valuation of truth: the first as that valuation's erroneous *presupposition*, namely Platonic metaphysics (and, in general, all morality structured by the ascetic ideal in its radical form), and the rest as that valuation's *consequences*, namely the progressive discrediting of man's highest traditional values.

8.2.1 'Nihilism (1)': The life-denying presupposition of the 'will to truth'

'Faith in truth', Nietzsche says, by affirming the unconditioned, necessarily affirms another world in just the way that Platonic/Christian metaphysics does, because 'this world' is inescapably a realm of the conditioned in that all things are essentially interconnected (e.g. *WP*, 584) and so possess a historical character. But since there is no (intelligible) realm of the unconditioned, to affirm it is quite literally to affirm what, for us, must be The Nothing ('Nothing' being capitalized in order to underline the active impulse to believe in what is not real and to deny the value of what is real). This manifestation of the

---

[4] This contrast between a nihilism that is destructive and a nihilism that is marked by mere indifference may approximately correspond to Nietzsche's distinction between, respectively, 'active' and 'passive' nihilism (e.g. *WP*, 22–3). In the secondary literature, Heidegger provides probably the most powerful interpretation of the stages or types of nihilism in Nietzsche—based, in particular, on extracts from *WP*, such as those I have just cited. (See his *Nietzsche*, i. 26–8, 156–61; ii. 172–5; iii. 201–8; iv, *passim*.) See also Alan White, 'Nietzschean Nihilism: A Typology', *International Studies in Philosophy*, 19/2 (1987), 29–44.

ascetic ideal's 'will to nothingness' is the first sense in which unconditionally valuing truth is nihilistic.

8.2.2 'Nihilism (2)': Loss of faith in God

Eventually, 'faith in truth' brings about the second stage of nihilism: the discrediting, to greater (e.g. Hume) or lesser (e.g. Kant) degrees, of belief in God and in direct divine authority for moral values, but *not yet* in the supremacy of certain of those values themselves, such as equality, pity, and truthfulness. These values continue to be ascribed absolute value, explicitly or implicitly, in people's ethical practices and beliefs, even when the theology which originally 'justified' that ascription is no longer believed. Indeed, in this stage of nihilism, *equality*, which was once parasitic upon a Christian conception of souls as equal before God (or, equivalently, in the quality-less subject which, by definition, is equal to all other such subjects), is espoused with ever greater fervour. *Pity* dominates morality, partially in virtue of this valuation of equality—because, being equal in this way, we take it that we can readily know the nature and causes of suffering in others *and* that we have a duty to ensure that they do not suffer more than we do.[5] *Truthfulness* is treated as unconditionally valuable even—or just—by those who have explicitly repudiated a metaphysical *conception* of truth or of the authority for values. That faith in truth discredits theology or metaphysics in this sense, but not key values originally justified by it, cannot, I take Nietzsche to suggest, be an oversight, but must flow from *the same* fundamental will that takes 'its direction from the ascetic ideal', namely *'a will to nothingness'* (*GM*, III, 28), a will that is sustained despite the massive scepticism directed by modernity against *all* its other expressions— sustained simply because no alternative meaning for life to one structured by the ascetic ideal has yet been found.

8.2.3 'Nihilism (3)': Making man insignificant

Eventually, the 'faith in truth' of modern science, being *structured* by the ascetic ideal, also has a practical *result* of the ascetic ideal: namely, to belittle man—first, like the old religious belief, by setting him over against the (unworldly) ideal of Truth[6] and second, unlike the old

---

[5] The pity of 'morality' standardizes the sufferer: 'strips away from the suffering of others whatever is distinctively personal' (*GS*, 338).

[6] i.e. a 'realm' of Truth which is felt to be purified of the world's flux and messiness.

religious belief, by 'naturalizing' him. For whereas the theological manifestation of the ascetic ideal had belittled man by making him the helpless 'child of God', the scientific manifestation does so by turning him into an animal, deprived of a divine soul. Thus 'all science . . . has at present the object of dissuading man from his former respect for himself'—an object which Nietzsche, in part, admires: 'for he that despises is always one who "has not forgotten how to respect" . . .'. And is not the result, Nietzsche asks, that man 'is slipping faster and faster . . . into nothingness? into a *"penetrating* sense of his nothingness"?' (*GM*, III, 25). Yet this naturalization of man, though it proceeds bitterly far, remains ascetically ideal, for it still conceives of everything as insignificant over against Truth; and, out of precisely this *religious* urge, it sacrifices God and everything else that was previously holy, even if, as a result, nothing is left (of the values and concepts that formerly structured people's lives). This is surely why Nietzsche says that the final rung of the 'great ladder of religious cruelty' is '[t]o sacrifice God for the nothing' (*BGE*, 55)—that, in effect, the religious instinct seeks its ultimate satisfaction in the sacrifice of God himself.

8.2.4 'Nihilism (4)': Loss of faith in morality's highest values

It is only in the fourth stage of nihilism that our unconditional truthfulness proceeds to call into question the value of morality's highest values—equality, pity, and, finally, 'will to truth' *itself*—by forcing us to see that they are not only life-denying in the ways outlined in this and other chapters, but also parasitic upon the erroneous idea of regarding timeless standards of value as intelligible. These are the inferences that the will to truth has resisted for so long, and that, when achieved, finally enable our valuation of truth to be honest. The last and most difficult of these inferences is against unconditioned truthfulness itself—and only when this has been made is belief in the possibility of timeless standards of judgement finally abandoned. And this event, in turn, marks the full recognition of the meaning of 'the death of God'.

In sum: the 'faith in truth' that originates with Plato is destined to bring about a progressively deepening condition of nihilism—beginning with a belief in The Nothing ('God', the 'Forms', etc.), proceeding to the 'death of God', but not yet of the 'highest' values formerly justified by him, subsequently cultivating a new conception of man's littleness, and then undermining the highest values of traditional morality including, finally, unconditioned truthfulness itself. Though Nietzsche sees these dramas of destructive nihilism as consequences of embracing the life-denying 'will to truth', his attitude to them, insofar as they are the fruits of rigorous honesty and the stimuli for a reinvigoration of man through the search for more life-enhancing values, is far from uniformly hostile. And he sees them as pursued only by the truthful few, those 'heroic spirits who constitute the honor of our age' (*GM*, III, 24). Nonetheless, to the extent that even these few fail to draw the final 'inference' against unconditionally valuing truth, they, too, remain infected by a 'will to nothingness'.

8.3 THE POVERTY OF SOME TRUTHS

An unthinking commitment to truth makes our estimation of particular truths undiscriminating, with the result that we have often valued truths of little value to 'ascending' life—such as (some of) those of the specialized sciences—while, by contrast, we have ignored others of inescapably great value to ascending life—such as 'laws of the order of rank' (*GS*, 373; *A*, 57), the value of our values (*GM*, I, 17, Endnote), and the 'eternal basic text of *homo natura*' (*BGE*, 230). And Nietzsche therefore calls on philosophy and 'physiology' to refocus themselves on precisely these sorts of issues—i.e. on a project for a naturalistic, but non-egalitarian, ethics (e.g. *GM*, I, 17, Endnote).

8.4 THE ELUSIVENESS OF TRUTH ABOUT THE 'DEEP' STRUCTURE OF REALITY; AND THE LOST RICHES OF THE 'SUPERFICIAL'

The value of truth, and of truth-seeking, is further limited by the fact, as Nietzsche sees it, that human beings have the greatest *aptitude* for the 'superficial'—for 'forms, tones, words' (*GS*, P, 4)—and the least for grasping the deep structure and tremendous complexity of reality. This latter is beyond our ken: 'nature has hidden behind riddles'; truth does not remain truth 'when the veils are withdrawn' (ibid.); and this is perhaps because we have no 'organ for knowledge'

(*GS*, 354)—a suggestion which is surely Nietzsche's variant of the old idea that the apparatus of perception and cognition deceives. And yet the 'will to truth' causes us obsessively to search for the deep and systematically to spurn the superficial—i.e. to expend our lives on what we are least good at and to ignore what we are best equipped for.

The handicap that places truth about the deep structure of reality beyond us is the limitation of 'consciousness', which is, with few exceptions, able to experience only a 'surface- and sign-world', and to re-present it only in terms of the greatly simplified[7] propositions that we call 'truths' (*GS*, 354). Such 'a "world of truth" that can [supposedly] be mastered completely and forever with the aid of our square little reason' degrades existence to 'a mere exercise for a calculator' and divests it of 'its *rich ambiguity*' (*GS*, 373)—in contrast to the reality and imagination expressible in art and action, in riddling rather than defining. This is just the sort of 'thoroughly artificial' world in which 'science at its best' keeps us (*BGE*, 24)—which is why a ' "scientific" interpretation of the world . . . might . . . be one of the *most stupid* of all possible interpretations of the world, . . . one of the poorest in meaning' (*GS*, 373). In short, propositional truths impoverish both the observed—which they strip of everything that cannot be generalized—and the observer, whose incommunicable uniqueness must be subordinated to the need to be universally comprehensible.

Crucially, this limitation on our capacity for grasping things in all their complexity applies not merely to knowledge of the 'outside' world but, as we noted earlier, also to knowledge of *ourselves* and our actions (*GS*, 335). And it applies in particular to the 'men of knowledge' who, in their need for generalizations and conceptualizations, are inevitably inattentive to the details of their own experience: their vocation for truth constitutionally unsuits them to self-knowledge, and therefore makes them 'necessarily strangers' to themselves (*GM*, P, 1). Moreover, the general limitation on self-knowledge has three important ethical implications which we discussed in Chapter 6.2.3.1: that an individual cannot know the maximum life-enhancement, or potentiality, of which he or she is capable; that the value of an agent's actions in promoting his or her good cannot be judged either by their

---

[7] To simplify is, however, not necessarily to falsify, unless one claims that one's beliefs and statements reflect reality in all its complexity—though in this passage Nietzsche seems to conflate simplification with falsification.

immediate consequences or by single rules or standards that pick out only particular causes or effects of them; and that the obstacles to accurate introspection inevitably limit the value of pity.

By contrast to the often-futile search for deep 'truths', what, Nietzsche asks, if 'the only thing that allowed itself to be grasped' were really the *opposite* of such truths: i.e. 'precisely the most superficial and external aspect of existence—what is most apparent, its skin and sensualization' (*GS*, 373)—as, he says, is probable? Real understanding would, then, stop 'courageously at the surface . . . to believe in forms, tones, words, in the whole Olympus of appearance' (*GS*, P, 4). It would recognize 'how much wisdom lies in the superficiality of men' (*BGE*, 59). It would, like the Greeks, be 'superficial—*out of profundity*' (*GS*, P, 4).

8.5 THE PARALYSING EFFECTS OF REFLECTIVE SELF-CONSCIOUSNESS

That the very activity of reflective self-consciousness may impede creativity is suggested by Nietzsche's interesting idea that it is 'almost the norm among fertile artists', such as 'the whole world of Greek art and poetry', that 'it never "knew" what it did' (*GS*, 369)—that 'a continually creative person, . . . one who knows and hears nothing any more except about the pregnancies and deliveries of his spirit [is] one who simply lacks the time to reflect on himself and his work' (presumably in the sense of judging the overall nature and value of art or artistic creation *as such*, rather than in the sense of reflecting on the conception and execution of works of art themselves).

This thought has at least two implications. First, a relentlessly self-conscious mode of relating to things (persons, events, objects, oneself) may be the *phenomenological* correlate of the unconditioned valuation of truth. In other words, if we incessantly ask about things whether they are truthful or express truth or what truths can be said of them, we may no longer be able to experience them innocently and in their many aspects. (Yet this self-consciousness is surely sustained, and even intensified, by Nietzsche's own concern with *value*: for to ask of everything—one's culture, one's history, one's art, one's values themselves—'what is its life-value?', and, to that extent, to experience it *as* value, is as 'uninnocent', as self-conscious, as to ask of everything 'what is its truth-value?') Second, there is an enduring tension—though not a contradiction—in Nietzsche's thought between the value and disvalue of truth-seeking: creativity will be hampered both by too little and by too much, but will be favoured by the right amount. Creativity will be hampered by too little because ignorance allows all sorts of life-denying illusions to flourish: hence we must discover in order to create; 'we must become *physicists* [i.e. seek knowledge] in order to be able to be *creators*' (*GS*, 335). Whereas too much self-reflection will paralyse creativity (*GS*, 369), which, as we have seen, is why it is strictly 'forbidden' to artists. I will pursue this theme further in the concluding chapter.

8.6 THE DANGER OF PREMATURE SELF-KNOWLEDGE

To know, or seek to know, the truth about 'what one is'—i.e. the 'organizing "idea"' (*EH*, II, 9) around which one's whole life will take shape—before one has lived and tested oneself sufficiently, threatens to arrest one's development and so one's very ability 'to become what one is'. I have already alluded to this interesting suggestion in Chapter 6.2.1, and will discuss it further in Chapter 10.4.2 below.

8.7 TRUTH OUT OF ERROR

The foregoing discussion suggests why the unconditional commitment to truth might arise from, and in that sense be parasitic upon, its very opposite, namely the 'will to deception'—and, if so, why such unconditionality may actually be impossible, not only in practice but in principle.

Nietzsche introduces this paradoxical nature of the 'will to truth' by asking: 'How *could* anything originate out of its opposite? for example, truth out of error? or the will to truth out of the will to deception? . . .' (*BGE*, 2). And he answers by speculating that the very *value* of 'the true, the truthful, the selfless' may lie in their being insidiously related to such 'wicked' things as 'deception, selfishness, and lust'. Such claims can strike one at first as exhibitionistic indulgence in hollow inversions—as a sensationalist mania for insisting that simply everything is the opposite of what it seems to be. Yet there are, I suggest, three serious points here.

First, truth might arise out of 'error' insofar as truth is fostered by 'the will to truth', which itself rests on two sorts of error discussed above: that of regarding truth as always more valuable than untruth and that of positing as absolutely true and valuable the unverifiable postulates of metaphysical dualism. And the will that drives us to espouse *just these* 'errors'—which are hardly arbitrary if, as Nietzsche claims, they are expressed throughout Western philosophy—is a 'will to deception'. For such errors arise neither from mere sloth nor from practical limitations, such as those of perception, cognition, or education, but rather from a deliberate attempt to see the world as it is not, that is, as conforming to values of permanence and impartiality. Thus, faith in God—the most conspicuous of all the symbols of permanence—is 'the subtlest and final offspring of the *fear* of truth, . . . the most consistent of all falsifications, . . . the will to the inversion of truth, to untruth at any price' (*BGE*, 59). In short, the will to 'untruth at any price' sustains the will to 'truth at any price'.

Second 'truths' depend, for their very formulation, on a litany of smaller 'fictions' that make the world tractable for us, such as 'substance', 'cause', 'unity', and 'identity' (e.g. *GS*, 111). These logical concepts are fictions, I take Nietzsche to be saying, in that there are no items to which they successfully refer.

The third sense in which truth may depend on falsity is captured by Nietzsche's claim that the intellectual *skills* required for truthfulness, namely, the skills of 'subtler honesty and skepticism', arose out of the need for an umpire between competing errors (*GS*, 110). Now this happened, it seems, either when these errors were of equal utility to life—specifically, 'wherever two contradictory sentences appeared to be *applicable* to life because *both* were compatible with the basic errors'—or when they were of no use to life but one needed, as it were, to categorize them (i.e. 'wherever new propositions, though not useful for life, were also evidently not harmful to life'). At first, these skills of truthfulness were 'intellectual play and impulse'—i.e. recreational—but later they became 'a profession, a duty, something dignified . . . and eventually . . . a need among other needs . . . A thinker is now that being in whom the impulse for truth and those life-preserving errors clash for their first fight, after the impulse for truth has proved to be also a life-preserving power.'

Nietzsche therefore suggests three senses in which truth or the 'will to truth' depend upon error or the impulse to falsify: first, the dependence of the 'will to truth' on the great ethical and ontological fictions of Platonism/Christianity; second, the dependence of truth-claims upon the specific 'fictions' of logic; and third, truth-seeking as a duty and a need, fostered by the requirement to adjudicate between 'errors' of equal or no utility. To the extent that these dependencies are necessary, truth cannot be unconditionally valuable—even to *its own* pursuit.

8.8 CONCLUSION

Taken together, these various points suggest that to value truth unconditionally or uncritically is to impoverish life in the following principal senses:

1. A flourishing life needs (some) untruth—both, externally, about the world and, internally, about ourselves.

2. Valuing truth unconditionally is nihilistic in the sense that it is structured by the ascetic ideal—and in three further (roughly, chronologically successive) senses towards which Nietzsche's attitude is complex: i.e. it discredits both Platonic metaphysics and belief in God; it generates a world-picture in which man is greatly diminished in stature, compared to his role at the centre of a divine creation; and it ultimately 'devalues' our highest traditional values, including itself.

3. Unconditional faith in truth has, so far, caused us to value many truths that do not enhance life (such as those of arcane scientific specialities that are merely narcotics or distractions) and to ignore others that can do so (such as genealogies of values).

4. We are, anyway, poorly equipped to comprehend deep truth, and so impoverish our lives by devoting them unthinkingly to its pursuit; whereas we are better equipped to discover the rich experience of the 'superficial', which we deny ourselves by focusing excessively on the relatively thin experience afforded by propositional truth. The 'superficiality' of 'the Greeks' (presumably those of a Homeric cast in Nietzsche's great Homer-versus-Plato stand-off—*GM*, III, 25) resided in their freedom from such a focus—a freedom which enabled them to achieve *real* profundity.

5. There are special problems with introspective truth-seeking—vital though that is in the right amount. First, it is particularly

unsuccessful (as evidenced by the opacity of the mechanism and significance of our individual actions). Second it can be inhibiting: creativity and reflective self-consciousness can be mutually antagonistic. And third, it can be premature—and will then thwart one's flourishing.

In sum: Nietzsche suggests that unconditionally to value truth is to deny the *nature* of human life (as something temporal and conditioned), the *needs* of human life (for untruth and the 'superficial'), and the *limitations* of human life (for gaining access to truth). It is, therefore, to sacrifice too much (life) for too little (life-enhancement). And to fail or refuse to see that this is so is, ultimately, to be indifferent to the value of truth itself.

9

The Unconditional Value of Truth:
An Assessment of Nietzsche's Critique

9.1 INTRODUCTION

The previous chapter attempted to set out the diverse elements of Nietzsche's 'experimental' questioning of the value of truth. We saw that this critique of the value of truth in the name of the value of truth—this claim that we have been untruthful about the nature and value of our valuation of truth—is one of the most pioneering and powerful aspects of his philosophy. For it is very plausible that on a short-term calculus of utility, untruth *is* frequently more useful than truth, while on a long-term calculus of utility or, indeed, on the basis of 'the character of existence' as such, we simply cannot say 'whether the greater advantage is on the side of the unconditionally mistrustful or of the unconditionally trusting' or whether '*[n]othing* is needed *more* than the truth' (*GS*, 344). Hence to suggest that the value of truth is unconditioned is simply to '*affirm another world* than the [real] world of life, nature, and history' and thus 'to negate . . . this world'. (Whether this negation precludes a flourishing life is, however, a further question.[1]) This means that we need to find another form of justification for the value of truth, such as the naturalized 'transcendental' form of argument which I suggested in Chapter 5.4: namely, that seeking or knowing or telling truths (at least to a particular degree of accuracy and over a particular range of truths) is—or, in some cases, must be believed to be—presupposed

---

[1] Once again, we confront that conundrum on which much of Nietzsche's critique of morality and metaphysics turns: namely, why illusions (in this case that truth is unconditionally valuable) that deny how the world actually is should be life-denying—or, conversely, why life-enhancement necessarily presupposes world-affirmation (see also Chapters 2.3, 5.5, and 6.4). We have seen that Nietzsche himself is ambivalent on this very question, sometimes asserting that illusions like the unconditional are essential for life (e.g. *BGE*, 4), at other times castigating them as life-denying. I return to this theme in closing Chapter 10.5.

by, or internally necessary to, certain practices or forms of life, such as scientific investigation, or the seeking of power over the world, or successful communication, or Nietzschean nobility.

This form of argument yields, I suggest, a wider range of justifications for valuing truth passionately than simply one structured by the ascetic ideal (and hence, for Nietzsche, characterized by world-denial). In this chapter I indicate three possible *world-affirming* justifications for passionately valuing truth: first, that truth-seeking gives man control over the world;[2] second, that truth-telling is crucial to communicative practice; and, third, that religious concepts *can* give science a form of justification that is world-affirming.

9.2 KNOWLEDGE AND CONTROL OVER NATURE

Nietzsche's claim that 'faith in science . . . cannot owe its origin to . . . a calculus of utility'—and that it must be a moral faith (*GS*, 344)—is belied by, for example, Bacon's valuing of science for the purpose of controlling nature, including sickness, hunger, and other such obstacles to flourishing. This 'mechanistic' justification for valuing truth (unappealing though it may be from, say, an ecological perspective) was prominent in the birth of science in the sixteenth and seventeenth centuries, and certainly does not fall into the category of diffident motives for science, such as boredom, curiosity, leisure, or knowledge as a means to virtue, that Nietzsche sometimes sees as the only alternative motivation to one structured by the ascetic ideal (*GM*, III, 23; cf. *GS*, 123).

Nietzsche's denial that science can be based on a 'calculus of utility' depends on his claim that science must rest on the 'unconditional faith or conviction . . . that truth is more important than any other thing, including every other conviction'. He adds:

To make it possible for this discipline to begin, must there not be some prior conviction—even one that is so commanding and unconditional that it sacrifices all other convictions to itself? . . . The question whether *truth* is needed must not only have been affirmed in advance, but affirmed to such a degree that the principle . . . finds expression: '*Nothing* is needed *more* than truth, and in relation to it everything else has only second-rate value'. (*GS*, 344)

---

[2] Such a goal is world-affirming in its motivation, even if, on other grounds, such as psychic, ecological, or economic welfare, it is to be repudiated.

Now Nietzsche is not simply suggesting that the principle '*Nothing* is needed *more* than truth' has, historically, accounted for the prestige of science, or that, philosophically, it is internal to science. He is advancing the more radical view that any attempt to justify the scientific enterprise as such cannot but appeal to this principle: that this principle is a condition for the possibility of science. And he is suggesting that, being unconditional, that principle, and hence science itself, cannot be prudential (for untruth is 'constantly' useful), and so must be moral. In other words, science's faith that nothing is needed more than truth is not a prudential value needed for its own success but is a special case of a moral maxim: ' "I will not deceive, not even myself" '.

Yet that there *can* be a motive for rigorous science other than valuing truth for its own sake—as a moral maxim—is, as I just suggested, demonstrated by the case of Bacon (and of his later disciples, for example among the *philosophes* of the Enlightenment). 'The true and lawful goal of the sciences', wrote Bacon, 'is none other than this: that human life be endowed with new discoveries and powers.'[3] As the historian Peter Gay points out, Bacon's summons is 'to enter into the "kingdom of man, founded on the sciences", and to enlarge "the bounds of Human Empire, to the effecting of all things possible." . . . To Bacon, all things possible meant better food, sounder health, greater kindness.'[4] Hitherto, Bacon suggested, human beings had underestimated their power—and this modesty the new science would show to be unwarranted. Mastery of nature will proceed from submission to knowledge; and this 'utilitarian empiricism', as Gay calls it, is advanced by Bacon and enthusiastically adopted by many Enlightenment figures as justifying the passionate valuation of truth. Successful mastery of nature does not, of course, show of the scientific theories explaining it that they are *true*; but it does constitute a motive or a justification for valuing the pursuit of truth and knowledge in the first place that, unlike the ascetic ideal, is explicitly world-affirming. Hence, though, over the centuries, the pursuit of science has, indeed, been motivated by more than an instrumentalist valuation of truth (and other motives undoubtedly include the moral, unconditioned valuation of truth targeted by Nietzsche), this does not mean that only the moral valuation can '*make it possible for*

---

[3] Francis Bacon, *The New Organon*, in *Works*, IV, 79; cited in Peter Gay, *The Enlightenment: The Rise of Modern Paganism* (New York: W. W. Norton, 1977), 312.
[4] Gay, *The Enlightenment*, 312.

this discipline to begin' or, conversely, that the instrumentalist valuation cannot justify that beginning.

9.3 TRUTH-TELLING AND SOCIAL RELATIONS

Nietzsche's critique of the value of truth (and truth-telling) seems largely to ignore the various ways in which it functions as a precondition for communicative practice—especially for mutual comprehension, reciprocal recognition, and the assumption of predictability that is necessary for trust. A detailed exploration of this type of reason for valuing truth—i.e. as a transcendental condition of communicative practice—would be entirely beyond the scope of this study, and is mentioned here only to flag Nietzsche's neglect of it. For example, 'social' honesty and transparency may be indispensable (*a*) to the friendship, love, cooperation, and reciprocal predictability within at least a restricted circle of people that most, if not all, individuals need in order to flourish; and (*b*) to the extent that the self is 'inter-subjectively' constituted through membership in a community, involving certain shared values, practices, and conventions, that makes the development of its individual identity, powers, and projects possible. Even if social relations in general and trust in particular also require self-deception about others and their relations to us, we cannot doubt the high value placed upon truth and honesty, transparency and predictability, in the phenomenology of trust. And here we need to avoid the conflation of truth-seeking and truth-telling that Nietzsche allows in *GS*, 344: for, in general, we may value the *truth* about others very differently—and perhaps rather less highly—in our relations with them than we value their *honesty*.[5]

In suggesting this, we are *not* standing on moral ground—for three reasons. First, we are not demanding unconditionally that ' "I will not deceive, not even myself" ': for some deception of oneself or others may be compatible with, or even essential to, stable social relationships (a conjecture which I shall not attempt to substantiate here). Second, we are not denying that living successfully demands

[5] Truth-telling and truth-seeking are evidently closely linked insofar as both are manifestations of a single ethical commitment to valuing truth and each depends upon the primitive virtues of that commitment, namely sincerity and accuracy. Though the precise relationship between truth-telling and truth-seeking is beyond the scope of this study, the point that is being flagged here is that, notwithstanding this inter-linkage, they may also possess distinct roles in communicative practice.

or involves much 'simulation, delusion', and the like—though Nietzsche's assertion that 'the great sweep of life has actually always shown itself to be on the side of the most unscrupulous *polytropoi*' (*GS*, 344) is, even if factually correct, no argument in itself that deception is life-enhancing by *his own* ethical standards. And third, to invoke the value of social cohesion is not to threaten Nietzsche's insistent individualism—because we can justify this value as a condition for the *individual's* preservation and enhancement.

9.4 LIFE-ENHANCING JUDAEO-CHRISTIAN REASONS FOR VALUING TRUTH

Finally, a Judaeo-Christian religious justification for the passionate valuation of truth—and hence for science itself—need not employ the ascetic ideal and thus need not be life-denying. Indeed, Christianity and its Judaic root supply other concepts that, if invoked to justify truth-valuing, can do so in a world-affirming way. Two such concepts[6] are suggested here: first, the idea that man is lord of nature (an idea closely allied to the notion that man participates in the divine capacity for free will); and, second, the view that the world is to be venerated as God's creation and that the injunction to love and know God as best we can is therefore an injunction to love and know nature as best we can. The effect of the first concept would be to sanction *control* of the world (and hence knowledge of it, to the extent that knowledge is required for control, or even is itself a form of control). The effect of the second concept would be to sanction *truth-seeking* about the world. To the extent that Judaeo-Christianity promulgates both concepts, it is capable of underpinning science (and technology) in a world-affirming way.

The point I am making here is philosophical, not historical: I am not competent to comment on the complex and controversial matter of how Christianity actually influenced the rise of science and technology. I am merely saying that insofar as concepts like these are part of the Christian armoury, as these two undoubtedly are, Christianity can underpin science in ways that do not picture the world exclusively as something to be overcome—i.e. in ways not structured by the ascetic ideal in its extreme form. But I would

---

[6] Both concepts are employed in the Baconian justification for science mentioned in section 9.2 above.

contend that Nietzsche's theory of the Christian-ascetic basis of science is *also* philosophical rather than historical—and, specifically, that the third essay of *On the Genealogy of Morals*, where this theory is most prominently articulated, is, like the first two essays, primarily advancing hypothetical rather than historical genealogies.

So how could these two ideas—that man is lord of nature *and* has a duty to know the world in order to know God—support science in a world-affirming way?

The first, that man is lord of nature, is aided by two other typically Judaeo-Christian conceptions: that God is all-powerful through a perfectly free will in which man to some extent shares; and (not a uniquely monotheistic idea[7]) that nature herself is not deified. Both concepts sustain a wide gap in power between man and nature: the former by reinforcing his putative power, the second by stripping nature of the power that, in certain animist views, makes her seem so awesome and ungraspable.

Second, if scientific investigation is conceived as a *duty*, as a way of honouring, knowing, and giving thanks to God for his creation, it need not be ascetic in the sense of regarding the complexity of the world as something to be transcended. (Such a conception, it has been argued, was espoused by Bacon, Newton, and Kepler and greatly enhanced by the Reformation and the various brands of Protestantism that followed it, especially those which emphasized the obligation, for everyone of sufficient talent, to study both Books of God—Scripture and Nature—without regard to the authority of either Church or Greek tradition.[8])

---

[7] But also held by, for example, an atomist like Democritus.

[8] For further details on this historical point, see R. Hooykaas, *Religion and the Rise of Modern Science* (Edinburgh: Scottish Academic Press, 1972), 105–6 and 109–14. Hooykaas also suggests three other reasons why, as a matter of historical fact, Christianity—or at least Protestantism—facilitated the rise of science: (1) The need to investigate nature by *observation* increases once she is conceived as created (and even, for, say, Berkeley, sustained in being) by a God who is all-powerful and need obey no laws of logical necessity uncreated by him. For then the only way to know the world is not by pure logical deduction—i.e. by what seems reasonable to man—but by descriptive empiricism. Christianity humbles man by teaching that he cannot master the world with reason or Platonic 'recollection'—but that he can know only by attentive 'looking'; and this gives truth-seeking fresh impetus. Hooykaas cites, for example, the empiricism of the agnostic scientist T. H. Huxley: 'Science seems to me to teach in the highest and strongest manner the great truth which is embodied in the Christian conception of entire surrender to the will of God: Sit down before fact as a little child, be prepared to give up every preconceived notion, follow humbly and to whatever abysses nature leads, or you shall learn nothing.' (T. H. Huxley to C. Kingsley, 23 Sept. 1860, quoted in Hooykaas, *Religion and the Rise of Modern Science*, 51–2). (2) The idea that everybody has their individual relationship to God—one

Concepts which assume, first, man's *right* to dominate nature—in virtue of his being placed above it in the 'order of existence'—second, his *duty* to know it—in virtue of its being created by God—and, third, his *capacity* to dominate and discover it—in virtue of his empowerment with a metaphysically free will and nature's disempowerment through its de-deification—such concepts would seem to underpin science without themselves being structured by the ascetic ideal in its extreme form. This sort of justification for science—and for valuing truth—would be world-affirming because it is about relating more fully to God's creation, rather than about transcending or devaluing it. (It is, of course, another matter whether dominion over the world is a 'healthy' way of relating to it, as many, from nineteenth-century Romantics to modern ecologists, have doubted.) This is why I suggest that Judaeo-Christianity bequeaths not merely the ascetic reason for valuing truth identified by Nietzsche—i.e. the repudiation of the flux of life by seeking Truth as something purified of, or transcending, it—but also a thoroughly unascetic reason: i.e. the binding of man to the world through comprehending and controlling it.

That a Christian justification for science and truth-valuing can be life-affirming merely exemplifies a wider thought[9] which can get lost in the noise and smoke of Nietzsche as 'anti-Christ': namely, that there is nothing *inherently* world-repudiating about worshipping gods, doing things for the sake of gods, seeing them as legislators or exemplars of the highest values, and attributing to them overriding power of causation. These attitudes only become life-denying where man sees the worship of gods as *entailing* the denial of life, where to do something for the sake of a god *just is* to turn one's back on the

origin of the democratic spirit so detested by Nietzsche—might have facilitated the (again, largely Protestant) notion that each person has the right and duty to discover God's creation for himself, free of entrenched human presuppositions; hence, that to repudiate the traditional natural philosophy that had so impeded science was to submit the more fully to divine authority. Hooykaas cites, in evidence of this view, the English Puritan Nathanael Carpenter: 'I am free, I am bound to nobody's word except to those inspired by God' (Hooykaas, *Religion and the Rise of Modern Science*, 113). (3) With the 16th century, the experimental method, and in general mechanical and manual work, shunned by Greek rationalism and its medieval embodiments as inferior to the pure thought of, for example, mathematics and geometry, is regarded as equally valid before God and thus receives its indispensable religious sanction (ibid. 92–6). Though these ideas are suggestive and interesting, I am not in a position to evaluate their historical accuracy as explanations of the rise of modern science.

[9] A similar point is made in Chapter 5.5 and 5.6 in discussing the conditions under which the ascetic ideal is life-denying.

world (even though one may do 'good works' in it), or where the trials of life are to be overcome for the sake of 'another life' rather than to flourish in this one. Thus, piety in general—i.e. reverent wonder at what seems larger in power, perfection, or complexity than ourselves (or, at least, than our understanding)—is life-denying only if it causes us to repudiate the remainder of experience or existence.[10]

9.5 CONCLUSION

An extremely important feature of Nietzsche's critique of the unconditioned value of truth is to remind us, first, that all practices or ways of life—including truth-seeking and the enterprise of science (in the broad sense of *Wissenschaft*)—are motivated and justified, implicitly or explicitly, by certain values;[11] second, that an evaluation of the nature and function of science demands that these values be themselves identified and justified; and, third, that, historically, the value of science, like that of truth and truth-seeking in general, has tended to be either unexamined or regarded as self-justifying.[12]

The main problem with this critique lies, however, in Nietzsche's claim that rigorous science is, in its essence, a *moral*, and to *that* extent life-denying, enterprise; and, specifically, that this is because it necessarily presupposes, and is motivated by, the belief that truth is unconditionally valuable. By contrast, I have proposed three pos-

[10] One may also conjecture that if the concept of a metaphysically free will has, indeed, been crucial to the birth of modern science and technology, both in making the world knowable only empirically (because purely willed by God rather than ordered by an a priori logic) and in empowering man to intervene in nature (such intervention being crucial both to experiment and to the application of knowledge), then it would turn out that metaphysical voluntarism, just like the ascetic ideal, is a conceptual buttress to scientific truth-seeking which is itself eventually destroyed by that very science. That, in a genealogy of the value of truth, metaphysical voluntarism might figure alongside the 'ascetic ideal' would be no coincidence. For both concepts are constitutive of the Judaeo-Christian idea of man's necessary relationship to God: in the case of 'free will', as partaking in one of his essential features; in the case of the 'ascetic ideal', as the necessary overcoming of (aspects of) the worldly for the sake of the divine.

[11] '[S]cience also rests on a faith; there simply is no science "without presuppositions"' (*GS*, 344).

[12] These concerns appear as early as *The Birth of Tragedy* where, as Nietzsche himself says in his late preface to that work, he asks about the '*whence*' and 'significance of all science, viewed as a symptom of life' (*BT*, 'Attempt at a Self-Criticism', 1). That science cannot be self-justifying, but must be justified in terms of other practices or needs or the values internal to them, is surely part of what he means by insisting that 'the problem of science cannot be recognized in the context of science' (ibid. 2).

sible justifications for valuing truth passionately that are not world-denying—indeed, whose common factor is that they are directed at, and implicitly affirm, human beings' interest in the world and in each other. These justifications concern control over the world, the presuppositions of human communication, and religious motivations for science that are world-affirming.

It is the case, however, that whether or not these three justifications are successful, they do leave standing the essential tension in Nietzsche's thought between the value of truth and the value of untruth in the life of a flourishing individual. On the one hand, Nietzsche values truth very highly for at least four reasons: first, in order to avoid the snares of *décadence, ressentiment,* and morality; second, in order to make the various explicit affirmations that he calls for, such as of 'Eternal Return'—which we could hardly do properly if we did not have knowledge of what we were affirming; third, because knowledge of our strengths and weaknesses is needed in order to create out of ourselves a 'whole' character with 'style'; and, fourth, simply because Nietzsche himself is still inextricably part of a millennia-old ethical culture that values truth as 'divine', so much so that he can question the value of truth only in the name of truth—that is, for the sake of exposing the errors in traditional conceptions both of what truth is and, more importantly to him, of how it is valuable. (In the next chapter, we will look more carefully at these reasons for valuing truth.)

On the other hand, untruth and deception (of ourselves and others) can also, in his view, be crucial—in at least the six specific ways outlined in Chapter 8.1.2. Of these ways in which untruth can be valuable, the most interesting to Nietzsche is what he takes to be a precondition for being able to affirm the world at all, *precisely* when one knows the truth about its terrible nature: namely, art. There are two points here (for a further discussion of which the reader is referred back to Chapter 3.1.3). First, the more we value truth and the more we look at the world as, in Nietzsche's view, it is—i.e. as a cruel, godless, purposeless place, in which the pervasive need for *untruth* makes pure truthfulness unattainable—the more we need the fictional (though life-enhancing) realm of art, where man can invent the harmony, beauty, teleology, and other forms of imagined or idealized order which the scientific spirit abolishes from nature. This is *not* to 'aestheticize' existence by seeing it *as* a work of art; it is precisely the counter-value to a thoroughly unaesthetic perception of existence: one which looks unadorned reality straight in the face. Art makes truth bearable—and so truthfulness more possible; for without art honesty 'would lead to nausea and suicide' (*GS*, 107). Indeed, Nietzsche suggests that this is, in a sense, so for whole epochs as well as for individuals: man in general would 'get a hold of the truth *too soon*' if he had not *already* become 'artist enough' and so 'strong enough' (*BGE*, 59).

Second, in order to be free to fictionalize, the artist must not 'lay hold of actuality'—his and, perhaps, the world's too (*GM*, III, 4)—in the sense of 'grasping' it through concepts, because, at any rate as I interpret Nietzsche, this would sterilize those powers of imagination by which he creates. Now since, as I have argued in previous chapters, these contradictory needs and capacities for truth and untruth, for conceptual and non-conceptual ways of affirming life, may be found in the same person—the 'philosopher' and the 'artist' who embody them are to be understood as 'types', just as 'slaves' and 'masters' are—there is here a tension in the soul that is ineliminable, part of what Nietzsche sees as the tragic nature of living.

One of the most interesting results of Nietzsche's critique of the 'will to truth' is, therefore, to show how dramatic and inescapable is this opposition between our needs for truth and for untruth—and to suggest that flourishing is, in some sense, dependent upon our capacity first to maximize and then to hold in balance these two extremes (cf. *BGE*, 212; *TI*, IX, 49–51). In other words, the 'highest' type of individual needs truth *and* art: his aim is not to replace truth-seeking with art-making. As this study has repeatedly underlined, truth *retains* a very high value in Nietzsche's own ethic; and, before closing, it remains to investigate further what sorts of insight into reality Nietzsche regards as most valuable to a flourishing life—at least in an age of *décadence* such as ours.

10

The Valuation of Truth in Nietzsche's Philosophy

... what one has forbidden so far as a matter of principle has always been—truth alone. (*EH*, P, 3)

In the light of this survey of both Nietzsche's general critique of morality and his specific attack on unconditional truthfulness, what conclusions can we draw about how truth is valued in his new ethic? My answer is that, for Nietzsche, the principal (but not the sole) value of truth is to overcome those life-denying 'errors' that morality perpetrates 'as a matter of principle'; that because morality, like any ethic, is, for him, an inextricably historical development, truth is valuable in this way not for anybody at any time, but only for a very particular sort of ethical community at a very particular time in its own history; and that, for those not afflicted by such errors, truth may be valuable in quite different ways.

The particular community in question comprises, of course, the ethical descendants of Platonism-Christianity at that point in their history when, motivated by the value they themselves attach to truth in virtue of that descendancy, they have disposed of enough of the errors employed by their morality, such as beliefs in an all-merciful God or in an anthropocentric universe, that they are finally capable of tackling the most basic of all their errors: namely, those postulates of the 'atomistic need' through which they (consciously or unconsciously) elevate the permanent, the unconditioned, the equal, and the unhistorical as such[1] and denigrate the becoming, the conditioned, the unique, and the historical—i.e. through which they continue to express the ascetic ideal. Nietzsche regards these errors as so deeply embedded in the structure of our valuing and thinking

---

[1] i.e. the transcendence not just of one's own particular history, tradition, and position in time, but of *any* history, tradition, and position in time.

that even those who dismiss as absurd any idea of unconditioned values or the metaphysical subject or the supremacy of the atemporal, and who explicitly repudiate the Platonic (and, in general, timeless) metaphysics which made of those errors a philosophical system, may nonetheless persist, in their *actual* ethical valuations and practices, in behaving *as if* those very errors were true. Indeed, a striking example of this persistence is the theme of this very case study: namely, the propensity to treat the value of truth as unconditioned. Another example is egalitarian and democratic belief, and its presupposition of some essential equality of human nature.

This largely unconscious hypocrisy is precisely what Nietzsche sees in the failure of modernity to comprehend the terrifying significance of the 'death of God' (a failure demonstrated, for example, by the atheists who ridicule the 'madman' for so hysterically announcing that event[2]). Typically, people see that 'death' simply as welcome relief from the dark forces of superstition and arbitrary authority, and as a delightful gift of personal empowerment and political liberty. Because they are ultimately untruthful about the value of truth—by ascribing it unconditioned value—they fail to understand that the deeper significance of the 'death of God' is to discredit any conception of rational or ethical or, indeed, artistic, standards as susceptible of timeless and permanent justifications. Moreover, they underestimate the courage needed for such understanding (or for translating such understanding into their ethical practices), and make the mistake of believing that its attainment will be vouchsafed simply by an end to clerical or secular despotisms or to other insidious 'structures' of power. In other words, they believe, with Kant, that '[n]othing is required for this enlightenment . . . except [such public] *freedom*'[3]—and ignore, as Kant ultimately did, his own injunction: '*Sapere Aude!*',[4] which, for Nietzsche, would demand, first and foremost, an attack on the despotism of the 'atomistic need'. Yet Nietzsche also holds that the personal courage, self-respect, and receptivity to truth that are required if the 'death of God' is to be properly understood are found only in certain 'types' of people. It is the task of these few to face the world with the reality that standards conceived as radically extrinsic to temporality,

---

[2] *GS*, 125.

[3] Immanuel Kant, 'An Answer to the Question: What is Enlightenment?', in *Perpetual Peace and Other Essays*, trans. Ted Humphrey (Indianapolis: Hackett, 1983), 42.

[4] 'Dare to know!' (ibid. 41).

history, or perspective *as such* have been deprived of any justification—i.e. that the assumptions which such justification necessarily
employs are no longer regarded as intelligible and thus as acceptable.
At this historical juncture—one marked by, roughly, the completion
of three out of the four stages of 'nihilism' that we reconstructed in
Chapter 8.2—truth can possess no higher value, in the terms of
Nietzsche's ethic, than to enable that very reality to be faced.

In addition, of course, there are various other ways in which truth
can be valuable for life-enhancement, to which I will refer: for example, in giving 'style' to one's character or in 'purifying' one's values. In
all cases, however, the task of getting away from universal and timeless prescriptions requires Nietzsche's readers not merely to define
what sorts of truth are valued within his ethic and why, but also *for
whom* and *when* they are valuable—i.e. for which particular *types* of
people and *stages* in the process of 'becoming what one is'. This 'what',
'for whom', and 'when' will be carefully distinguished in this chapter.[5]

10.1 GROUNDING NIETZSCHE'S VALUATION OF TRUTH

My account of Nietzsche's valuation of truth must begin with the
particular end and virtues which, in his ethic, condition its value.

10.1.1 The purpose of valuing truth

The general end which conditions the value of truth in Nietzsche's
ethic is clearly 'life-enhancement'—i.e. the maximization of power,
sublimation, and 'form-creation' that invites love of life. Specifically,
the value of truth must be considered in relation to the three types
of form-creation which he most esteems: creating new life-affirming
values, creating great art, and giving 'style' to one's character.

All three types of form-creation demand the perfection of self-
legislation or of the capacity to 'promise' oneself, which Nietzsche
equates with genuine freedom. Now Nietzsche's very modern
conception of freedom—as self-responsible commitment to the
'necessity'[6] embodied or expressed in one's will[ing]—does in one

---

[5] The further question of where knowledge is *not* valuable—i.e. useless or harmful—
has already been addressed in Chapter 8.1.2.

[6] Very roughly, for Kant it is the necessity of reason, while for Nietzsche it is the necessity of nature, and specifically of a certain individual past and 'type'.

sense go further than Kantian autonomy in terms of independence
from constraints (since Nietzsche's self-legislation is clearly uncon-
strained by anything like universalizability, or duty to the moral law,
or the metaphysical reality underlying Kantian freedom); but in
another sense it takes a step back from Kantian autonomy by thinking of an individual's possible good(s), and thus of the values that
she legislates for herself, as 'fated' by how things are in nature—the
world's and ours as individuals.[7] There is no contradiction here:
though, for Nietzsche, the individual's 'highest' needs and aims are
the only authority for values, those needs and aims are determined
by the nature, nurture, and life-circumstances which make her what
she is, and which are, in turn, expressions of a certain history.
Whether or not Nietzsche conceives that history as contingent, in
that it could have been otherwise, it seals the individual's fate. In
other words, an individual's history determines what Nietzsche calls
her 'necessity'; and it is a condition for her freedom and life-
enhancement that she achieve full-blooded mastery and expression—
i.e. 'willing'—of that necessity (*BGE*, 213).[8] Conversely, it is
weakness to interpret every ' "psychological necessity" ' as 'unfreedom' (*BGE*, 21).

Now, for Nietzsche, the most fundamental of all the errors of
morality is its denial of two key facts implicit in this account of the
authority for values: first, that such authority resides solely in the
individual's conditions for flourishing; and, second, that those conditions, and hence that authority itself, are determined by the individual's particular history. Morality denies the first fact by positing
an ethical order given by God, Reason, or other authorities for values conceived as transcending the nature and needs of the individual. And it denies the second fact by attributing to man an explicitly
unhistorical essential nature or, at least, 'moral' nature—i.e. com-
prising what is deepest and best in man as such or what pertains
most directly to his ethical practices—which is eternal and universal
and endowed with a 'free will' that putatively chooses his values.
Both sorts of error are consequences of the 'atomistic need', to which
we will return below. They are, for Nietzsche, crucial to the life-
denying nature of morality. Moreover, they are not arbitrary, but

---

[7] In this latter sense, Nietzsche is a recognizably 'ancient' thinker. The combination of
the ancient and the modern in Nietzsche's ethics is well brought out by Peter Berkowitz
in *Nietzsche*, e.g. 266–7, and I am indebted to his work for this point.

[8] This point is explained in more detail in Chapter 2.4.

arise from 'not *wanting* to see at any price how reality is constituted fundamentally' (*EH*, IV, 4), by pursuing 'untruth at any price' (*BGE*, 59). Their overcoming depends on 'supreme self-examination on the part of humanity' (*EH*, IV, 1).

By contrast, a life-enhancing ethic must be attuned to both the cardinal facts that morality falsifies. This means, above all, that it must accept that the individual is entirely natural and so historical. Indeed, Nietzsche says, to 'translate man back into nature' and recognize again 'the basic text of *homo natura*' is the best answer to the question: ' "why have knowledge at all?" ' (*BGE*, 230). In order to achieve this, such an ethic must affirm, or at least not deny, certain general features of nature and history, notably temporality, flux, the interconnection of all events, and the absence of eternally valid standards given by any authority conceived as transcending individual human needs and historical traditions. Given, as we have seen, how subtle the ignoring, in practice, of such facts can be—for example, by positivists who continue to value truth unconditionally, or by anti-metaphysicians who still posit continuants, such as atoms or egos, that 'hold fast' in this world of flux—such realism will be hard to achieve. It results, however, in the immoralist who 'conceives reality *as it is*', who 'is not estranged or removed from reality but is reality itself and exemplifies all that is questionable and terrible in it—*only in that way can man attain greatness*' (*EH*, IV, 5).[9]

My suggestion, therefore, is that the principal value of truth in Nietzsche's ethic is in enabling us—i.e. the descendants of Platonic-Christian morality—to understand that morality falsifies these two key facts, and hence to overcome the obstacles created by the anti-historical ambitions of morality to willing the fate determined by our individual history. (In addition, of course, truth is also internally valuable to certain specific ends or practices, such as scientific investigation and individual or social relationships, which were touched on in Chapter 9.2–3.) Since most of Nietzsche's key ethical

---

[9] Nietzsche's paradigmatic immoralist would appear to be Goethe, who maximally affirms the necessity that he finds both in external reality and in himself—i.e. who, crudely put, achieves in his mature period a synthesis of the objective and the subjective, of the *Aufklärung* and of '*Sturm und Drang*'. This is the Goethe who strove for 'universality in understanding and in welcoming, letting everything come close to [him]self, an audacious realism, a reverence for everything factual'. His '*amor fati*' reflects a thoroughgoing realism (*TI*, IX, 50; cf. 49, 51). For a good summary of the mature Goethe as a paragon of *Deutsche Klassik*, see R. B. Farrell, in J. M. Ritchie (ed.), *Periods in German Literature* (London: Oswald Wolff, 1966), 99–120.

objectives demand the capacity to will one's individual necessity or fate, truth turns out to be instrumentally crucial to living by his ethic—at least for the inheritors of morality. Such objectives include 'becoming what one is', affirming 'Eternal Return', '*amor fati*', expressing one's 'will to power', and attaining 'redemption'—which, for Zarathustra, is 'to re-create all "it was" into a "thus I willed it"' (*Z*, II, 20).

This account of the value of truth has two implications. First, it means that such truths about—i.e. explicit propositional knowledge of—the individual as part of nature and as determined by a specific history *need not* be sought by an ethical community, like 'the Greeks', that does not deny them in the first place, and *should not* be sought by those, namely 'artists', who must remain estranged from at least their own reality if they are to be true to it.

Second, if truth is valuable primarily insofar as it 're-attunes' us to these fundamental facts, then its job—at least at this juncture in our ethical history—consists principally in the 'negative' task of identifying and disposing of those confusions and deliberate falsifications that stand in the way of such an attunement, rather than in the 'positive' task of, say, understanding exactly who we, as individuals, are, or defining our maximum 'good', or establishing the means for attaining it, or evaluating the worth of our actions. Indeed, as I indicated in previous chapters, Nietzsche is distinctly sceptical of the value *and* the possibility of attaining these latter kinds of knowledge.

10.1.2 Virtues of the truth-valuer

Knowledge can have value for life—and, also, will be successfully secured—*only* if the knower displays two attitudes (characteristic of a 'noble' ethic): first, one of audacious engagement with the reality he describes, and, second, one of reverence for himself.

On the first, though Nietzsche's 'conception' of truth is, as argued in Chapter 7, broadly empirical, the business of finding and facing it differs markedly from many traditional conceptions thereof. First, such truth can be ugly (rather than Platonically beautiful); second, it can be discovered only by 'living dangerously' (and not by will-less contemplation, which is no better for securing truth than for winning a woman);[10] third, it can arise out of evil and untruth (not out of love of the good); fourth it must be felt—not merely conceptual-

---

[10] *BGE*, P.

ized—if the reality it describes is vividly to be apprehended; fifth, to find and face it demand Homeric virtues of hardness, courage, cunning, and 'trusting fatalism' (not the urge for comfort and predictability—*TI*, IX, 49; cf. *BGE*, 39); and, sixth, these virtues are best sustained by the faith 'that all is redeemed and affirmed in the whole [person or life that one becomes]' (*TI*, IX, 49)—a faith that denotes Nietzsche's later conception of 'Dionysian'.[11] Those capable of such fortitude are Nietzsche's 'free spirits' in general (clearly nothing to do with *laissez faire*), and the tragic Greeks and Goethe in particular (*TI*, IX, 49–51). Indeed, one measure by which Nietzsche evaluates people is how much truth they can face—in exactly this manner of unvarnished, direct confrontation with reality.[12]

The second attitude essential to conferring value on truth is the respect for himself typical of a 'noble' nature—one who numbers himself among the *esthloi* (the good): i.e. as possessing being and reality (*GM*, I, 5) and, as the ultimate mark of self-respect, capable of the sovereignty to 'make promises' (*GM*, II, 1). For only self-respect—the 'fundamental certainty that a noble soul has about itself' (*BGE*, 287)—sustains the fortitude to face the nature of existence directly and truthfully (though to tolerate such insight one might, through art, falsify much else). Without self-respect, one is at best an excellent gatherer of small truths but will lack the stomach for the big truths—and in particular, for the two cardinal facts that morality falsifies (i.e. for fully grasping the implications of the 'death of God').[13] This is just the attitude exemplified by the

---

[11] Thus, Nietzsche's later conception of the Dionysian (e.g. *TI*, IX, 49; *BGE*, 295) denotes the wholeness and multiplicity of an individual, his successful integration of a complex 'soul'—in contrast to his early conception in *The Birth of Tragedy*, where the god represents the formless, intoxicated, uncontrolled, innermost depths of nature, as distinct from the form-creating, controlled, art-making force of the Apollonian (e.g. *BT*, 5–7, *passim*).

[12] I interpret the epigraph to *GM* III as referring precisely to these virtues of the truth-seeker. Wisdom, this enigmatic epigraph suggests, can be secured only by full-blooded engagement with life, in which cautious reason is supplemented by 'unconcern', veneration of nature by 'mockery', and contemplation by 'violence'. Truth yields not to the purely detached, but to those who confront reality with all their artfulness, passion, and cunning. In short, this epigraph exemplifies the '*different* kind of spirit' (*GM*, II, 24) which Nietzsche seeks, the '*opposing will*' which he demands (*GM*, III, 23 and 25)—in contrast to the sombre, pious spirit animated by the ascetic ideal, whose many expressions are listed in *GM*, III, 1.

[13] Note that the 'noble's' identification of himself with truth and truthfulness functions only as a *condition* for it to be valuable to value truth—not as a *reason* to value truth (in the sense of truth-seeking or truth-knowing). In other words, the noble's self-image as the

diligent scholar, the 'objective spirit', who 'has lost any seriousness for himself' and so can be no more than 'an instrument, . . . a mirror' in the service of knowledge (*BGE*, 207).

10.2 *WHAT* TRUTHS ARE VALUABLE?

Having pointed out, first, the end and, second, the virtues which, for Nietzsche, condition the value of truth-knowing and truth-seeking, I shall now focus a little further on *what* truths and truth-seeking are required for attuning oneself to the fundamental reality that values are 'authorized' by the individual's conditions for life-enhancement and are determined by his specific past.

10.2.1 *Overcoming the 'atomistic need'*

Most fundamentally, attunement to this reality requires one's ethic to free itself from—i.e. requires one to understand that there is no warrant for calling 'true'—the postulates generated by the 'atomistic need', at least in its more metaphysical guises (*BGE*, 12). This need, we recall, is to make permanent or 'hold fast' reality by positing standards or ontologies conceived (implicitly or explicitly) as radically immune to contingency as such—i.e. as transcending 'becoming', temporality, and the seamless causal relatedness of all objects and events. The atomistic need also evinces the urge to explain or justify in terms of those standards all our values and beliefs and practices (and, *pari passu*, to explain in terms of those ontologies all objects and events).

Now, in the Platonic-Christian ethical community, the most obvious manifestation of the atomistic need, so I take Nietzsche to suggest, is the 'metaphysical need' (*BGE*, 12). This posits, for example, overtly metaphysical continuants (viz. ultimate substances, subjects, and first causes such as, respectively, atoms,[14] the Christian 'soul',

possessor of truth does not commit him to seeking or formulating truths. One might even read Nietzsche as suggesting that the whole urgency of the search for truth is itself a sign of some basic distress or dis-ease in man, that in a condition of ease and satisfaction with himself truth would not be valued in so marked or explicit a fashion (a point that Nietzsche seems to make in the last paragraph of *GS*, 120). Thus, when the Greeks were healthy, they remained 'superficial' (*GS*, P, 4), creating without knowing, and without trying to know, what they were doing (*GS*, 369). When they became decadent and distressed, *then* they turned to truth—and to Socrates (*TI*, II, 9–11, *passim*).

[14] Or some sort of irreducible particles.

and absolute 'free will'—e.g. *BGE*, 12 and 21); the 'good as such'—which denies perspectivism, 'the basic condition of all life' (*BGE*, P); the monotheistic god; the metaphysically structured interpretations of suffering (as punishment for essential guilt, or as redeemable in the beyond); and, in general, the unconditioned. These beliefs are, in turn, employed to justify our failure to take responsibility for ourselves as 'sovereign' individuals—i.e. those who can legislate for and so 'promise' themselves, rather than looking 'reactively' to universal or unconditioned values for guidance. And such failure, in its turn, means that we refuse to allow others to take responsibility for themselves, which motivates the sort of pity endorsed by morality.

But the atomistic need is *not* overcome merely by discrediting the Platonic type of metaphysics. It continues to be expressed through such covertly atomistic beliefs as the essential equality of all human beings (in virtue of certain invariant and constitutive features); through, more generally, the very notion of the 'identical';[15] through conceiving individual actions as self-contained units of ethical evaluation; and, most widely, through conceptual or aesthetic forms that posit 'eternally enduring' order. When Nietzsche says that the 'total character of the world' is 'in all eternity chaos' (*GS*, 109), he means, I suggest, that we lack grounds for assuming that *anything* about the universe can thus be held fast (or can be absolutely identical to anything else)—i.e. can be taken as unchangingly conforming to certain anthropomorphic models of order and permanence fashioned by our conceptual and aesthetic preferences.

The overcoming of the atomistic need, at least in its overtly metaphysical manifestation, therefore involves first and foremost the end of all values and practices that depend upon belief in absolute and timeless standards or entities and upon a phenomenology of standing 'extrinsically' over against life or temporality as such. (Such an overcoming is, it would seem, part and parcel of the 'death of God'.) And it is, consequently, the end not only of such beliefs, such as those of Christianity, but also of the prior *questions* to which they constitute responses. For these questions, I suggest, presuppose the same fundamental values and concepts that structure their responses, in just the way in which the question 'what is the meaning of man, the human *animal*?' presupposes the metaphysical dualism that infects its ascetically ideal answer (see Chapter 5.7), or in which the

---

[15] Which, again, presupposes 'atomistic' features in virtue of which two things or actions are the same (rather than merely similar; cf. *GS*, 111).

envy-laden questions fostered by *ressentiment* presuppose the same notion of essential human equality that structures *their* answers (see Chapter 3.3). And it is because the atomistic need is the bedrock of the concepts and categories of morality that it is, as I read Nietzsche, the only motive or value for which he sees no life-enhancing application whatsoever and to which his opposition is therefore total.[16]

Yet we come here to a dilemma at the heart of Nietzsche's philosophy. On the one hand, Nietzsche declares 'war unto death' on the atomistic need (*BGE*, 12), and insists that the 'total character' of the world is in all eternity 'chaos' (*GS*, 109). Thus, he not only sees belief in fixed constants as 'false', but also, to a very extreme degree, wishes to overcome such belief and the 'need' underlying it. On the other hand, he knows that belief in such constants is, to some extent, indispensable to life: indeed, that 'every skeptical tendency constitute[s] a great danger for life' (*GS*, 111), and that judgements like the synthetic a priori 'must be *believed* to be true, for the sake of the preservation of creatures like ourselves' (*BGE*, 11). Ultimately, however, Nietzsche cannot press both these claims to their extremes; he has to relent on one of them. For, at the limit, it is contradictory to claim that the world's 'total character' is chaos (which, at first glance, looks like a culmination of German Idealism that leaves only arbitrary 'interpretative' acts of will) and, in concluding this same passage, to hope that we 'begin to "naturalize" humanity'—i.e. to see humanity as wholly a part of nature. Indeed, if the world's total character is chaos, we end up with Stanley Rosen's conjecture that Nietzsche 'seems to have deprived himself of the ability to explain the presence of a world' at all;[17] and it is then hard to see what it would be for man to be 'naturalized'. Similarly, it is unintelligible to suggest that we can *altogether* avoid concepts which 'hold fast', and which therefore effectively strive to immunize from contingency, certain putative aspects of reality; and, at the same time, claim that life needs such constants. The reality is that Nietzsche has to relent on the first claim in the dilemma: he has to allow that life—and, specifically, all experience, understanding, speech, and communication—requires constants which cannot be experienced as merely theoretical or provisional. (Indeed, Nietzsche's own conception of the fundamental structure of the world as 'chaos' is itself a unified

---

[16] Evidence for this total opposition is presented in Chapter 3.2 (last paragraph).

[17] Stanley Rosen, *The Ancients and the Moderns: Rethinking Modernity* (New Haven: Yale University Press, 1989), 214.

interpretative structure, which cannot be characterized as 'chaos'.[18])
And the upshot of this reality is that, insofar as such constants, such
attempts to hold fast, are 'shadows of God' (*GS*, 109), it is unlikely
to be possible[19] to 'complete our de-deification of nature' (ibid.) and
thus, in a sense, to complete the death of God.[20]

10.2.2. Ethical deliberation

In addition, in order not to succumb to life-denial, Nietzsche
demands of a *décadent* like himself—i.e. of most of his sympathetic
readers (though, again, not necessarily of those who are free from the
falsifications of morality)—a process of ethical enquiry that, to summarize the matter very considerably, investigates the value of one's
own individual values in a three-stage process. The first stage is to
discover the highest values one intuitively holds, which tells one
something about what one really is;[21] second, one sifts out those values that are conducive to making just such a type of person strong
or life-affirming; and, finally one attempts to specify and understand
ever more precisely the nature and value of these values. All three
stages presuppose prolonged encounter with the obstacles, by-ways,
dilemmas, and other 'hard cases' of real experience, which makes
possible an ever more precise specification of values and the conditions for their success in life-enhancement. These stages can, therefore, occur only at an appropriate point in the individual's life (see
10.4 below).

That deliberation has a central role within a Nietzschean ethics in
enabling one to identify, specify, and confirm or discard one's innate
values is strongly suggested, first, by Nietzsche's clear expectation
that genealogical analysis, driven by the 'will to truth', will have

---

[18] I find this problem of self-reference harder (and more interesting) than the parallel
issue of how Nietzsche's perspectivism could itself be a perspective.

[19] Or, as we argued in Chapter 5.6, desirable.

[20] In a similar spirit, MacIntyre rightly asks whether the narrating of any intelligible
genealogy does not inescapably involve the genealogist in commitments to certain timeless
standards of truth, reference, logic, rationality, and selfhood (especially the selfhood of the
genealogist)—standards which are 'independent of the particular stages and moments of
the temporary strategies through which the genealogist moves his or her overall projects
forward'. In other words, MacIntyre suggests, such commitments are essential to the intelligibility of a genealogy, even if it is the declared aim of the genealogist to abolish them
(Alasdair MacIntyre, *Three Rival Versions of Moral Enquiry* (London: Duckworth, 1990),
54–5).

[21] See *BGE*, 6. In particular, where one stands on the value of suffering (*BGE*, 270),
rank, and reverence (*BGE*, 263) is a litmus test of the 'type' of person one is.

precisely this result (cf. *GM*, III, 27);[22] second, by his recognition that '[l]earning changes us' (*BGE*, 231); third, by his specific request that we discover all that is lawful in the world *in order to* purify our valuations (*GS*, 335); fourth, by his insistence on systematic research into the function of values (see *GM*, I, 17, Endnote: 'the determination of the *order of rank among values*'; cf. *GS*, 345); and, fifth, by his emphasis on the great danger of prematurely seeking truth about our 'organizing "idea"' (*EH*, II, 9)—a danger that can exist only if he believes that truth has the power to change us. These points alone quash any suggestion that Nietzsche is an obscurantist for whom knowledge is irrelevant to life-enhancement.

10.3 *FOR WHOM* IS TRUTH VALUABLE?

All 'life-enhancement' requires us to face the world aright in the minimum way sketched above. But these generalizations about the value of truth need to be further qualified because, for Nietzsche, everything is valuable in different ways for different types of people. Since, according to our reconstruction of his typology of people, the latter are to be classified, first, by their *degree* of life-enhancement (i.e. how much they can express power, sublimation, and form-creation that seduces to life), and, second, by their *type* of life-enhancement (i.e. to which of the three kinds of form-creation most valued by Nietzsche they are suited), we need now to indicate how, according to this classification, the value of truth is determined by *who* is pursuing or espousing it.

10.3.1 *Degrees of life-enhancement and the value of truth*

The degree of life-enhancement of which one is capable reflects one's position in the 'order of rank' (*A*, 57), and to this, in turn, is correlated 'an order of rank of problems' (*BGE*, 213), which governs the kind of knowledge to which an individual is suited. This correlation is one of those natural laws that, for Nietzsche, traditional morality and its 'democratic' instinct have ignored, and that his ethic explicitly recognizes. Thus every soul is disposed to certain 'predeter-

---

[22] Indeed, for Nietzsche, knowledge of the functions of values can precipitate action with almost Kantian automaticity—at least in its capacity to discredit old values (by providing convincing reasons for their life-denying functions which shatter our faith in them), if not in compelling us to adopt new, putatively life-enhancing, values.

mined decision[s] and answer[s] to predetermined selected questions' (*BGE*, 231); its values, affirmations, and denials grow out of [it] with the 'necessity with which a tree bears fruit' (*GM*, P, 2); and those whose soul is not of the requisite rank will be repulsed 'mercilessly' by problems that they are not 'predestined' to solve: 'the primeval law of things takes care of that' (*BGE* 213). In short, there is, for Nietzsche, a fixed correlation between, on the one hand, kinds of problems and knowledge and, on the other hand, types of 'soul' that are able to understand, employ, *and respect* them properly.

Those individuals—and, indeed, ages—which, for Nietzsche, possess a feeble capacity for 'life-enhancement' are distinguished by their manner of valuing truth and by the types of truths they value— i.e. by valuing truth as an end in itself (as an escape into the safety of the unconditioned) and by valuing 'small and common facts' (*BGE*, 253, *passim*). They approach 'higher' truths—such as about the nature and value of values—clumsily and irreverently, because they have no real sense of their subtlety or significance. England supplies Nietzsche's paradigms of such individuals and ages. Thus Darwin[23] and John Stuart Mill—those whose extraordinary brilliance gave huge historical impetus and fresh justification to the old 'democratic spirit' nourished by Socrates and Christ—are lambasted as mediocrities; while the eighteenth century was a period in which the 'aridity' of 'English' truth-seeking gained the upper hand throughout Europe (*BGE*, 253). By contrast, 'spirits of a high type' have the courage and power to create new forms, and to value truths only as a means to this end. But they also have the nobility—as expressed in an '*instinct of reverence*' (*BGE*, 263)—to *do justice* to higher truths.

[23] Nietzsche's understanding of Darwin is, in many places, confused (e.g. *TI*, IX, 14 or *WP*, 685, both entitled 'Anti-Darwin'). For example, he takes Darwin's notion of 'survival of the fittest' to mean survival of the 'highest', 'stronger', 'better constituted', or most exceptional. He accuses Darwin of not understanding that the 'highest' and the 'lucky strokes' are the most vulnerable, because the most risk-taking and complex in needs, and that it is the majority who survive because they fit in rather than stand out (e.g. *BGE*, 201–3). Yet Darwin would have agreed completely with this: the 'fit' are not the 'highest' but the *best adapted* to their environment; and one's adaptability presumes nothing about one's sophistication or strength, let alone about the cultivated life-enhancement that is Nietzsche's primary interest. Indeed, Darwin would have concurred with any gardener that, unprotected, the exquisite plants will always be stifled by the commonplace. Nietzsche's aim is, of course, to criticize the supposed unconcern of Christian morality and its modern 'democratic' descendants with the 'highest' cultural types, but his attack on Darwin in this context is largely misplaced.

Between these two extreme types—between those who merely 'know' and those who 'can' (i.e. create or embody new values)—there is, Nietzsche suggests, a 'chasm' that is 'greater, also uncannier, than people suppose' (*BGE*, 253). This chasm is between the Christian-scientific-democratic and the Nietzschean-aristocratic ways of valuing truth—between, to put the matter very telegraphically, the unselective and ascetically ideal pursuit of truth and the highly discriminating and life-enhancing manner of employing it. It is a chasm because on the one side is embodied the very ethic that Nietzsche repudiates (at least for 'higher' souls), while on the other side is the life-enhancing ethic which marks a revaluation of all values.

10.3.2 Types of life-enhancement and the value of truth

In addition, and more interestingly, Nietzsche advances a clear distinction between his three favoured types of life-enhancement—i.e. of form-creation that maximizes power and sublimation and that invites love of life—in terms of their need and aptitude for propositional truth. These types of form-creation, we recall, are philosophy (creating new values), art (beautifying the world), and giving 'style' to one's character (thus making it affirmable).

In an age of '*décadence*', it is really the job of philosophers (or *Wissenschaftler* in general) to steer humanity away from the life-denying errors of morality and to legislate new values. Insofar as both tasks demand truth-seeking in the ways we have outlined, philosophers' cardinal virtue is clearly honesty or truthfulness (*GM*, I, 1; *BGE*, 39; or, for Zarathustra: *EH*, IV, 3). Indeed, Nietzsche values the capacity for insight into reality as the supreme mark of 'rank': even suffering is valued by him primarily because it enables one to know '*more* than the cleverest and wisest could possibly know', to become 'the elect of knowledge' (*BGE*, 270). Thus: 'How much truth does a spirit *endure*, how much truth does it *dare*? More and more that became for me the real measure of value . . . error is *cowardice*' (*EH*, P, 3).

Second, for the 'artist', dedication to truth-seeking, in the sense of *formulating truths*, is both difficult (as a matter of temperament) and damaging (to the falsifying capacities needed to create beauty). There are three areas, we recall from Chapter 3.1.3, in relation to which Nietzsche appears to suggest that propositional truth-seeking is damaging to the artist: her 'inner' reality in particular; the overall (ethical) value of her work; and, perhaps, 'external' reality in general. Nonetheless, as we also discussed there, the artist must have had, at some point, a very thorough confrontation with reality because her creativity, as Nietzsche describes it from *The Birth of Tragedy* onwards, depends upon the violence of her *reaction* to reality. In other words, if she is to falsify powerfully, she must first have seen powerfully (though this falsification has nothing to do with that of morality because its underlying function, as in Greek Tragedy, is to affirm life, despite and including its horror).[24]

Third, for giving ' "style" to one's character' (*GS*, 290), the last of the three types of form-creation most highly valued by Nietzsche, knowledge of 'the strengths and weaknesses' of one's individual nature is, as we have seen, essential. But the overall controller of this style is—like the 'organizing "idea"' (*EH*, II, 9) that marks one's individual destiny—really an innate, though only gradually evolving and discernable, 'taste' (*GS*, 290), in the formation and discovery of which propositional truth-seeking or -knowing, or direct introspection, has, at most, a secondary role. This taste, whose nature becomes evident only when its 'work is finished' (ibid.), employs knowledge about one's strengths and weaknesses in shaping one's character much like a master chef uses his knowledge of the nature and possibilities of various ingredients in creating the dish—i.e. what drives the integration of the personality is not the truth about what makes it most powerful but the 'artistic plan' of giving it 'style'.[25] Here truth-seeking (both to know what elements we are made of and how much knowledge of them we can bear) is followed by art-making. Ironically, however, artists themselves are likely to be particularly unsuited to such artistry of character, both because they are poor at introspective truth-seeking and because their energies are diverted into external creation.

In a very general sense, then, 'becoming what one is', whether through philosophy, art, or giving style to one's character, is begun

[24] For an excellent account of Nietzsche's conception of how tragedy enabled 'the Greeks' to affirm life, see M. S. Silk and J. P. Stern, *Nietzsche on Tragedy* (Cambridge: Cambridge University Press, 1981), esp. chapters 4, 6, and 8.

[25] Habermas suggests that 'Nietzsche enthrones taste, "the Yes and the No of the palate", as the organ of a knowledge beyond true and false, beyond good and evil', though I would prefer to use the word 'decision' (or even 'conscience'!) here rather than 'knowledge' (Habermas, *The Philosophical Discourse of Modernity*, 96). It is worth recalling in this context that Nietzsche's ultimate opposition to Christianity is a matter of taste and 'no longer' of reasons (*GS*, 132).

by living fully (this is the prerequisite for developing both strength and knowledge), developed by attentive 'looking' (albeit with different requirements for propositional truth-seeking of each of the three activities), and completed by form-creation.

10.4 *WHEN* (OVER A LIVED LIFE) IS TRUTH VALUABLE?

We have touched at several points on Nietzsche's suggestion that successfully to seek, formulate, and tolerate great truths—for example, about the fundamental character of reality or about 'what one is'—demands considerable experience and maturity, and that to pursue them too hastily can arrest one's maturation, thus stymieing one's capacity both to understand the world and to 'become what one is'. There are two ways in which such truths can be premature: first, they can destroy us (or, at least, our development) if we have not developed sufficient strength for them—for which reason, Nietzsche says, the *homines religiosi* have always understood that great truths must not be grasped '*too soon*' (*BGE*, 59); and, second, real understanding—which Nietzsche presents as a sort of gelling of many different powers or insights—is not available to us until we have separately and sufficiently developed those individual powers and insights. Moreover, there appears to be both a general and a specific sense in which truth-seeking can be premature. The former relates to *complex* knowledge (of, one supposes, ethical matters, in particular) and the latter, as we mentioned earlier, relates to *self*-knowledge.

10.4.1 *The general sense: attaining complex knowledge*

The attainment of complex knowledge, Nietzsche suggests, presupposes a three-stage emotional development in which rival 'instincts' develop separately, then clash, and finally (though rarely) reach an accommodation (*GS*, 333). Understanding is 'the form in which we come to feel' that accommodation—i.e. the settled relationship between our dominant instincts, each of which possesses its own particular perspectives on objects or events. Since only the accommodation—i.e. the third stage—is conscious, we wrongly suppose 'that *intelligere* must be something conciliatory, just, and good—something that stands essentially opposed to the instincts, while it is actually nothing but a *certain behaviour of the instincts toward one another*' (*GS*, 333).

This model of thinking, though threadbare, clearly reflects Nietzsche's general picture of the 'self' as a collection of warring drives that reach accommodations under the influence of dominant drives. It tentatively suggests two conclusions indicated by Nietzsche, and a third not mentioned by him:

1. Understanding, far from being distinct from the emotions or demanding their suppression, is structured by a certain order in the emotional economy.

2. If peace and consciousness characterize only the final accommodation between the 'instincts', while the first two stages involve much restlessness and conflict and are unconscious, then quietude is not the sole, or even the main, condition for fertile thought. Indeed, quietude is necessary only for the final, 'cream skimming', act of forming conscious understanding. (On this view, 'living dangerously' nourishes thought both by bringing the agent into proximity to reality, and by arousing her instincts to life and battle.)

3. To seek at least complex truths too early—i.e. before the three stages have had time to play themselves out—can result in a truncation of that process of emotional development and hence of one's powers of understanding.

10.4.2 The specific sense: 'becoming what one is'

'Becoming what one is' is, I argued in Chapter 6, the new ideal that best embodies Nietzsche's ethic of life-enhancement. It is a long process, which, in terms of the value of truth to it, can be conveniently divided into two stages.

In the first stage, there is one type of knowledge that is essential and another that must not be sought.

The essential knowledge (for those afflicted by '*décadence*') is of the fact that we each have an individual 'necessity' which is historically determined. This knowledge, deeply grasped, enables us to face the world aright, to avoid the pitfalls of *ressentiment*, and so to create healthy conditions for the development both of our single qualities and powers and of the 'organizing "idea"' (*EH*, II, 9)[26] which will, later, mark their integration into a whole self.

---

[26] Or 'personal providence' (*GS*, 277), 'single taste' (*GS*, 290), 'granite of spiritual *fatum*' (*BGE*, 231), etc.

The dangerous knowledge which we must *not* seek in the first stage is of the precise nature of this 'organizing "idea"'—and attempts to define the latter could stymie its development. This, at any rate, is how I interpret passages like the following:

'My thoughts', said the wanderer to his shadow, 'should show me where I stand; but they should not betray to me where I am going. I love my ignorance of the future and do not wish to perish of impatience and of tasting promised things ahead of time.' (*GS*, 287)

Truly high respect one can have only for those who do not *seek* themselves. (*BGE*, 266)

To become what one is, one must not have the faintest notion *what* one is. (*EH*, II, 9)

The point here, to which I alluded earlier, is that the premature attempt to understand one's 'organizing "idea"' would make impossible two crucial preparatory phases: first, the innocent, unimpeded experience that comes from forgetting, misunderstanding, and narrowing oneself and, second, the development of '*single* qualities and fitnesses' free from the straightjacket of overall goals or meanings (*EH*, II, 9). In these preparatory phases the potentiality of the Nietzschean self—which, as we have mentioned, is not a single fixed *telos* waiting to be actualized, but rather a set of potentialities that themselves evolve under the pressure of changing nurture and life-circumstances—is gradually enriched. The danger of prematurely attempting to define 'what one is' is to arrest the accumulation or evolution of these potentialities and therefore to fail to discover what one could have been. Moreover, the road to 'becoming what one is' is usually not straight, and involves blunders and wrong turns, 'wasted' energy, protective misunderstandings, and self-narrowing. Hence, we must keep the 'whole surface of consciousness . . . clear of all great imperatives'; be alert to the 'many dangers that the instinct comes too soon to "understand itself"'; and '[b]eware even of every great word . . . [and] pose' (*EH*, II, 9).

The second stage begins when we reach that 'high point in life' (*GS*, 277) at which our organizing idea or personal providence will have sufficiently formed within us to guide us to becoming what we are—i.e. to actualizing certain potentialities which we have then accumulated. This is the time when 'form-creation' can begin in earnest.

In sum, both the general and the specific senses in which truth-seeking can be premature have weight for Nietzsche because the knowledge he most values—notably about the fundamental character of existence, about the value of values, and about our strengths and weaknesses—presupposes intense experience, long emotional development, and the subconscious formation of ideas, all processes which premature truth-seeking can arrest. Hence, in general, if we value truth, especially of this complex kind, we should avoid seeking it too early; and, in particular, if we are to be truthful *to* ourselves, we must be cautious in seeking the truth *about* ourselves. This is, in turn, part of a larger theme in Nietzsche's writing: that in the interests of being true to oneself certain knowledge must be regarded as not merely premature, but as generally harmful or useless. Thus, he remarks, 'the creative may possibly have to be lacking in knowledge' (*BGE*, 253).

10.5 CONCLUSION

To embrace the unconditioned, Nietzsche's critique of morality suggests, is to wish to escape not merely the particular history that has made each individual what he or she is, but history and temporality *as such*. This is impossible, and even unintelligible, because the past inevitably conditions our values in three senses. First, it conditions which values *can 'enhance'* any given individual. It does so because the nature, nurture, and life-circumstances that have made an individual what he is are products of a certain past, with the result that the values which can 'enhance' him are themselves conditioned by that same past. Second, historical events condition which values an individual *actually pursues*. They do this both specifically, in virtue of the ethical inheritance bequeathed by that individual's unique past and life-circumstances and, generally, by determining the dominant values that he imbibes from the wider culture or ethical community of which he is a member—such as, in the Platonic-Christian tradition, the propensity to value truth highly. Third, both these senses also apply to a culture or epoch as a whole: the particular history that has made it what it is conditions both which values it actually espouses and their value to it. This is just the sense in which truth about the value of truth is valuable to us, the inheritors of Platonic-Christian morality at this particular stage in our history, in a way in which it would not have been valuable to the Homeric Greeks, who were unburdened by the errors fostered by the 'atomistic need'.

Now the first two of these senses in which our values are historically conditioned can, of course, conflict: the conditions for the
enhancement of any particular individual may run counter to the values which he actually pursues or which dominate the ethical tradition—of family or society—into which he is born. That opposition
is, for Nietzsche, potentially empowering in that it pits the individual against his culture, thus inducing him to specify and take responsibility for his ethical allegiances, with all their implications. Yet, I
take Nietzsche to be suggesting, in such a confrontation the individual is unlikely entirely to *jettison* his ethical inheritance—at least in
the shape of its highest values: i.e. those that most decisively inform
its identity and practices. Because that inheritance is, in part, *what
he is*, he will tend to oppose its values in the name of its values; and,
as a result, he will, at most, respecify or re-employ such values
according to standards which are themselves likely to develop out of
that inheritance, without being able to step outside the latter altogether. This is, of course, how Nietzsche portrays the upheavals of
the Christian West: science attacks religion, religion attacks science,
and Nietzsche attacks both, all in the name of one value: that of
truth. Similarly the French Revolution attacks (among other institutions) the old religious order in the name of the very egalitarianism
which that order, in the shape of its conception of the 'soul' and of
universal values, promotes. Moreover, such ethical conservatism is
reflected in the fact, as I see it, that Nietzsche does not repudiate any
traditional values as such (except for the atomistic need which
underlies morality), but insists only on *redeploying* traditional values
for life-enhancing ends. True revolution against an ethical heritage,
in the sense of overthrowing its entire set of highest values, is, on
this view, immensely difficult—which may be why Nietzsche
demands, first and foremost, the 'purification' (*GS*, 335) or revaluation (*EH*, IV, 1) of our traditional values, but not their replacement
as such.

Though the individual's highest values are inevitably conditioned,
in all three senses, by a past, there are, as we have seen, types and
features of human nature that, for Nietzsche, are universal and,
hence, values—i.e. conditions for their enhancement—that are
unhistorical in the sense that they are not specific to a *particular* ethical tradition or epoch. This is so, for example, of values conducive
to the flourishing of the types of form-creator that he most esteems,
such as the philosopher and the artist, or, more broadly, to re-

expressing the 'eternal basic text of *homo natura*' (*BGE*, 230). But this does not, of course, make these values unhistorical in the sense that Nietzsche finds unintelligible: i.e. in the sense that they supposedly transcend—are immune to or unconditioned by—not this or that history, but history or temporality *as such*. In short: the value of a value is conditioned by a whole spectrum of facts about human nature and its needs, ranging from the most general (those putatively common to people, or types of people, in all historical cultures and epochs) to the most specific or local (those evinced by a particular person at a particular time in a particular culture).

Nietzsche's critique of the value of truth illustrates the breadth of this spectrum. Thus, the value of truth is *'unhistorical'*—i.e. determined by universal features or needs of man, rather than by those specific to a particular culture or historical situation—insofar as, for example, it is valuable to giving style to one's character. And its disvalue is 'unhistorical' insofar as, for example, seeking or knowing truth limits the creativity of the artist, or one's ability to 'become what one is', or one's capacity to experience the 'superficial'. In thus alluding to the dangers of truth, as he sees them, Nietzsche seems to be giving a modern twist to the old idea of forbidden knowledge (represented in the Christian world by the story of Eden and in the ancient world by the story of Prometheus). In particular, the knowledge for which we must not be impatient is precisely of what most matters to Nietzsche, namely the nature of *'what* one is', the secret, as it were, of one's power.

By contrast, Nietzsche's principal example of the *historically specific* value of truth concerns the overcoming of *décadence*. For a culture in this condition, propositional knowledge about the basic character of reality—such as its freedom from qualities postulated by the 'atomistic need'—is vital, as is examining the functions of (and so 'purifying') our highest values, and explicitly affirming 'Eternal Return' or other (for him) crucial tests of life-enhancement, all of which can be achieved only if one faces the world as it really is. The idea here, then, is that propositional truth, at least of such matters, is essential only for those (people, civilizations, ethical communities) who falsify reality in ways harmful to life—in just the way that, for Nietzsche, Platonic-Christian morality does; and, conversely, that an overriding emphasis on, and talent for, such truth-seeking is not required when one is properly attuned—i.e. stands in an honest relationship—to these features of reality and so need not strive explicitly to affirm them. In such a state, which was that of 'the Greeks', it is possible 'to stop courageously at the surface' (*GS*, P, 4)—possible, in other words, to do without our tremendous emphasis on truth-seeking because one's relationship to reality is, in just these essentials, *already* truthful.

These contrasts between the value and disvalue of truth (or truth-seeking) constitute a tension central to Nietzsche's thought, of which we have encountered at least three expressions. The first is that though truth can be an indispensable medicine for a life-denying culture, it, like many powerful and life-saving medicines, has dangerous side-effects—notably insofar as (in Nietzsche's view) seeking it limits the richness of experience and the power of artistic creativity. Second, though to look at life honestly may be essential to becoming strong, one also needs to beautify (which, for Nietzsche, is to falsify) life in order to flourish, which means that one needs art as well as truth—and, indeed, art *in order* to sustain truthfulness. Third, though artists need 'eternal unreality' (at least in relation to their own natures) in order to be creative, this, if true, renders them especially vulnerable to the dangers against which knowledge can protect—notably the seduction of *décadence*, as witness the case of Wagner, as Nietzsche sees it. Moreover, this unreality handicaps their ability meaningfully to affirm 'Eternal Return' and *amor fati*, since such an affirmation demands great clear-sightedness if it is to be a genuine ethical test. Thus to the extent that knowledge 'redeems', such redemption is beyond the grasp of what is undeniably one of Nietzsche's highest 'types'. Only in the unity of a personality which embraces the 'artist'- and the 'philosopher'-types, and so accommodates the pursuit of truth and falsehood, can the value to life of both the latter be reaped.

These points suffice to refute two views that might be taken of Nietzsche's attitude to the value of truth: either that he values principally introspective knowledge (as a guide to 'self-realization') or that he is, quite simply, hostile to truth-seeking. The former view is ruled out by Nietzsche's insistence that one should not seek prematurely to know what one is, that artists in particular must observe this prohibition, that reflective self-consciousness can paralyse creativity, and that, in any case, the significance of our actions (which includes our thoughts) is ultimately opaque. The latter view is discredited by Nietzsche's whole genealogical project, which presupposes that impulses to life-denial, and the values and errors which they employ, are undermined precisely by truthfulness about their functions rather than by retreating into militant obscurantism. In other words, though Nietzsche regards the particular 'faith in truth' of, say, the Enlightenment as unwarranted by his standard of life-enhancement, and all claims to have overcome myth and prejudice as absurd, he, unlike some of his postmodernist followers, holds that these beliefs can be overcome only by *more* rather than by less enlightenment.

Yet courageous though Nietzsche's evaluation of the value of truth is, it places in question, once again,[27] a central assumption of his whole philosophy: that it is necessarily life-denying to ignore or falsify reality in the ways that Platonism or Christianity does—and specifically to affirm as real what is unreal or unverifiable or even unintelligible, namely the proposition that our highest ethical, epistemological, and artistic standards are timeless standards radically external to any history, contingency, and ordinary practices. In short: it begs the question why life-enhancement necessarily requires world-affirmation—at least in the very senses that, according to Nietzsche, Christianity ineluctably opposes; why, in other words, *precisely those* errors propounded by the 'atomistic need' are necessarily life-denying, whether they take theological form (such as the Christian God or soul) or are also susceptible of secular expressions (such as the metaphysical subject). The proposition that, on the contrary, such 'errors' *can* be life-enhancing—short of their employment to justify abdication and resignation of the will—not only has the weight of Western cultural wealth on its side, but, as I argued in Chapters 5.5 and 9.4, is supported by the idea that belief in a god in whose divinity one shares—or, more generally, in a transcendent reality or absolute Being that justifies or empowers one's values and practices—*can* stimulate the very individual creativity that Nietzsche seeks. To say this is not, of course, to say that we have a *choice* between accepting or repudiating the particular fictions of the 'atomistic need': we have no such choice if, in practice, the authority of our standards of value or rational acceptability or warranted assertibility is, to put the matter in Nietzschean terms, overwhelmingly dictated by our own nature, nurture, and life-circumstances—i.e. by the conditioning of a particular past.

---

[27] I have, using various formulations, opposed this assumption in Chapters 2.3, 5.5, and 6.4.

To sum up: on the one hand, Nietzsche's great achievement is to force us to recognize that some of our actual ethical practices are deeply incoherent or hypocritical: that, for example, many in our age who have repudiated as unverifiable or unintelligible such postulates as the unconditioned, the metaphysical subject, or the universal prescriptivity of the good, continue to regard, say, truth or pity or equality as intrinsically valuable. He shows us that central to this failure to follow through our repudiation of a metaphysics of atemporality to its bitter end in the undermining of the unconditional valuation of truth itself is that we have, in effect, lacked the courage of our conviction in that very value. And since that value is one of our highest values, and hence defines, in part, of 'what we are', this lack of courage, he implies, means that we fail fully to 'become what we are'—i.e. fully to actualize one of our potential *telē*, which means fully to live out the consequences of the highest values implicit in that *telos*. In other words, we neglect genuinely to live that 'form of life' of which truthfulness is a (or even the) defining value. On the other hand, whether this neglect is really so disastrous, judged by Nietzsche's *own* standard of life-enhancement, remains an open question which, I have suggested, he does not convincingly answer. Yet it is in forcing us to *face* this neglect—and, in doing so, to evaluate for ourselves the value of what is arguably our most sacred and unquestioned value, namely that of truth—that one of Nietzsche's most original, powerful, and enduring contributions to philosophy may ultimately lie.

Bibliography

1. PRIMARY SOURCES

The English translations of Nietzsche's works to which I have referred are listed below. The German original may be found in Friedrich Nietzsche, *Sämtliche Werke: Kritische Studienausgabe*, ed. Giorgio Colli and Mazzino Montinari, 15 vols., Berlin: de Gruyter, 1980.

The Antichrist (1888), trans. W. Kaufmann, in *The Portable Nietzsche*, ed. W. Kaufmann, New York: Viking, 1954.

Beyond Good and Evil (1886), trans. W. Kaufmann, New York: Vintage, 1966.

The Birth of Tragedy (1872), trans. W. Kaufmann, New York: Vintage, 1966.

The Case of Wagner (1888), trans. W. Kaufmann, New York: Vintage, 1966.

Daybreak: Thoughts on the Prejudices of Morality (1881), trans. R. J. Hollingdale, Cambridge: Cambridge University Press, 1982.

Ecce Homo (1888), trans. W. Kaufmann, New York: Vintage, 1967.

The Gay Science (1882; Part 5: 1887), trans. W. Kaufmann, New York: Vintage, 1974.

Human, All Too Human (1878), trans. R. J. Hollingdale, Cambridge: Cambridge University Press, 1986.

On the Genealogy of Morals (1887), trans. W. Kaufmann and R. J. Hollingdale, New York: Vintage, 1967.

Thus Spoke Zarathustra (1883–5), trans. W. Kaufmann, in *The Portable Nietzsche*, ed. W. Kaufmann, New York: Viking, 1954.

On Truth and Lies in a Nonmoral Sense (1873), in *Philosophy and Truth: Selections from Nietzsche's Notebooks of the Early 1870s*, ed. and trans. Daniel Breazeale, Atlantic Highlands, NJ: Humanities Press, 1979.

Twilight of the Idols (1889), trans. W. Kaufmann in *The Portable Nietzsche*, ed. W. Kaufmann, New York: Viking, 1954.

The Will to Power (Notes from the 1880s), trans. W. Kaufmann and R. J. Hollingdale, New York: Vintage, 1968.

2. SECONDARY SOURCES

ALDERMAN, HAROLD G., *Nietzsche's Gift*, Athens, Oh.: Ohio University Press, 1977.

ALLISON, DAVID B. (ed.), *The New Nietzsche: Contemporary Styles of Interpretation*, Cambridge, Mass.: MIT Press, 1985.

ANSELL-PEARSON, KEITH, *An Introduction to Nietzsche as Political Thinker: The Perfect Nihilist*, Cambridge: Cambridge University Press, 1994.

—— and CAYGILL, H. (eds.), *The Fate of the New Nietzsche*, Aldershot: Avebury, 1993.

BARKER, STEPHEN, *Autoaesthetics: Strategies of the Self after Nietzsche*, Atlantic Highlands, NJ: Humanities Press, 1992.

BERDYAEV, NICHOLAS, *Dostoevsky*, trans. Donald Attwater, Cleveland: The World Publishing Company, 1957.

BERGMANN, PETER, *Nietzsche: 'The Last Antipolitical German'*, Bloomington, Ind.: Indiana University Press, 1987.

BERKOWITZ, PETER, *Nietzsche: The Ethics of an Immoralist*, Cambridge, Mass.: Harvard University Press, 1995.

BERMAN, DAVID, 'Nietzsche's Three Phases of Atheism', *History of Philosophy Quarterly*, 5 (1988), 273–86.

BERNSTEIN, JOHN ANDREW, *Nietzsche's Moral Philosophy*, Rutherford, NJ: Fairleigh Dickinson University Press, 1987.

BLONDEL, ERIC, *Nietzsche, The Body and Culture: Philosophy as a Philological Genealogy*, trans. Seán Hand, Stanford, Calif.: Stanford University Press, 1991.

CARTWRIGHT, DAVID E., 'Kant, Schopenhauer, and Nietzsche on the Morality of Pity', *Journal of the History of Ideas*, 45/1 (1984), 83–98.

CLARK, MAUDEMARIE, *Nietzsche on Truth and Philosophy*, Cambridge: Cambridge University Press, 1990.

—— 'On *Truth and Lie in the Extra-Moral Sense*', *International Studies in Philosophy*, 16/2 (1984), 57–66.

COLLINS, DEREK, 'On the Aesthetics of the Deceiving Self in Nietzsche, Pindar and Theognis', *Nietzsche-Studien*, 26 (1997), 276–99.

COPLESTON, FREDERICK, *Friedrich Nietzsche: Philosopher of Culture*, 2nd edn., London: Search Press, 1975.

DANNHAUSER, WERNER J., *Nietzsche's View of Socrates*, Ithaca, NY: Cornell University Press, 1974.

DANTO, ARTHUR C., *Nietzsche as Philosopher*, New York: Macmillan, 1965.

DELEUZE, GILLES, *Nietzsche and Philosophy*, trans. Hugh Tomlinson, London: Athlone Press, 1983.

DERRIDA, JACQUES, *Spurs: Nietzsche's Styles*, trans. Barbara Harlow, Chicago: University of Chicago Press, 1979.

DETWILER, BRUCE, *Nietzsche and the Politics of Aristocratic Radicalism*, Chicago: University of Chicago Press, 1990.

DÜRR, V., GRIMM, R., and HARMS, K. (eds.), *Nietzsche: Literature and Values*, Madison: University of Wisconsin Press, 1988.

FERRY, LUC, *Homo Aestheticus: The Invention of Taste in the Democratic Age*, trans. Robert de Loaiza, Chicago: University of Chicago Press, 1993.

—— and RENAUT, A. (eds.), *Why We Are Not Nietzscheans*, trans. Robert de Loaiza, Chicago: University of Chicago Press, 1997.

FOUCAULT, MICHEL, *The Foucault Reader*, ed. Paul Rabinow, New York: Pantheon, 1984.

GAY, PETER, *The Enlightenment: The Rise of Modern Paganism*, New York: W. W. Norton, 1977.

GEUSS, RAYMOND, 'Nietzsche and Genealogy', *European Journal of Philosophy*, 2/3 (1994), 274–92.

GILLESPIE, M. A., and STRONG, T. B. (eds.), *Nietzsche's New Seas: Explorations in Philosophy, Aesthetics, and Politics*, Chicago: University of Chicago Press, 1988.

GOETHE, J. W., *Faust I*, in *Goethes Werke*, iii, 6th edn., ed. Erich Trunz, Hamburg: Christian Wegner Verlag, 1962.

GOLOMB, JACOB, *In Search of Authenticity: From Kierkegaard to Camus*, London: Routledge, 1995.

—— 'Nietzsche on Authenticity', *Philosophy Today*, 34 (1990), 243–58.

GRIMM, RÜDIGER H., *Nietzsche's Theory of Knowledge*, Berlin: Walter de Gruyter, 1977.

HAAR, MICHEL, *Nietzsche and Metaphysics*, ed. and trans. Michael Gendre, Albany, NY: State University of New York Press, 1996.

HABERMAS, JÜRGEN, *The Philosophical Discourse of Modernity*, trans. Frederick Lawrence, Cambridge, Mass.: MIT Press, 1987.

HALES, STEVEN D., 'Was Nietzsche a Consequentialist?', *International Studies in Philosophy*, 27/3 (1995), 25–34.

HARPER, RALPH, *The Seventh Solitude: Metaphysical Homelessness in Kierkegaard, Dostoevsky, and Nietzsche*, Baltimore: Johns Hopkins University Press, 1965.

HATAB, LAWRENCE J., *A Nietzschean Defense of Democracy: An Experiment in Postmodern Politics*, Chicago: Open Court Press, 1995.

HAVAS, RANDALL, *Nietzsche's Genealogy: Nihilism and the Will to Knowledge*, Ithaca, NY: Cornell University Press, 1995.

HEIDEGGER, MARTIN, *Nietzsche*, ed. David Farrell Krell, San Francisco: Harper & Row, 1979–87; reprinted as HarperCollins Paperback edn., 1991, vols. i–iv (vols. i and ii: trans. David Farrell Krell; vol. iii: trans. Joan Stambaugh, David Farrell Krell, and Frank Capuzzi; vol. iv: trans. Frank Capuzzi).

HEIDEGGER, MARTIN, *The Question Concerning Technology and Other Essays*, trans. William Lovitt, New York: Harper & Row, 1977.

HELLER, ERICH, *The Importance of Nietzsche: Ten Essays*, Chicago: University of Chicago Press, 1988.

—— *The Poet's Self and the Poem: Essays on Goethe, Nietzsche, Rilke, and Thomas Mann*, London: Athlone Press, 1976.

HOMER, *The Odyssey*, trans. E. V. Rieu, London: Penguin, 1985.

HOOYKAAS, R., *Religion and the Rise of Modern Science*, Edinburgh: Scottish Academic Press, 1972.

HOULGATE, STEPHEN, *Hegel, Nietzsche and the Criticism of Metaphysics*, Cambridge: Cambridge University Press, 1986.

HUNT, LESTER H., *Nietzsche and the Origin of Virtue*, London: Routledge, 1991.

IBANEZ-NOE, J., 'Nietzsche and the Problem of Teleology', *International Studies in Philosophy*, 29/3 (1997), 37–48.

JASPERS, KARL, *Nietzsche: An Introduction to the Understanding of his Philosophical Activity*, trans. Charles F. Wallraff and Frederick J. Schmitz, Tucson, Ariz.: University of Arizona Press, 1965.

—— *Nietzsche and Christianity*, trans. E. B. Ashton, Chicago: Henry Regnery (Gateway edn.), 1961.

JUNG, C. G., *Nietzsche's Zarathustra*, ed. James L. Jarrett, Princeton: Princeton University Press, 1988.

KAHN, CHARLES H., *The Art and Thought of Heraclitus*, Cambridge: Cambridge University Press, 1979.

KANT, IMMANUEL, 'An Answer to the Question: What is Enlightenment?', in *Perpetual Peace and Other Essays*, trans. Ted Humphrey, Indianapolis: Hackett, 1983.

—— *Groundwork of the Metaphysic of Morals*, trans. H. J. Paton, New York: Harper & Row (Harper Torchbooks), 1964.

KAUFMANN, WALTER, *Nietzsche: Philosopher, Psychologist, Antichrist*, 4th edn., Princeton: Princeton University Press, 1974.

KLOSSOWSKI, PIERRE, *Nietzsche and the Vicious Circle*, trans. Daniel W. Smith, London: Athlone, 1997.

KOELB, CLAYTON (ed.), *Nietzsche as Posmodernist: Essays Pro and Contra*, Albany, NY: State University of New York Press, 1990.

KOLAKOWSKI, LESZEK, *Modernity on Endless Trial*, Chicago: University of Chicago Press, 1990.

KRELL, DAVID FARRELL, *Infectious Nietzsche*, Bloomington, Ind.: Indiana University Press, 1996.

LAMPERT, LAURENCE, *Nietzsche and Modern Times: A Study of Bacon, Descartes and Nietzsche*, New Haven: Yale University Press, 1993.

—— *Nietzsche's Teaching: An Interpretation of* Thus Spoke Zarathustra, New Haven: Yale University Press, 1986.

LEA, F. A., *The Tragic Philosopher: A Study of Friedrich Nietzsche*, New York: Barnes & Noble, 1973.

LEITER, BRIAN, 'Nietzsche and the Morality Critics', *Ethics*, 107/2 (1997), 250–85.

—— 'Morality in the Pejorative Sense: On the Logic of Nietzsche's Critique of Morality', *British Journal for the History of Philosophy*, 3/1 (1995), 113–45.

—— 'Beyond Good and Evil', *History of Philosophy Quarterly*, 10/3 (1993), 261–70.

LEVINE, PETER, *Nietzsche and the Modern Crisis of the Humanities*, Albany, NY: State University of New York Press, 1995.

LOUDEN, R. B., and SCHOLLMEIER, P. (eds.), *The Greeks and Us: Essays in Honor of Arthur W. H. Adkins*, Chicago: University of Chicago Press, 1996.

LÖWITH, KARL, *Nietzsche's Philosophy of the Eternal Recurrence of the Same*, trans. J. Harvey Lomax, Berkeley and Los Angeles: University of California Press, 1997.

—— *From Hegel to Nietzsche*, trans. David E. Green, New York: Columbia University Press, 1991.

MACINTYRE, ALASDAIR, *Three Rival Versions of Moral Enquiry*, London: Duckworth, 1990.

—— *After Virtue: A Study in Moral Theory*, 2nd edn., London: Duckworth, 1985.

MAGNUS, BERND, 'Perfectibility and Attitude in Nietzsche's *Übermensch*', *Review of Metaphysics*, 36/3 (Mar. 1983), 633–59.

—— *Nietzsche's Existential Imperative*, Bloomington, Ind.: Indiana University Press, 1978.

—— and HIGGINS, K. M. (eds.), *The Cambridge Companion to Nietzsche*, Cambridge: Cambridge University Press, 1996.

—— MILEUR, J.-P., and STEWART, S. (eds.), *Nietzsche's Case: Philosophy as/ and Literature*, New York: Routledge, 1993.

MARTIN, GLEN, *From Nietzsche to Wittgenstein: The Problem of Truth and Nihilism in the Modern World*, New York: Peter Lang, 1989.

NEHAMAS, ALEXANDER, *Nietzsche: Life as Literature*, Cambridge, Mass.: Harvard University Press, 1985.

NUSSBAUM, MARTHA C., 'The Transfigurations of Intoxication: Nietzsche, Schopenhauer, and Dionysus', *Arion*, 1/2 (May 1991), 75–111.

—— *The Fragility of Goodness: Luck and Ethics in Greek Tragedy and Philosophy*, Cambridge: Cambridge University Press, 1986.

O'FLAHERTY, J. C., SELLNER, T. F., and HELM, R. M. (eds.), *Studies in Nietzsche and the Judaeo-Christian Tradition*, Chapel Hill, NC: University of North Carolina Press, 1985.

—— —— —— *Studies in Nietzsche and the Classical Tradition*, 2nd edn., Chapel Hill, NC: University of North Carolina Press, 1979.

OWEN, DAVID, *Nietzsche, Politics and Modernity: A Critique of Liberal Reason*, London: SAGE Publications, 1995.

PARKES, GRAHAM, *Composing the Soul: Reaches of Nietzsche's Psychology*, Chicago: University of Chicago Press, 1994.

—— (ed.), *Nietzsche and Asian Thought*, Chicago: University of Chicago Press, 1991.

PIPPIN, ROBERT B., *Modernism as a Philosophical Problem*, Oxford: Basil Blackwell, 1991.

POELLNER, PETER, *Nietzsche and Metaphysics*, Oxford: Clarendon Press, 1995.

PUTNAM, HILARY, 'Pragmatism', *Proceedings of the Aristotelian Society*, 95 (1995), 291–306.

QUINE, W. V. O., 'Two Dogmas of Empiricism', in *From a Logical Point of View*, 2nd edn., New York: Harper & Row (Harper Torchbooks), 1963.

RICHARDSON, JOHN, *Nietzsche's System*, New York: Oxford University Press, 1996.

RITCHIE, J. M. (ed.), *Periods in German Literature*, London: Oswald Wolff, 1966.

RORTY, RICHARD, *Contingency, Irony, and Solidarity*, Cambridge: Cambridge University Press, 1989.

ROSEN, STANLEY, *The Mask of Enlightenment: Nietzsche's Zarathustra*, Cambridge: Cambridge University Press, 1995.

—— *The Question of Being: A Reversal of Heidegger*, New Haven: Yale University Press, 1993.

—— *The Ancients and the Moderns: Rethinking Modernity*, New Haven: Yale University Press, 1989.

SALLIS, JOHN, *Crossings: Nietzsche and the Space of Tragedy*, Chicago: University of Chicago Press, 1991.

SANTAYANA, GEORGE, *Egotism in German Philosophy*, New York: Haskell House Publishers, 1971.

SCHACHT, RICHARD, *Making Sense of Nietzsche: Reflections Timely and Untimely*, Urbana, Ill.: University of Illinois Press, 1994.

—— (ed.), *Nietzsche, Genealogy, Morality: Essays on Nietzsche's Genealogy of Morals*, Berkeley and Los Angeles: University of California Press, 1994.

—— *Nietzsche*, London: Routledge & Kegan Paul, 1983.

SCHATZKI, THEODORE R., 'Ancient and Naturalistic Themes in Nietzsche's Ethics', *Nietzsche-Studien*, 23 (1994), 146–67.

SCHELER, MAX, *Ressentiment*, trans. W. Holdheim, New York: The Free Press, 1961.

SCHOPENHAUER, ARTHUR, *The World as Will and Representation*, trans. E. F. J. Payne, vols. i and ii, New York: Dover, 1969.

SCHRIFT, ALAN D., *Nietzsche and the Question of Interpretation: Between Hermeneutics and Deconstruction*, New York: Routledge, 1990.

SCHUTTE, OFELIA, *Beyond Nihilism: Nietzsche without Masks*, Chicago: University of Chicago Press, 1984.

SEDGWICK, PETER R. (ed.), *Nietzsche: A Critical Reader*, Oxford: Basil Blackwell, 1995.

SHAPIRO, GARY, *Nietzschean Narratives*, Bloomington, Ind.: Indiana University Press, 1989.

SILK, M. S. and STERN, J. P., *Nietzsche on Tragedy*, Cambridge: Cambridge University Press, 1981.

SLEINIS, E. E., *Nietzsche's Revaluation of Values: A Study in Strategies*, Urbana, Ill.: University of Illinois Press, 1994.

SOLOMON, ROBERT C. (ed.), *Nietzsche: A Collection of Critical Essays*, Garden City, NY: Anchor Press, 1973.

—— and HIGGINS, K. M. (eds.), *Reading Nietzsche*, New York: Oxford University Press, 1988.

SORABJI, RICHARD, *Matter, Space, and Motion: Theories in Antiquity and their Sequel*, London: Duckworth, 1988.

—— *Time, Creation, and the Continuum: Theories in Antiquity and the Early Middle Ages*, London: Duckworth, 1983.

STACK, GEORGE J., *Nietzsche: Man, Knowledge, and Will to Power*, Wolfeboro, NH: Hollowbrook Publishers, 1994.

STATEN, HENRY, *Nietzsche's Voice*, Ithaca, NY: Cornell University Press, 1990.

STERN, J. P., *Nietzsche*, London: Fontana Press, 1978.

STRONG, TRACY, *Friedrich Nietzsche and the Politics of Transfiguration*, expanded edn., Berkeley and Los Angeles: University of California Press, 1988.

TAYLOR, CHARLES, *Sources of the Self: The Making of the Modern Identity*, Cambridge: Cambridge University Press, 1989.

TEJERA, V., *Nietzsche and Greek Thought*, Dordrecht: Martinus Nijhoff, 1987.

THIELE, LESLIE PAUL, *Friedrich Nietzsche and the Politics of the Soul: A Study of Heroic Individualism*, Princeton: Princeton University Press, 1990.

WARREN, MARK T., *Nietzsche and Political Thought*, Cambridge, Mass.: MIT Press, 1988.

WESTPHAL, KENNETH, 'Was Nietzsche a Cognitivist?', *Journal of the History of Philosophy*, 22/3 (1984), 343–63.

WHITE, ALAN, *Within Nietzsche's Labyrinth*, New York: Routledge, 1990.

—— 'Nietzschean Nihilism: A Typology', *International Studies in Philosophy*, 19/2 (1987), 29–44.

WILCOX, JOHN T., *Truth and Value in Nietzsche: A Study of his Metaethics and Epistemology*, Ann Arbor: University of Michigan Press, 1974.

WILLIAMS, BERNARD, *Shame and Necessity*, Berkeley and Los Angeles: University of California Press, 1993.

WILLIAMS, BERNARD, *Moral Luck: Philosophical Papers 1973–80*, Cambridge: Cambridge University Press, 1981.

WINCHESTER, JAMES J., *Nietzsche's Aesthetic Turn: Reading Nietzsche after Heidegger, Deleuze, Derrida*, Albany, NY: State University of New York Press, 1994.

YOUNG, JULIAN, *Nietzsche's Philosophy of Art*, Cambridge: Cambridge University Press, 1992.

YOVEL, YIRMIYAHU (ed.), *Nietzsche as Affirmative Thinker*, Dordrecht: Martinus Nijhoff, 1986.

Index